Peasant Uprisings in Japan

PEASANT UPRISINGS

A Critical Anthology

THE UNIVERSITY OF CHICAGO PRESS

Chicago & London

IN JAPAN

of Peasant Histories

Edited and Translated by

ANNE WALTHALL

Anne Walthall is associate professor of history at the University of Utah.

The University of Chicago Press, Chicago 60637
The University of Chicago Press, Ltd., London

Library of Congress Cataloging-in-Publication Data

Peasant uprisings in Japan : a critical anthology of peasant histories /
edited and translated by Anne Walthall.
   p.   cm.
   A selection and translation of original Japanese texts.
   Includes bibliographical references and index.
   ISBN 0-226-87233-5 (cloth). — ISBN 0-226-87234-3 (paper)
   1. Peasant uprisings—Japan—History. 2. Japan—History—
Tokugawa period, 1600–1868. I. Walthall, Anne.
   DS871.5.P44 1991
   952'.025—dc20   91-9362
                                                CIP

Title page illustration: detail of "Edo Riot" by Hosoya Syomo. Edo Period. Ink painting on paper. 126.3 x 27.2 cm. Courtesy of the Tokyo National Museum.

Contents

Acknowledgments   vii

Introduction   1

O N E

The Sakura Sōgorō Story   35

T W O

A Record of How the Four Orders of People in Mimasaka
Ran Riot   77

T H R E E

A Thousand Spears at Kitsunezuka   119

F O U R

A Tale of a Dream from the Fox Woman Plain   169

F I V E

A Tale Told in a Dream of a Eulogy to Filial Piety   193

S I X

Rereading Peasant Histories of Peasant Uprisings   217

Notes   233

Index   259

Acknowledgments

L IKE ANYONE WHO ACCEPTS the challenge of Japanese history, I am primarily indebted to the Japanese scholars without whose meticulous research this study would not have been possible. Those who edited and published the texts I have translated are listed in the endnotes. I am especially grateful to Hosaka Satoru, who not only lent me his copy of the Sakura Sōgorō story but spent many hours checking my reading of it, often on trains on our way to see memorials to peasant martyrs. For many years he sustained a research group on peasant uprisings—the Hyakushō ikki kenkyūkai—where I learned much about the dangers of overly inflating the significance of texts. Its members too have contributed in tangible and intangible ways to this study. I have also depended greatly on Fukaya Katsumi for his insights into the structure of the relations between lord and peasants and more generally for his encouragement and support of this and many other projects over the years. For leading me beyond the field of peasant studies, I thank Takayama Yoshiki and Suemoto Yōko. For the many kindnesses they have shown me and for the help they have provided that goes far beyond the requirements of scholarship, I thank the Kitajimas—Manji, Eiko, Hideki, and Shigeki.

The final shape of this project owes much to Herman Ooms, whose initial doubts forced me to sharpen my arguments for doing it. Helen Hardacre generously lent her expertise on Japanese religion to the chapter on Sōgorō. Maria Dobozy, Kathryn Stockton, and Peggy Pascoe led me to folklore studies and feminist theory. Henry Whiteside and Pat Briggs offered editorial advice. For their help and friendship I express my thanks. Those who critiqued the manuscript for publication, Harry D. Harootunian, Stephen Vlastos and Gail Bernstein, have my sincere gratitude for their efforts. My thanks go also to the copy editor, Kathryn Gohl. A generous sabbatical leave awarded me by the College of Humanities at the

University of Utah made it possible for me to finish this manuscript. Both the dean, Norman Council, and my former department chair, Larry Gerlach, have created an environment that facilitates research and writing. To them and my friends and colleagues at the University of Utah go my appreciation and thanks.

Introduction

PEASANT PROTESTS IN EARLY MODERN JAPAN numbered in the thousands. Many were modest in scale, consisting of little more than rumblings of discontent. Violence was avoided, for the most part, by spokesmen for the community, who humbly petitioned the ruling authorities for tax exemptions or famine relief. Sometimes peasants acted on their own, quarreling with village officials and rioting. By the dawn of the modern era, every region of Japan, with the exception of southern Kyushu, had been rocked by at least one large-scale uprising in which peasants marched en masse to present their demands to the authorities and to destroy the property of commoners who had done them wrong.[1]

The aim of this book is to allow the peasants to speak for themselves in histories of protest. Five texts written primarily in the early nineteenth century have been selected, providing a chronological sweep from 1600 to 1868. We begin with Sakura Sōgorō, a peasant martyred in the middle of the seventeenth century who lived not far from what is now Tokyo International Airport. Like other representations of his deeds, this story seeks to placate vengeful ghosts and explain how a local shrine came into existence. The second chapter of this volume presents the earliest history of a peasant uprising which is sympathetic to the participants; it originates in the Tsuyama domain of western Japan, where in 1726 the peasants opposed the domain's taxation policies. Written soon after the uprising was suppressed, the text draws heavily on Japanese classical tradition. Later, in 1764, peasants marched on Edo (present-day Tokyo) to protest a change in the transportation system. The text translated in chapter 3 was copied in 1874; it presents the perspective of village officials caught between their communities and a ruling class no longer able to guarantee public order. In 1804, the transportation system provided another excuse for an attack on the property of men deemed selfish by their neighbors. One text from 1863, presented in chapter 4, incorporates local legends and

1

folklore to recount the origin of place-names. Chapter 5, the last translation, returns us to Tsuyama, where in 1866 peasants demanding reforms in domanial policy once more attacked village leaders and other wealthy men whose interests conflicted with their own. This history is centered not on the man accused of leading the riot, however, but on his daughters.

Using these texts for a perspective on peasant culture raises a number of issues. They were created by and for people whose worldview was a product of the nineteenth century, not the twentieth, in a country so different from our own that it has been described as inscrutable. I would not want to imply that peasant uprisings as empirical events do not really exist except as "texts" masquerading as "the real," and therefore the only object worthy of study is the text itself. Instead my object is threefold:

In his essay on ethnographic authority, James Clifford argues that as long as ethnographers impose their own narrative on the native, they are privileging their interpretation of culture over that of their object. The same can be said of the relationship between the historian and the document. One way for ethnographers to abrogate this authority is to present as many large chunks of data as possible, even if they do not completely understand the data's meaning.[2] For that reason, I have presented translations of these histories in their entirety.

Presenting complete texts, however, suggests that the knowledge found in them is a given: it is already constituted, it is self-contained, and it is completly intelligible. The histories of peasant uprisings tell a seemingly coherent story, one that by its very coherence establishes closure. This closure is reinforced when a text is simply translated. To disrupt this illusion, I have drawn on critical theory for its insights into language and the diverse voices that inform the text. Finally, I am aware that this kind of theorizing can all too easily lead, as Bryan Palmer has said, to "a hedonistic descent into a plurality of discourses that decenter the world in a chaotic denial of any acknowledgment of tangible structures of power."[3] To avoid this danger, I keep my eyes focused firmly on power relationships within a changing historical context.

To what extent did the histories of peasant uprisings incorporate the concerns and assumptions of the peasants who participated in these events? The peasant population included such a diverse range of social standings and economic classes that some historians might question whether the term *peasant* applies at all. In a largely illiterate society, documents necessarily had to come from people whose wealth allowed them to achieve a level of education unimaginable by the average peasant, but who were unlikely to approve of peasant violence. Nevertheless, too much must not be made of the gulf between learned and peasant culture. Within a village, degrees of literacy stretched along a continuum. The man who wrote "A Thousand Spears at Kitsunezuka" appropriated much more of the elite tradition than did the author of "A Tale of a Dream from the Fox Woman Plain." Like pastors in medieval Europe, these writers adapted to their audiences by writing in a "comprehensible and simple language, resorting to familiar images, . . . referring to folktales, and even making use of the stylistic features of tales and story."[4] They needed to make less effort at adaptation than an urban or samurai intellectual, moreover, for they grew up in daily interaction with their less-advantaged neighbors.

The historian may still question the validity of my enterprise on the grounds that these texts misrepresent the most prevalent forms of conflict in early modern Japan. This chronology of peasant uprisings makes it appear that after the first nonviolent protests, uprisings escalated rapidly into destructive riots. Such was not the case. Most contention between commoners and rulers continued to take the form of petitionary protest. What caught the attention of writers, however, was large-scale and massive unrest. For the most part, their texts were inspired by the effort to explain extraordinary outbursts of disorder, not the ongoing struggle over village administrative practices or taxation policies that rarely resulted in loss of life. To capture the extraordinary nature of the former events, they relied on enthusiastic descriptions of imaginary battles that say more about the tools they had to think with than the historical facts of the case. Men who lived sometimes a hundred years or more later and miles away did not necessarily know what actually happened. It is not the argument of this book that these texts reflect an objective reality; rather they show how various sectors of the rural population re-created the past to represent their contemporary concerns and fears.

Politics and Peasant Protest

Political power in early modern Japan was restricted to members of the ruling class. These were the samurai, whose public possession of sword and surname distinguished them from the rest of society. Pre-eminent among them was the shōgun, a title monopolized between 1600 and 1868 by the Tokugawa family. Holding office as a grant from the emperor who lived cloistered in Kyoto, the shōgun ruled directly over one-fourth of Japan. The rest of the country was divided among 240 to 260 daimyō or lords, some of whom led a relatively autonomous existence far from the center of power while others found their fortunes in the Tokugawa bureaucracy. Most samurai served either the shōgun or daimyō. They practiced the martial arts, staffed the bureaucracies, or led lives of idle poverty when official positions were unforthcoming. But whatever they did, they lived in castle towns and cities at a distinct remove from the peasants over whom they ruled.

During the seventeenth century, in a long drawn-out process never completely finished, the ruling class tried to perpetuate the status of every member of this society through heredity.[5] The samurai, some 6 percent of the population, held the dominant position because they had conquered the country by force of arms, but they misrepresented themselves as the exemplars of virtue. Because they trafficked in intangible qualities as compared to everyone else who trafficked in material goods, the samurai conferred a moral superiority on themselves. The peasants made up approximately 85 percent of the population and were the most regularly exploited segment of society. Because they produced the basic necessities of life, they were given pride of place among the commoners. Confined to the cities were two other groups: the artisans, who created objects for others, and the merchants, officially despised because they produced nothing. Fitting with difficulty within this status system were *rōnin* (masterless samurai), who might make a living by telling tales or teaching school, *gōshi* (country samurai), who were neither peasants nor warriors, plus priests, monks, doctors, and scholars, who lived their lives entirely in the countryside but who did not farm, pay land tax, or share the communal obligations and rights that accompanied landholding. Outside the status system altogether were the *hinin*, the nonpeople, many of them impoverished peasants or townspeople turned beggars. In the 1866

Tsuyama riot, the peasants called themselves beggars. Finally, there were the outcasts *(eta)*—those assigned tasks so loathsome that no one else would do them. One of these was to execute peasants who protested.

The nature of the Tokugawa state has long been the subject of debate among historians. James White has argued that the shōgun's house government, the *bakufu,* can be compared to the absolutist states of early modern Europe because, like them, it controlled the legitimate use of physical force.[6] The bakufu regulated many other areas that also impinged directly on the peasants' everyday life. After it proscribed Christianity and some militant Buddhist sects, it required all Japanese to register at an approved Buddhist temple. Although it allowed the daimyō to issue paper certificates backed by rice for use solely within their own domains, it monopolized the coinage in a trimetallic system. The most valuable coin was the gold *ryō,* the least was the copper *mon,* and the ratio between them was approximately 4,000 to 1. The silver *monme,* worth one-sixtieth of a *ryō,* circulated in western Japan. A boon for historians, the bakufu established an official calligraphic style, the *o-ieryū,* as a means of imposing its own worldview on the populace. Through the Imperial Court it issued a calendar based on the lunar cycle, and it approved the selection of auspicious era names to keep track of the years.[7] Its authority over the transportation system transcended that of local rulers. Occasionally peasants overcame domanial distinctions to protest bakufu commerical policies en masse. Nevertheless, the bakufu never managed to tax the peasant producers outside its own lands. Peasants who lived in the domains of the daimyō could not use the bakufu as a higher juridical court of appeal.

Peasants tended to personify the authorities.[8] In this way they supported the fiction that their lord, called by his official name (for example, Hotta Kōzuke no suke), or the shōgun, referred to as O-uesama (the honorable high one), took an active interest in their welfare. Those who made the decisions, however, were always bureaucratic functionaries. Senior councillors *(rojū)* who set policy for the bakufu, the house elders *(karō)* who did the same in the domains, the Kantō *gundai* who administered the region around the shōgun's castle at Edo, and the intendants and magistrates who implemented policy seldom came in direct contact with the peasants. Communications were delivered by lower-ranking officials such as the inspectors *(metsuke).* Often the means of these messages was a

Introduction

clerk employed privately by the higher official to speak in the name of his master, a distinction ignored by the peasants. When the haughty Ina Hanzaemon, the Kantō *gundai*, revoked a bakufu decree to increase the number of villages supplying peasant porters in 1764, the peasants asserted that Ina himself had come to meet them—an assertion, denied in official records, that they were worthy of his presence.

The samurai seldom needed to appear in the countryside, for the peasants ran their own affairs. The village constituted a corporate unit with common lands and the responsibility to pay taxes and keep the peace. Membership in the community was held as a hereditary right only by the *honbyakushō* or landholding peasants, who spoke in village assemblies and monopolized the village offices. Nevertheless, the village was neither undifferentiated nor homogeneous. Among the *honbyakushō* were families wealthy enough to seek the civilization of cities and others so poor they were compared to the beasts in the field. Below them were families without shares *(kabu)* in the village corporation, denied a voice in village affairs, and able to draw on the village commons only through their peasant masters. The authorities found it easier to tax an entire village as a unit than to tax individual holdings, but collective responsibilities brought in their train a high degree of cohesiveness. Hilton L. Root has pointed out that English peasants were difficult to mobilize en masse because, unlike their Burgundian counterparts, "they had neither a village assembly to represent them nor collective rights and properties to unite them."[9] As in France, so in Japan: protest was always collective.

Over the course of the Tokugawa period, relations within the village changed. Village membership continued to be limited to those with shares, but these shares could be traded if a *honbyakushō* family found itself habitually unable to contribute to the village tax assessments. The subordination of nonshareholders became less intensely personal, but their economic viability also became increasingly precarious. As Thomas C. Smith has pointed out in what is still the best book in English on the history of Japanese agriculture, "there were in many Japanese villages suppressed hatreds that merely needed some shock . . . to send them boiling to the surface."[10] The basic building block for uprisings remained the village, but by the nineteenth century, the upper stratum was more often the target than the leader of attack. The histories of peasant uprisings demonstrate as much conflict within the various segments of the peasant population as between peasants and officials.

Regardless of how removed the upper stratum in the village became from the ordinary peasants, it continued to monopolize village office. Unlike Germany, where the most important official, the headman, was elected for life, in Japan the position was usually hereditary.[11] In some parts of Japan the headmen were the descendants of warriors who chose to rusticate following the sword hunts of the 1580s. Underlying the violence done in Tsuyama in 1726, for example, was resentment against the privileges acquired by the country samurai *(gōshi),* whose authority over a number of villages either as deputy district headmen *(chūjōya)* or league headmen *(ōjōya)* enabled them to exploit the trade in rice certificates. Although the headmen's economic and social positions often brought them into conflict with the ordinary peasants, they continued to identify strongly with the village and to claim that their interests were identical with those of the community. While forced to admire a headman like Sōgorō who sacrificed his life for others, fellow headmen preferred not to emulate him.

Within the village were other officials, some with hereditary claim to office, others not. The elders *(toshiyori)* assisted the headmen, and when the office rotated, it was usually among their number. The ruling authorities required that group leaders *(kumi-gashira)* oversee the moral conduct of every family in the group. Were a peasant to be summoned before the magistrate, his group leader would have to accompany him. Toward the last half of the Tokugawa period, some villages managed to establish a peasants' representative *(hyakushōdai)* to oversee the interests of the landholders in the village officials' councils, those held to divide the village tax assessment being considered the most crucial. Caught between their obligations to their rulers and their responsibilities to their fellow peasants, village officials also had to guide their family fortunes through changes in the economy.

Economic Development

The chief mediation between villages and the state was the payment of tribute or taxes. In theory the taxes were paid in kind as a percentage of the harvest. Thus the size of a village was calculated not in terms of area but in terms of its putative yield. Even the size of a domain was measured not by the number of acres it covered but by its income. The standard unit of measurement was the *koku*, 5.1 bushels, enough rice to feed one man for one year. All daimyō had lands worth at least ten thousand *koku*, but many peasants never saw as much as one. They measured their harvest in terms of *to* (10 percent of a *koku*), *shō* (10 percent of *to*), and *gō* (10 percent of *shō*). Peasants whose land was unsuitable for rice cultivation either had to buy rice with which to pay their taxes or petition to be allowed to pay taxes in cash. They were also subjected to a variety of miscellaneous taxes *(komononari)*, extraordinary levies on demand *(goyōkin)*, and the corvée. In return, they enjoyed the bounty of the "great peace" imposed by the Tokugawa, and they might receive loans in aid *(ō-sukui)* were their situation truly desperate.

Peasants in Tokugawa Japan were undoubtedly exploited by the state, but the degree of exploitation is often debated. The rulers believed that they extracted every bit of surplus for the peasants' own good, with tax rates of 40 to 60 percent and sometimes higher. (Wealth left in the villages would corrupt the peasants' moral fiber, and they would become indolent.) Herbert Bix has concluded that this was indeed how much tax was collected, an oppressive burden.[12] Some Japanese historians assume that peasants on land held directly by the bakufu paid out less than 30 percent of what they actually harvested.[13] Philip Brown has demonstrated that the tax rates were derived from wildly inaccurate land surveys.[14] William Kelly's detailed comparison of production versus the tax base in Shōnai in 1800 and 1820 suggests a tax rate of about 22 percent. Ancillary taxes were heavy, but the peasants also had access to nonagricultural and nontaxable handicraft income.[15] Tax rates were probably higher early in the Tokugawa period, before peasant production increased beyond the ability of rulers to tax it. Nevertheless, the situation compares favorably with early modern Germany, where approximately 30 percent of what the peasants produced was taken from them in kind by the political authorities and church tithes.[16] It is doubtful these figures would have consoled a peasant forced to mortgage his land after a poor harvest.

Whatever the surplus left to the peasants, it was not, of course, distributed equally. As in Burgundy, collective agriculture, collective tax responsibility, and village assemblies did not ensure the redistribution of wealth or the leveling of inequalities, nor did they

guarantee subsistence.[17] In a largely agrarian economy, survival
was precarious for those whose holdings were too small to generate
a surplus during years of plenty. Many village headmen either paid
no taxes or had their tax burden lightened to compensate for the
weight of their official responsibilities, but they expected the ordinary peasants to pay everything they were supposed to, and
sometimes more. In the seventeenth century, peasant landholders
who worked large plots with crews of hereditary dependents kept a
disproportionate share of the harvest for the main household. Even
after tenants started renting land in the eighteenth century, landlords had a much better sense of harvested yields than did samurai
in the castle towns, and they made sure that they got their 50 percent. Those with extra lent to those without. Despite governmental
fiats to prohibit the alienation of land, some peasants found themselves forced to relinquish their holdings to their creditors.

The Tokugawa period saw the transformation from subsistence
to commercial agriculture and from a system that relied primarily
on barter to one that emphasized monetary exchanges. The process
was a long one left incomplete when the shōgun resigned his office
in 1868, and it began in different areas of the country at different
times. It was just taking hold in Tsuyama when the peasants there
rose in protest against the monetarization of the rice trade through
the use of rice certificates. Even in the 1760s, peasants who lived far
from the post stations still worked as porters rather than hiring substitutes. But by the time peasants closer to Edo protested a change in
the transportation system in 1804, it had become customary for
them to evade at least some of their obligation for moving baggage
by paying others to do it. In 1866 Tsuyama, the circulation of money was taken for granted.

One unanticipated effect of the status system was that urban
merchants in Japan did not control the spread of commercial opportunities. Forbidden to communicate with the peasantry except at
carefully regulated markets, they dealt with the producers through
middlemen who took advantage of their position to develop their
own enterprises. By the late eighteenth century, rural handicrafts
and trade had begun to blur the distinction between the worthy
peasant and the ignoble businessman or the less ignoble craftsman.
Other peasants became wealthy by exploiting their tenants and
developing new agricultural techniques. With few exceptions,
peasants who made their fortunes this way tended to keep both

their residences and their capital in the village.[18] Economic development in early modern Japan thus took a different road from that of the West, where the entrepreneurs and their money tended to concentrate in the cities.[19]

Commercial agriculture and the circulation of money did not obviate insecurity. Peasants continued to rely on what they grew for what they ate, but they also began to produce goods to sell. Instead of sleeping or simply engaging in idle chatter, they used their evenings and the winter months to work on handicrafts. Combs or sandals could be made by tenant farmers, but they might still be endebted to the landlord or a money lender for the wherewithal to buy raw materials. By the end of the Tokugawa period, new forms of economic subordination were sometimes replacing, sometimes supplementing, the earlier forms of personal subordination found in peasant villages. When peasants felt that they were being exploited unjustly, they might attack in riots aimed at the destruction of ill-gotten gains.

The heterogeneity of the Japanese village community made economic change possible. As in Burgundy, communal property relations did not prevent the peasants from preferring market production to subsistence. In fact, wealthy peasants actually exploited collective rights so that they could produce commerical goods more readily.[20] They were the ones with the wherewithal to experiment with multiple crops, new varieties of seeds and plants like the sweet potato and corn, and commercial crops like the mulberry leaves fed to silk worms. They were the first to invest in commercial fertilizers, dried sardines being the most popular. They developed or encouraged new technology to thresh and winnow grain. They studied and wrote detailed handbooks designed to promote more effective agricultural practices across Japan. Despite their achievements, however, their position in the status system forced them to bow and scrape to the samurai, men they were increasingly less likely to see as their betters. Faced with the lessening effectiveness of the political elite and the tensions engendered by new forms of exploitation, some of them turned to the study of peasant life, religion, and local history.

The Structure of Peasant Life

Understanding peasant society does not end with defining the forms of exploitation practiced by the state and the economy. Peasants worked hard, but their work was inherent in the practice of peasant life. In some parts of Japan, they shoveled away the snow each spring to let the sun warm the soil. They carefully mixed a soup of fertilizer (often including night soil), dirt, and water for the rice seedling beds, plowed and irrigated the fields, transplanted the rice, hoed and weeded it, spread oil to control insects, and watched the skies, praying for just the right amount of rain during the growing season and clear skies for the harvest. The ripe grain had to be cut, threshed, winnowed, and dried, then inspected for quality, packed into straw bales weighing sixty pounds or more, and carried perhaps to a storehouse but more likely to a landlord or tax collector at the end of the year. Two months later, the cycle started again. Punctuating the daily round of agricultural tasks were seasonal rituals and festivals.

Japanese peasants drew on an eclectic religious tradition. Each village was attached to a Buddhist temple, where it registered births and performed burials. Different sects predominated in different regions; for example, Pure Land Buddhism, which taught faith in the saving power of the Amida Bodhisattva, spread along the Japan Sea, and Zen Buddhism was common in the mountains of central Japan. Regardless of the sect, however, Buddhist priests were subjected to two kinds of control. They were licensed by the headquarters of their sect, and they had to report any change of residence to the ruling authorities. Peasants also assumed that the priests' special status gave them a privileged access to the ruling authorities to be used for the welfare of their parishioners. In the village, the priest was expected to provide memorial services for ancestors. Sutras had to be read to propitiate unquiet spirits, to ward off sickness, and to prevent disasters. The peasants respected these religious and even magical practices. Some histories of peasant uprisings suggest that the peasants could be anticlerical, but their criticisms of the clergy did not imply an opposition to the Buddhist orthodoxy.[21]

Buddhist temples coexisted with Shintō shrines. Each village contained at least one shrine for its local tutelary deity. Here the villagers prayed for good harvests and entertained the gods and themselves with festivals (which became increasingly elaborate by the early nineteenth century). The prevalence of sumō wrestling, the puppet theater, and Kabuki suggests that what the rulers feared had indeed happened: the surplus of wealth left in the countryside was encouraging the spread of leisure-time pursuits. Peasants also used the shrine precincts and other sacred places on the margins of human habitation for village assemblies. Meeting in the presence of the gods was believed essential if human beings were to reconcile their differences and reach a consensus because it seemed to take a miracle for unanimity to be reached. It was claimed that this sign of a divine presence made the decision legitimate, whether it was to contribute village funds for rebuilding the Grand Shrine at Ise or to protest a change in taxation policy.[22]

In some ways Buddhism and Shintō were so intermingled that to worship in one mode was to include elements of the other. According to Japanese Buddhist teachings, the Japanese deities or *kami* were considered the avatars of particular Buddhas or bodhisattvas who were their original substances. Shintō priests reversed the relationship, claiming that the *kami* preceded their Buddhist avatars. Both *kami* and Buddhas were ranked, conforming to the vertical hierarchies in human society. At the top was the *gongen* or *dai-gongen*, the title by which Ieyasu, the founder of the Tokugawa state, was known after his death. *Dai-gongen* was the Buddhist equivalent to *dai-myōjin* or Great August Deity in the Shintō pantheon. In both cases the titles were supposed to be limited to those important spirits who protected the entire country or the world or who in life had done great deeds. To call a peasant a *myōjin* after death was as incongruous as calling him a general *(taishō)* in life, but in histories of uprisings, peasants did both, manipulating the status hierarchies to bestow honor on themselves.

Buddhist, Shintō, and folk beliefs did not constitute distinct layers or separate compartments in the Tokugawa mind.[23] The *yamabushi*, mountain priests or shamans, practiced ritual ascetic and occult exercises in the mountains to acquire power over spirits. They guided the pious in their pilgrimages to holy places, took young men into the mountains for initiation ceremonies, and traveled to the other world to communicate with the beings there. Dressed in costumes that marked them as "the other," they were strangers who visited villages in much the same way as the gods. The peasants feared and respected the shamans and other itinerant ascetics whose lives differed so greatly from their own sedentary existence. During riots, however, they borrowed the accoutrements of "the other" to sanctify their attacks. Blasts from conch shell trumpets heralded extraordinary events. In some records from the post station riot of 1764, it was reported that the peasants carried the *bonten* of the *yamabushi,* a long pole topped with a mane of white paper streamers used to drive away insects, illness, and evil.

The religious practices described above were primarily group activities performed from time immemorial at the village level. Prayers to the tutelary deity for a good harvest and sutras read at the local temple to ward off insects aided the community as a whole. Festivals may have become more elaborate in the early nineteenth century, but the essential kernal of age-old beliefs remained. The dominant Buddhist concerns of earlier ages—the evanescence of existence, its travails and miseries, and the theory of karma—continued to haunt early modern peasants, but the peasants also placed new emphasis on this-worldly benefits. Instead of listening to Buddhist priests expound on the mysteries of the universe hidden deep in the sutras, peasants preferred simple formulas with magical efficacy. Like French peasants before 1750, they believed that "the universe was neither totally good nor totally bad, but entirely peopled with ambivalent forces which could be oriented, captured, or warded off by magic."[24] Pollution and crimes could be overcome through rites of purification and the saving power of the gods. This consciousness affirmed the world as it is and celebrated its growth and development.[25] Many peasants assumed that affairs in the invisible world were in some way analogous to those in the visible world, or at least that the spirits over there were vitally interested in what human beings did. Even the belief in the power of angry or jealous spirits (for example, the revenge of Sakura Sōgorō) was harnessed to explain political events in the here and now.

The new emphasis on worldly benefits accompanied the spread of popular cults centered on deities providing services to individuals and their families. These cults depended for their membership not on the prior existence of community ties, but on the creation of confraternities *(kō)*. The eminent scholar of popular religion, Miyata Noboru, has argued that for individuals to offer prayers that benefited themselves was an urban phenomenon arising out of the insecurities and alienation of city life.[26] Nevertheless, the confraternities spread rapidly in the countryside as well, where they provided a new mechanism for social networks. The early nineteenth century saw them in bewildering proliferation. Some, like the Fuji-kō, taught their believers the fundamentals of diligence, frugality, and fortitude; others collected money for group pilgrimages. Others had evolved into revolving credit associations, while others held all-night vigils to prevent the worms that inhabit the body from reporting its misdeeds to the king of heaven. Among the Shintō-Buddhist deities around whom the cults were centered were Jizō, the guardian for dead children, Daikoku, one of the gods of wealth, and Inari, the goddess of rice. Foxes, the messengers of Inari, played a role in histories of the post station riot of 1804. Just as the Inari cult invaded the cities, confraternities dedicated to Daikoku attracted peasants who sought success in business. The way this practice appears in the history of the post station riot of 1764, however, suggests that at least some peasants saw the harm done to the community by the self-centered pursuit of wealth.

Histories of Peasant Uprisings: The Context

No matter how disruptive of local society, the destruction of property hardly rendered peasant uprisings sufficiently notable to be represented in local literature. For centuries before their deeds began to be encapsulated in narratives, peasants had protested their relations with the ruling authorities. What was needed was the justification to validate their experiences and pasts on their own terms and to conceptualize peasants as actors. Harry Harootunian has argued that some members of rural society found this justification in nativist thought—the belief in a distinct, sacred, and uniquely Japanese identity, which brought to the fore people and interests heretofore marginalized in political discourse.[27] Whereas eighteenth-century nativists sought to regain Japan's idealized past and "engaged in a quest for meaning, wholeness, and solace in what they perceived to be disordered times,"[28] their nineteenth-century counterparts looked to their immediate environment to explain what it meant to be Japanese and to find a solution for their problems. This nativist effort to plot a cosmic narrative made no mention of rebellions, yet, like the histories of peasant uprisings, it centered the lives of peasants and encouraged agricultural productivity. What both discourses shared was not simply a valorization of daily life, but, ironically, a list of grievances that needed correction. In

14

both cases this resulted in social and political criticism of the established arrangement of authority and the principles legitimating it.[29] By the last five years of Tokugawa rule, it was becoming increasingly apparent that the verities of the past would no longer hold. Confronted with the breakdown of political controls, the men who wrote or copied "A Thousand Spears at Kitsunezuka" or "A Tale of a Dream from the Fox Woman Plain" looked back to a time when unrest ended with the reestablishment of order. They openly expressed their contempt for ruling-class officials, but whatever doubts they felt about the stability of the political regime were buried under a need for strong local government run by men like themselves. This worldview focusing attention on peasants can thus be identified in a much broader segment of the population than that which explicitly embraced nativism.

By the early nineteenth century, the rural elite could employ a wide variety of intellectual offerings to construct its worldview. Confucian scholars in the cities attracted disciples who visited them rarely but who corresponded avidly. Eclectic thinkers such as Ninomiya Sontoku (1787–1856) and Ōhara Yūgaku (1797–1858) roamed the countryside, accepting room and board from village officials in return for instruction in conventional morality and the techniques of reviving depopulated villages. Suzuki Bokushi (1770–1842), a rich peasant-entrepreneur from the mountains high along the Japan Sea, sought intellectual stimulation and training in painting and poetry from his neighbors, traveling professionals, and teachers in Edo and Osaka. After forty years of fruitless effort, in 1837 he managed to publish an ethnographic survey of peasant life and customs in the snow country.[30] He carefully avoided forbidden topics like taxation policies and social protest, but he shared a common concern for local affairs with rural nativists and the men who wrote histories of peasant uprisings. Like them he put peasant life and the peasant experience at the center of his discourse, but he appropriated his language from many of the intellectual traditions available in the Japan of his day.

As Herbert Bix has pointed out, another context for peasant histories of peasant uprisings is the literary underground of Tokugawa Japan.[31] In contrast to those writings signed by authors, that circulated publicly with permission of the authorities, were others, often written anonymously, that passed clandestinely from one hand to another. Herman Ooms has pointed out that "Mikawa monogatari," a history of how the Tokugawa gained control of Japan, was never allowed to be published.[32] Nevertheless, it and texts based on it did circulate among the samurai and townspeople.[33] A copy must have reached Shinpū Kenchiku-ō, author of "A Record of How the Four Orders of People in Mimasaka Ran Riot," for he quotes it in his prologue. Another author whose works were never published was Andō Shōeki (1703–62), an iconoclastic doctor in northern Japan, whose radical rejection of religion and the state led him to develop his own theory of the universe.[34] Equally sensitive—although their criticism of the polity was never more than implied—were the histories of peasant uprisings. Banning these writings enhanced their value. In a society like that of Tokugawa Japan, where certain texts were proscribed and the memory of past events suppressed, simply to know something kept secret was power.[35]

Not all peasant writings and not all histories were suspect. From the end of the seventeenth century, textbooks on agronomy began to appear in Japan. The first were written by samurai, but by the eighteenth century, literate peasants were making their own contributions to the spread of technological advances. In 1784 a rich peasant from what is now Wakayama prefecture published in Osaka his "Precepts for Farm Families" *(Nōkakun),* which even included instructions on how to raise children.[36] Histories like that of the Tokugawa house *(Tokugawa jikki)* were published because rather than "name power [they] constructed events as the natural victory of the virtuous over evil."[37] Peasant writings in themselves or history in general was censored or forced underground only when it exposed, however subtly, the contingent nature of political authority.

Peasant histories of peasant uprisings tell the tale of underground heroes, men whom the ruling authorities tried to erase from popular memory. Like the monuments to peasant martyrs that had to be erected in secret, these histories constitute ambiguous portrayals of men who disrupted the social order. It sometimes happened that after an uprising, its leaders would be forgotten until a natural disaster recalled them to mind. Then, fearing that an angry spirit was at work, peasants would erect a memorial or a shrine to placate the *onryō.* In such cases, it is hard to argue that peasants admired without qualification the sacrifices made for them. On the other hand, even if Sōgorō came to be seen more as a protective deity than as a rebel, he must be included in the pantheon of heroes whose representations remained problematical—men like Taira no Masakado (?–940), who rebelled against the emperor; Yoshitsune (1159–89), the luckless brother of the first shōgun, Minamoto no Yoritomo (1147–99); Kusunoki Masashige (1294–1336), idolized by imperial loyalists; Yui Shōsetsu (1605–51), who led masterless warriors against the Tokugawa bakufu; and Amakusa Shirō (1621–38), the symbol of peasant resistance in the Shimabara Christian rebellion of 1637.[38] Despite its attempts to substitute its own ideology for history, the ruling class in Tokugawa Japan was never able to eradicate the memory of dissent. Perhaps it is because they spoke against this silence that underground heroes were so compelling.

Despite the pressure of censorship, the underground histories of peasant uprisings did not remain completely unknown. Within a year after the Shimabara rebellion, the court noble Karasumaru Mitsuhiro (1579–1638) had written the first of a number of books about this event, all of them cast in the guise of the war tale, with an emphasis on battles and military strategy.[39] Songs about Sakura Sōgorō spread as far south as Kyushu. One copy of "A Tale of a Dream from the Fox Woman Plain" circulated so widely that its owner worried about getting it back. Even "A Record of How the Four Orders of People in Mimasaka Ran Riot" contains indications that it was meant to be performed orally, probably before an audience. In a society with only a few literate members, texts were often read aloud. Suzuki Bokushi recalled fondly how he had read war tales to his mother, including the entire 360 sections of the *Shinsho taiheiki,* a tale of treachery and revenge.[40] The all-night vigils described in "A Thousand Spears at Kitsunezuka" provided additional opportunities to hear stories both oral and written. Whether it remained within the family or was extended to include a group of neighbors, the audience was clearly diverse, learning from a wide variety of texts, and involving a multiplicity of interests—male and female, rich and poor.

Histories of Peasant Uprisings: The Genre

The audiences and the authors of the histories of peasant uprisings utilized specific narrative structures to bring verisimilitude to these accounts of the past. One means of representing the inequalities and animosities generated in the practice of everyday life was the folktale. Folktales are built on social and moral dichotomies—the weak versus the strong, the good versus the bad, the rich versus the poor. The power relationships subsumed in these dichotomies are often overcome and reversed in the course of the telling. Thus the poor but honest man is able to gain great fortune while his greedy neighbor repeats his actions but ends up with nothing. Like legends, folktales mix the miraculous with the natural, the near with the far, and the ordinary with the incomprehensible to depict a world subject in fantasy to the control of human beings. They do not teach people how to function better in their communities. Instead they provide a means to express the frustrations and resentments that seethe beneath the surface of apparent harmony. Unlike the histories of peasant uprisings, they have no overt political dimension and are seldom situated in a specific locality; the events they relate could happen anywhere, to anyone, at any time.[41] Nevertheless, folktales and histories of peasant uprisings share similar structures. Both use conventional themes and stylistic devices and make no effort to disguise their conventional quality. In episodes strung together without climax, the rich and exploitative get their comeuppances; the ways men suffer and die are presented in all their unvarnished horror.

Folktales were not the only tools available to peasants to shape their experiences. Again and again the histories of uprisings evoke the literary ancestor in the Japanese tradition which informs all subsequent stories of strife—*The Tale of the Heike*. This work is a set of oral narratives first composed early in the thirteenth century about the rise and fall of Taira no Kiyomori (1118–81) and his clan. It and the other war tales *(gunki monogatari)* are derived, perhaps, from the *shinobi-koto*, a kind of eulogy offered to potentially evil spirits, in this case fallen warriors, as a means of placating them.[42] These war tales are central to the Japanese "great" tradition. Common currency among the literate and leisured in Japan's ruling-class circles, they told the deeds of men and women far removed from the world of the peasants. But was it so extraordinary that peasants knew these stories? As in preindustrial Europe, the relationship between oral and written culture was one of circularity: reciprocal influences traveled from low to high as well as from high to low.[43] Margaret Spufford has pointed out in another context that "right through to the nineteenth century, the Carolingian epic of noble dealings . . .

demonstrating . . . military virtues in splendid hunting-parties and jousts dominated the historical reading of the poor in France."[44]

This genre of war tales, to which the histories of peasant uprisings are most closely related, comes under the category of "historical tales" *(rekishi monogatari)* that describe aristocratic society, "material that leans toward the historicoliterary rather than the more strictly literary spectrum."[45] According to Earl Miner, the function of these tales is to name and use historical personages. The tales tell us "something of the nature of actual people" by emphasizing actions that entailed a series of consequences involving human relationships. The doings of these historical individuals, whether real like Minamoto Yoshitsune (1159–89) or fictional like Kuribayashi Yoshinaga, have an affective import that is enhanced because they can be attributed to figures who actually existed.[46] Through these tales we are left to understand what real people do and "how the same events might move us," what Aristotle called a "catharsis of pity."[47] By teaching about people, the histories of peasant uprisings adapt an inherited theme to their audience "so that the specificity of time and place shows through the universality of the topos."[48]

The evocation of war tales in the histories of peasant uprisings provides a clue to the nexus between the little tradition and the great tradition, an issue I deal with throughout my analysis of these texts. For the men who wrote these histories, the construction of a narrative discourse forced them to rely on previous models. Rather than assume that the peasants were passively influenced by the literature of the warriors, however, I argue that they appropriated motifs wrenched out of context from the classical tradition to create a new kind of hero. Here, as in the larger Japanese literary world, producers borrowed liberally and literally from other texts; indeed, allusive variation was a highly prized art. As Akiko Hirota has pointed out, the goal was the perfection of the producer's own aims and expression, not plagiarism.[49]

The histories of peasant uprisings are linked intertextually to the war tales because no text can ever be completely free of those that precede and surround it, but at the same time, these histories rewrote scenes from the war tales in terms of peasant perspectives and peasant concerns. It is not enough to say that the popular culture embedded in these texts is antagonistic to ruling-class values, contradicts ruling-class ideology, and seeks to undermine it, because the relationship between the two is much more complex than that of any antithetical polarity.[50] Bits and pieces of battle sets were rearranged to make a new meaning out of the situation and to provide a new significance for the readers. They provided tools to think with that the authors used in seeking to grasp the reality of riots. By translating the war tales into peasant discourse, the texts made an implicit critique of the premises of the classics produced for an aristocratic, leisured class. The great tradition reserves subjectivity to the rulers; histories of peasant uprisings bestow it on the peasants.

The range of selections made by peasants from what they were offered by elite and urban traditions was as diverse as rural society itself. The author of "A Thousand Spears at Kitsunezuka" could quote (albeit inaccurately) the poetry of Sugawara no Michizane (845–903). The author of "A Record of the Watanabe Doheiji Riot" relied entirely on the most popular motifs found in war tales to describe scenes of destruction and tied them together in a plot structurally similar to folk tales. "A Clamor of Ducks" *(Kamo no sawadachi)* summoned the night attack in "A Treasury of Loyal Retainers *(Chūshingura)*, the Tokugawa theatrical equivalent of medieval war tales, to its depiction of the 1836 Mikawa riot.[51] It ranked the ringleaders according to sumō wrestling terminology. Another list, "The Sumō Rankings of Conspicuous Villains" *(Kanzoku midate sumō bansuke-hyō)*, circulated among village headmen following the Tsuruda riot of 1868–70 in Mimasaka province.[52] A refusal to accept the dominant literary forms wholesale was balanced by an inability to reject them out of hand. Like the elaboration of folk songs in the eighteenth century and folk dances in the nineteenth, the histories indicate both an attraction and an opposition to the arts of the urban elites. Writing these histories was not simply an intellectual exercise to fit local happenings into the literary mold of the times, but an articulation of a worldview that deliberately centered peasant life as the object of concern.

Selecting Texts

Scattered throughout the vast documentary record of peasant uprisings during the Tokugawa period are narratives that represent themselves as a complete explanation for what had happened. The eminent social historian Aoki Michio believes they were written for almost all the large peasant uprisings. Copied repeatedly and handed down from one generation to the next, the narratives occasionally turn up in the surveys made of private collections.[53] For example, some years ago I visited a village high in the mountains of Nagano prefecture where a team of college students was cataloging farm records. In the papers of two different families they found versions of the Sakura Sōgorō story dating from the 1860s.

Given the wide range of histories of peasant uprisings, I developed the following criteria to help me select the five histories I present in this volume. One criterion was length: some histories about protest would fill a book. "A Tea Canister in the Rain" *(Uchū no kanzu),* which relates how the townspeople of Fushimi liberated themselves from the city magistrate in 1782, is a beautifully crafted tale deeply embedded in the elite literary tradition, but it and the other histories published in "Historical Materials for the Lives of Japanese Commoners" *(Nihon shomin seikatsu shiryō shūsei)* are too long to fit in an anthology. Even "A Tale Told through the Night at the Shrine to Jizō" *(Jizōdō tsuya monogatari)* about Sakura Sōgorō would require at least 150 pages in a complete English version. The availability of a complete, unabridged version constituted another consideration. In the modern period, some editors have deliberately and explicitly omitted what they considered to be wild exaggerations, falsifications of facts, and irrelevant material, precisely the kinds of fictive elements I find most fascinating.[54]

My criteria for selection emphasize variety of motifs rather than political considerations. All of the texts I have translated originate either in Tsuyama in western Japan or the Kanto hinterland to Edo, and the ruling authorities were either allies of the bakufu or the bakufu itself. Some impressive insurrections have been left out, the Bushū outburst of 1866 among the most notable.[55] Political scientists may be uncomfortable with the way I have ignored questions of geographical spread and the differences between domanial relations with the bakufu. For my purposes, however, these distinctions are less important than issues of textual production and content. I readily admit that I have made no effort at scientific sampling. Like Natalie Zemon Davis in her study of pardon tales, I prefer to encompass diverse elements, no matter how rare.[56]

Given the plethora of stories and the paucity of conventions, I thus decided to exclude a number of tales which repeat similar motifs. Like the histories translated in chapters 2 and 3, "A Record of the Watanabe Doheiji Riot" about an attack on sake brewers in 1787 and "A Clamor of Ducks" about the 1836 Mikawa riot represent the destruction of property as the clash of battle. War tales are evoked in the titles of *Hoei taiheiki* (Hoei period: 1704–10), which depicts the 1709 conflict in the Mito domain,[57] and "The Record of the Great Pacification of the Peoples' Disturbances in Inaba and Hōki" *(Inbaku minran taiheiki)*, which takes up a peasant uprising in the Tottori domain in 1739. Like other texts, the latter exists in multiple manuscript versions. The author's pen name, Totchō-dō, means "one who listens to talk," and he explains his choice by stating that every night he wrote down conversations he had heard. He is critical of his sources, quick to inject a note of personal comment in a vein similar to that of the author of the Sōgorō story, who disbelieved part of his own tale. Like "A Record of How the Four Orders of People in Mimasaka Ran Riot" (chap. 2), most of the text was written soon after the event, in the spring of 1740.[58] Neither *Hoei taiheiki* nor "The Record of the Great Pacification of the Peoples' Disturbances in Inaba and Hōki" describes the peasants as persons outside of the social acts defining their function in the riot. Both texts have enticing titles, but I decided against including either in order to encompass as broad a chronological sweep as possible.

In order to examine how peasants constructed their collective past, I have avoided accounts written by individuals who participated in the events they described. Imprisoned in 1822 for his role in a riot near Maebashi, Hayashi Hachiemon wrote a long testament ruminating on his experiences, entitled "Precepts for an Encouragement of Farming" *(Kannō kyōkun roku)*, but there is no indication that he ever expected anyone outside of his family to see it.[59] After the Shibusome uprising of 1856 near Okayama, two leaders wrote reports of their prison experiences.[60] One man who escaped punishment for his role in the 1863 riot in the Yashiro district of Yanezawa, Hoshi Ukichi, compiled a long manuscript recounting the events, which he carefully documented with petitions and government papers. He also included a copy of the petition attributed to Sakura Sōgorō.[61] Perhaps the most famous prison writer was Miura Meisuke (1820–64), who led the 1853 uprising in the Nanbu domain. He, too, possessed enough literacy to explain and justify his actions.[62] These documents would repay a careful analysis of how uprising leaders justified themselves, but that is not the intent of this study.

All histories of peasant uprisings share certain structural similarities. Villains are created to personify the issues, then either individual heroes act to save the peasants or crowds sweep across the domain, attacking other commoners and challenging the officials. The explanations for protest are always parsimonious and in themselves uninteresting. The texts chosen for the anthology collectively cover the major constituents of their genre and also include statements on religion, folklore, money, and women that in my judgment provide perspectives on the totality of the peasants' worldviews and suggest ways that social concerns changed over time and varied according to class. Rather than repeat too many histories that draw on the dominant motifs found in war tales, I have included texts with rarer elements as well. The histories of the Ushiku post station riot in 1804 are the only ones to my knowledge that incorporate folktales; the only text in which women assume the roles of progatonists is "A Tale Told in a Dream of a Eulogy to Filial Piety."

My choice of "A Tale Told in a Dream of a Eulogy to Filial Piety" might be seen as arbitrary. The selection is admittedly informed by present-day concerns, but I argue that the text can be read as a "break text"—"a narrative that pushes the conventions of its genre to the limit and in the process affords the reader a perspective . . . across the genre's historical development."[63] The histories of peasant uprisings which had replaced the warriors and aristocrats with peasants at center stage now highlight another seemingly passive and indeed often absent segment of the population—women. In so doing this history allows room on the margin for a new voice and a new set of issues within the parameters of the conventional morality of the Tokugawa period, and it incorporates a still more unlikely hero.

The Author and the Text

Like many war tales, most histories of peasant uprisings were written anonymously, and there is no such thing as an original text. Only one version out of almost one hundred for *The Tale of the Heike* can be attributed to an itinerant storyteller named Kakuichi. The authors of the earliest of the war tales, the *Shōmonki* or the story of Masakado's rebellion, are similarly unknown.[64] Judging from the frequency with which it was cited, the *Taiheiki* (Chronicle of Great Pacification) was perhaps the war tale most popular among the peoples of the Tokugawa period. It too passed through many hands before reaching its present form late in the fourteenth century.[65] A single event, of course, could give rise to more than one history. Just as the "Record of the Rise and Fall of the Minamoto and Taira" *(Gempei seisuiki)* contains a longer account of the incidents that fill *The Tale of the Heike,* so too do "The Child from Abeno's Questions" *Abenodō jimon)* and "A True Account of Endō from Western Bizen" *(Seibi Endō jikki)* provide variant perspectives on the 1786 peasant uprising in Fukuyama. Herbert Bix believes that the author of the former text was a Confucian scholar, possibly a bureaucrat, who larded his narrative with literary allusions and assumptions regarding the social order which were more representative of the worldview of rulers than of peasants.[66] The number of texts with indefinite attributions makes determining their author's identity difficult.

Many if not most histories of peasant uprisings were written by members of the ruling class who sought to understand the meaning of disorder by crafting a narrative of what had happened. The earliest versions of the Sakura Sōgorō story were written by samurai. Other histories appropriated the form of the war tale while bestowing honor on the samurai who suppressed unrest. The "Record of the Kurume Uprising," for example, emphasized the reform of the government from within and the warrior virtue of loyalty. In an episode found in none of the peasant histories I have seen, the ringleader proves his loyalty by committing suicide.[67]

Warrior histories of peasant uprisings encompass a much broader range of vision than those written by peasants. "A Record of the Beggars' Riot in Mimasaka" *(Sashū hinin sōdōki)* about the 1866 Tsuyama riot begins with Commodore Perry's visit to Japan in 1853, continues with the factional disputes within the bakufu, the bakufu expeditions against Chōshū, and the death of the shōgun. In contrast, "A Tale Told in a Dream of a Eulogy to Filial Piety" focuses unremittingly on events within Tsuyama. Even in texts sympathetic to the peasants' grievances, rioters are more likely to be branded as evil than they are in peasant texts, where their portrayal is much more ambiguous. Another difference between warrior and peasant histories lies in the roles assigned to women. For the most part, women in the former, if they appear at all, are depicted as seductresses, whereas in the latter they appear almost invariably and in guises that allow them virtue. The relations between peasant husband and peasant wife, analyzed in the conclusion to this book, find no place in samurai histories.

Just as histories written by peasants expose the various strata among the peasantry and exhibit their different attitudes, so too do histories written by the samurai expose the factions within the ruling class.[68] "The Ueda Broken Plaid" *(Ueda jimakuzure gōshi),* for example, which begins with a history of the domanial rulers, admitted that the peasants were justified in their anger.[69] Both elite and popular cultures borrow from each other, evoke each other, carry on a dialogue with each other, and thus relate in a dialectical manner. When the ruling class includes the interests and experiences of subordinate classes within its ideology, however, some experiences are transformed, while others (here I would point specifically to the practices of everyday life) are "excluded, suppressed, and socially devalued."[70] In the Tokugawa political order, peasants were viewed as passive and marginalized as objects of concern. In their own histories, they subverted this order by representing themselves differently from the way they were represented by the authorities.[71] Their concerns, their assumptions, their beliefs, and their values are what give meaning to these texts.

In selecting texts for this anthology, I have avoided those whose authors were obviously members of the ruling elite. For this reason I rejected two histories written by a samurai and a deputy district headman about the 1866 riot in Tsuyama. Both histories also neglected to include women and family life. The *Tenpō taiheiki* (Tenpō period: 1830–43), about an uprising in 1833 in Obama, was discarded despite its attractive title because it was found in the library of the Sakai family, lords of the Wakasa domain.[72] "A Tale Told through the Night at Nayadera" *(Nayadera tsūya monogatari),* about an uprising in 1712, has been lauded by Hayashi Motoi as one of the earliest examples of the peasant histories of peasant uprisings, but it was written or at least copied by a warrior in Daishōji, a branch of the Kaga domain, and circulated as much among the ruling class as among the peasants. One version of this text, subtitled *Kanō taiheiki* (Kanō is a place-name), ends with the admonition, "It is forbidden to show this secret writing to others."[73] This version begins with a

history of the Naya temple to explain how the place-name originated. Like "A Tale of a Dream from the Fox Woman Plain," the text
ends with a genealogy of the ruling family. Whether written by the
samurai or the local intellectuals, these texts share a similar structure; they probably circulated in that gray area where the line
between the subordinate and the ruling classes was indistinguishable.

Some authors were neither warriors nor peasants. The Shintō
priest Watanabe Masaka (1776–1840), who wrote "A Clamor of
Ducks" about the 1836 Mikawa riot, appropriated much of his material from another text probably written by a traveling play-
wright.[74] Shinpū Kenchiku-ō, author of "A Record of How the Four
Orders of People in Mimasaka Ran Riot," was a local intellectual,
possibly of *rōnin* extraction. Like many other histories, his text drew
on Buddhist imagery to express human suffering. The intertextual
context was limited to the Japanese classics, texts that circulated secretly among the samurai, and the early history of the Tokugawa
period. By the nineteenth century, the variety of men capable of
writing histories had grown much greater as literacy spread
throughout the village official class. For those who accept the
stereotype of the unlettered, silently suffering peasant, however, it is
difficult to imagine that peasants wrote history.

Some historians, challenging the assumption that peasants
could not have authored histories of peasant uprisings, have tried to
define to what extent peasants were literate and how much literacy
these texts required. Whether it was because Tokugawa rulers recognized the coercive power of the word or because they simply
wanted to circumscribe the warriors' range of contacts, directives to
the peasantry were transmitted not orally but in writing.[75] In the
1830s, there were over sixty-three thousand villages in Japan, each
with peasant officials responsible for reading the dictates of the
rulers and for paying taxes calculated on written land registers.
Mastery of communication with the dominant class came to distinguish the rural elite from the rural masses. Even ordinary
peasants might receive some education to help them do their accounts or participate in lawsuits. After the middle of the seventeenth century, the bakufu allowed peasant complaints against
unjust officials if the peasants followed proper procedures, but it expected written proof to back up the allegations. For both political
and economic reasons, people who could find someone to teach

them—Buddhist and Shintō priests, family elders, or retired village officials—sought to learn at least the rudiments of writing. Fukaya Katsumi has estimated that by the end of the Tokugawa period, the head of the average peasant household was probably literate.[76]

The increase in rural literacy was in part stimulated by a florescence of literary activity during the Bunka-Bunsei period (1804–29), when the arts escaped from the elite connoisseurs *(tsū)* of Edo to fall into the hands of country bumpkins *(yabo)*, artisans who created beauty out of the materials of their own lives and originated what are known today as Japan's traditional folk arts *(mingei)*.[77] Many factors were at work. First, between 1788 and 1793, the ruling authorities issued four decrees for the repatriation of Edo vagrants to their home provinces, and these people returned with a taste for urban attractions.[78] Next, domanial policies to encourage the development of products marketable in other areas included inviting urban artisans to the castle towns (from whence their skills diffused into the surrounding villages). In addition, so many writers and artists competed for a living in Edo and Osaka that they were forced to peddle their wares and talents in outlying areas as well. There they met eager audiences. By the 1830s, the spread of urban luxuries had become so obvious that laws designed to prevent this spread were making it difficult for peasants to satisfy their desire for novelty.

Degrees of literacy in rural areas varied enormously. Village headmen might send their sons to private academies in the castle towns for advanced study in the Chinese and Japanese classics; tenant farmers were fortunate to learn how to write their names and do numbers. One treatise written by a village official in the early nineteenth century urged peasants to learn "some poetry, linked verse, and song. Though common people in trade and agriculture can get along without such knowledge, it will help a little in keeping them from gambling."[79] Standard texts in village schools were usually the Chinese classics—the "Great Learning" and the "Classic on Filial Piety"—or texts derived from these using Japanese examples. Virtuous sons and daughters abound in histories of peasant uprisings, suggesting that the lessons learned in these texts were to be applied in the peasants' everyday lives. But whereas "A Thousand Spears at Kitsunezuka" includes allusions to Japanese literature that only an erudite peasant could have known, the vocabulary, tissue of references, and narrowness of vision in "The Sakura

Sōgorō Story" suggest a much lower level of achievement. Even more restricted in its field of vision is "The Military Chronicle of a Quarrel" *(Deiri gunhōki)*, the fictionalized account of conflict between the headman and peasants of Shimomuroga village, written by one of the peasants.[80] It thus appears that the educational background of the authors of these tales reflects some of the diversity of the rural population itself.

The Study of Histories of Peasant Uprisings

The historian of popular consciousness, Yasumaru Yoshio, fitted histories of peasant uprisings into his overall interpretation of peasant beliefs and attitudes. Peasants took the political arrangements implicated in the existing status order as a given and worked within them to bring about change. Diligent, hardworking, and honest, under ordinary circumstances they branded the destruction of property as a self-evident evil. Once an uprising was over, even the participants could not imagine what the exhilaration experienced during the event was like. Thus narratives were constructed to shape a complex historical event into a coherent and totalizing representation that explained how unarmed but suddenly self-confident men could oppose warriors. Scenes of crowd action were not necessarily untrue, but to capture the totality of the event, it was necessary to borrow the power of fiction.

Yasumaru argued that peasants never developed a revolutionary ideology. Legends created long after the event coalesced around emblematic figures such as Sakura Sōgorō. In lauding the heroic efforts of an individual, the potential for massive destruction was effectively denied. Village headmen who feared violence more than injustice were unlikely to have depicted the activities of the insurrectionary crowd. Only a liberated imagination inconceivable to the peasants could grasp a new historical possibility—a reversal of the social order. Thus most writers of histories of peasant uprisings were probably local intellectuals (doctors, priests, and scholars) so far removed from the status order that they could feel astonishment. Their writings represented a consciousness of the crises facing rural society without including the perspective of the rioters. Nevertheless, in deeming destruction the will of the gods and including stories of insurgent leaders who sought vengeance even after their deaths, the authors acquiesced in the sense of righteousness claimed by the crowd.[81] While recognizing the importance of the fictive elements in these histories, Yasumaru defines the range of their authorship too narrowly and leaves little room for different voices to appear within the text.

In his essay "Buried Literary Possibilities" *(Horobita bungakuteki kanōsei),* the historian and social critic Sugiura Minpei claimed that the content of histories of peasant uprisings was warped by government suppression. In 1758, for example, the Osaka city magistrate executed a professional storyteller named Baba Bunkō for having recited a tale about a peasant uprising in Mino. (According to other historians his crime was that of lèse-majesté for having exposed the secrets of a succession dispute in a daimyō family.)[82] Even treatises written by administrators as object lessons could not be published for they vitiated the official denial that uprisings happened. Since stories about uprisings could only circulate secretly in manuscript, they never escaped what Sugiura calls the Kabuki model. The lord is always virtuous, but, misled by syncophants, he dismisses loyal retainers and establishes new exploitative policies. A self-sacrificing individual appeals for a return to the old laws. He succeeds, but brings death on himself. A variation on this theme includes depictions of insurrections in which the crowd becomes bold and insolent, mocking warrior officials come to pacify them or running riot through houses. Without pursuing its implications, Sugiura noted that these vivid descriptions of action are missing from stories about uprisings written by intellectuals in the modern period.[83] By raising the issue of difference, however, he locates these texts in a body of experience foreign to his contemporaries.

The prolific scholar of peasant martyrs, Yokoyama Toshio, on the other hand, emphasizes continuity in the history of the Japanese struggle against oppression. Unlike Yasumaru, he finds in popular consciousness an antiauthoritarian streak that is exposed at times of social disorder and in the histories of peasant uprisings. In his view, these texts must be analyzed critically because, depending on who wrote them and when, they may make protest less meaningful than it actually was. This is especially true of the Sakura Sōgorō story. In the eighteenth century it was promoted by village officials who, when they began to lead large-scale uprisings, claimed peasant martyrs as their ancestors. In the nineteenth century, the descendants of these same officials tried to ignore the legends and play down incidents of violence which threatened their authority. Nevertheless, Yokoyama believes that through these histories, present-day readers can enter into the thoughts of men who expressed the will of the masses.[84] Even today, people in rural Japan remember the deeds of their ancestors, the peasant martyrs, and commemorate them in festivals complete with parades and drums.[85] Yokoyama would like to read in these histories the materials for the formation of a revolutionary class consciousness. As I argue in chapter 6, however, I see in these histories a call for social reform.

American historians of peasant uprisings have paid much less attention to these histories than have their Japanese colleagues. William Kelly provides little critical analysis of his sources. Stephen Vlastos dismisses these texts, saying, "the authors of chronicles of peasant uprisings tended to exaggerate and romanticize peasants' behavior, particularly their bravery and daring." Yet he accepts the pronouncement of Sasaki Junnosuke that "the first record of peasants using *yonaoshi* [world rectification] as a unifying force and source of authority is the uprising that took place in the Kamo region of Mikawa province in 1836,"[86] an assumption based on one of the most deliberately literary histories in the canon, "A Clamor of Ducks" *(Kamo no sawadachi)*.

More sensitive to textual nuances and more tolerant of literary embellishments is Herbert Bix. Given the heavy censorship that prevailed throughout the Tokugawa period, histories of peasant uprisings deliberately mixed fact and fiction, both for moral exhortation and the author's self-protection. Nor is it surprising that the unknown authors drew on theatrical conventions and evoked war tales such as *The Tale of the Heike*. "What better way was there to heighten popular emotions than by magnifying gestures or by pitting bare human passions against the oppressive feudal authorities in a striking tableau?" he asks.[87] True to the spirit of the times and to certain values of the classes they depict, the narratives afforded consolation, pleasure, and instruction to contemporary readers. For posterity they recorded the emotions of the people before and after their defeat.[88] Despite all evidence he musters to the contrary, however, Bix tends to treat the depictions of crowd action inscribed in these narratives as fact rather than as text.

According to Bix, even sympathetic histories of peasant uprisings were limited by the class background of their authors. By emphasizing Tokuemon's samurai birth and extraordinary talents,

the author of "A Record of How the Four Orders of People in Mimasaka Ran Riot" unrealistically transformed him into a hero
incapable of becoming a true class representative of the peasants.
No documents explain the 1761 uprising in Ueda from the view-
point of the people. Narratives that present a holistic account of the
riot support the status quo, suggesting that they were written by village officials, priests, or perhaps low-ranking samurai. Accounts of
the 1866 uprising in Tsuyama were written by a samurai doctor and
possibly by a village official. Insofar as they depict the peasants in
servile submission to virtuous samurai officials, however, the accounts betray the class interests of the peasantry.[89]

These Japanese and American historians have emphasized the
difficulty of assigning a political weight to the histories of peasant
uprisings. In all cases, the focus has been on how these texts depict
relations between the peasants and the authorities to the exclusion
of other considerations. Ignored has been what they have to say
about the family and the community, an issue I address in the conclusion of this book.

My previous work on peasant protest concentrated on textual
analysis. My book on social protest in the 1780s compared histories
of peasant uprisings with the other types of documents generated by
these events. Unlike the realistic and precise chronicles written by
village headmen for their families, the tales deliberately drew on
folkloric conventions to heighten their emotional impact. They
have a quadripartite structure: The prologue provides an essential
point of departure with a platitude, a short essay on good government, or scenes of plenty. Justice and prosperity are disrupted by a
villain who personifies exploitative political policies or the unequal
opportunities afforded by a market economy. The response summons heroes and heroic deeds to punish the villains or sends a
peasant army rampaging across the landscape and attacking the
warriors. Finally closure brings the deaths of the heroes and the restoration of governmental authority, usually in a benevolent guise.
These tales evoke an emotional attachment to an imaginary homogeneous community formed through horizontal bonds in which all
fulfill the responsibilities of their occupations, whereas in real life
villages were riven with tensions. Regardless of whether these tales
rely more on fiction than fact, they bring peasants marginalized in
the official discourse to center stage.[90]

My article entitled "Narratives of Peasant Uprisings in Japan" took a structuralist approach to the study of this genre. Concentrating on the distinction between story and plot, it showed commonalities between war tales, folktales, and local legends that relate the origin of place-names.[91] By applying the theories of the anthropologist Victor Turner and folklorists such as Axel Olrik, I demonstrated how the sequence of events was subordinated to a pattern imposed by the requirements of the narrative form. Flights of fancy enabled the peasants to create heroic actors out of insurgent leaders. Those frustrated by a politically repressive system could escape their limitations by imagining confrontations with the authorities which were unthinkable in real life. The lesson taught by the narratives was that disorder did not change the system. Nevertheless, later protests occasionally recalled earlier ones. For this approach, questions of content were privileged over the issue of authorship. But to dismiss the identity of the writer as irrelevant, as I did, because he was simply an amanuensis for the peasant bearers of oral tradition overlooks the importance of textual intent, its ideological stance, its inherent contradictions, and the relations of domination and subordination between author and audience.

Texts which purport to present a holistic and comprehensive history of peasant uprisings are more diverse and problematic than I first thought. As I have argued above, men from a variety of economic classes and statuses wrote histories of peasant uprisings, and their authorial intent must be seen in interaction with the diverse voices that inform the texts. Those written by village officials, who self-consciously and arbitrarily identified themselves with the peasantry, implicate in one way or another people who exercised domination over their fellows. Only by examining a number of stories written by men from various backgrounds is it possible to glimpse the ways in which "villagers presented the flow of social processes and the nature of social relations to themselves and among themselves."[92] To privilege the author over the text, however, imposes a limit on the ability of readers to make what they will of it.[93] Regardless of who wrote them, the histories have to make sense to those outside the authors' class. Like the communities from which they come, these histories contain unresolved contradictions only half alloyed with classical allusions and metaphors drawn from the war tales. A comparison of how I have read them with the conclusions drawn by Bix and Yasumaru suggests that while we have all recognized their inherent fictions, we have assigned different values to them and identified different structures of meaning.

The diversity of histories of peasant uprisings necessarily frustrates attempts to encompass them with a single explanation. When I first decided to translate these texts into English, I assumed that they could speak for themselves and, by so doing, would explain for any reader anywhere the world of peasants in the Tokugawa period. Some years later I have come to realize that this was merely an assumption based on common sense. The truths told by histories of peasant uprisings are not self-evident, nor do they reflect in any unmediated way the reality of experience for their authors and audience. In the introduction to each translation, I have suggested some of the ways in which it can be read. Some readers may decide to turn to the last chapter to find out what it all means without reading the histories themselves. This I would discourage, for the readings I offer are of necessity partial. I assume that other readers will bring their own perspectives to bear, which will lead them to their own conclusions.

Any translation project is itself fraught with danger. If the text is perceived as an object that should only produce a single invariant reading, any deviation on the part of the translator transgresses against it, but for all texts there are as many ways of translating as there are translators. No two languages are ever sufficiently similar to be considered as representing the same social reality, even when they coexist in the modern world. A translation is not the text translated. As Mark Morris put it, "a reader's effort to contact *Genji monogatari* by way of *The Tale of Genji* represents an always-already-doomed yearning after originary presence."[94] To transform a text written in early modern Japanese into twentieth-century English requires interpreting an alien code into one that makes sense here and now. The most that can be hoped for is an interpretation that represents a reading accessible to this day and age without violating the essence of the text.[95]

Some things are inevitably lost in translation. I have not reproduced the additive rhetoric of the texts, a rhetoric characteristic both of oral culture and of manuscripts never meant to be published. Instead of allowing ideas to pile on each other, in other words, I have made them relational, substituting *while, when, thus,* for *and, and, and.* I have, however, retained some practices important for people living in early modern Japan. Chapter titles even for short sections and the elaborate table of contents for the Sakura Sōgorō story that help make the structure of the narrative explicit for an audience hearing the story have been left as the authors had them. Lists of names and places which bestowed veracity and fixed the text in a specific place and time are included, even though the modern reader soon grows impatient with them. I have not abbreviated, eliminated, or shortened the many episodes included in texts like "A Thousand Spears at Kitsunezuka." Walter J. Ong has pointed out that whereas oral cultures construct stories episodically, written and especially published stories build to a climax.[96] For modern readers accustomed to a strictly linear plot development, its absence in these texts may cause discomfort. I hope so, for out of discomfort arises a consciousness of difference.

O N E

The Sakura Sōgorō Story

N O HISTORY OF PEASANT UPRISINGS IN JAPAN would be complete without Sakura Sōgorō. Sōgorō, or Kiuchi Sōgo as he is sometimes called, is the archetype of the peasant martyr, a man who deliberately sacrificed himself on behalf of his community. Even today most Japanese know the story of how he took pity on peasants driven to the verge of starvation by the cruel and rapacious taxes levied by Hotta Masanobu, villainous lord of the Sakura domain. Sōgorō appealed repeatedly to the officials for mercy in governing the people. When all his efforts failed, however, he dared petition the shōgun, even though he knew he would lose his life for this impropriety. By accepting death in remonstrating to his ruler, he forced Masanobu to remit the harsh taxes; peace and prosperity returned to the land. Over the course of time Sōgorō has remained a symbol of resistance to tyranny; the farmers who opposed the expropriation of their land for the Tokyo International Airport at Narita claimed him as their ancestor.[1]

For many Japanese, the legend of Sakura Sōgorō represents the entire body of peasant uprisings in the Tokugawa period. No matter that the legends do not agree on when he died, that no contemporaneous document proves his existence, or that according to the historical record, in 1660 Hotta Masanobu (1632–80) lost the domain he had inherited from his father only nine years earlier for having himself petitioned the shōgun to act benevolently toward samurai and commoners alike. Sōgorō has become synonymous with the rectification of government from below. He is the one to whom the other three hundred or so still-remembered peasant martyrs are most commonly compared. "Why is Sōgorō so famous?" wonders an old man living near the monument to Kainuma

35

Kyūhachi, who was executed in 1695. "Our Hachiman was equal to Sōgorō, but nothing was ever written down about him."[2]

Sōgorō is the only peasant to have gained nationwide fame in Japan's early modern era. A hundred years or so after his death, a temple erected in his memory became a pilgrimage site for peasants living on the Kanto Plain, where he was worshiped as a high-ranking Shintō deity *(dai-myōjin)*. Nursery rhymes, songs, stories, and religious pamphlets spread his fame from the northern part of Japan's main island to Shikoku and even to villages near the Amakusa Islands in Kyushu.[3] One song sung during the spring planting in the Kawakami district of Okayama prefecture sketched a fragment of the legend:

> Sōgorō, rather than see the hardships of the peasants, took
> their sufferings upon himself and presented a petition.
> Sōgorō, his petition stuck in a split bamboo, approached the
> lord's palanquin, and thrust it in.
> Sōgorō, tortured with water and fire and the rack, saw his
> innocent children burned with moxa.[4]

Most stories claim that his innocent children were beheaded before his eyes. The song nevertheless evokes the pain and suffering all too readily feared by the peasants.

The parallels between the Sōgorō story and that of other peasant martyrs are too close to be coincidental. "A Daily Record of the Riot over Ten Thousand *Koku*" *(Mankoku sōdō nichiroku)*, written anonymously in 1783, relates the efforts by headmen living near present-day Tateyama city in 1711 to revoke new taxes instituted by an upstart bureaucrat, Kawai Tōzaemon. Three headmen were beheaded, but in so outrageous a violation of procedures that the bakufu had to investigate. The bakufu executed Kawai and his son, dismissed local officials, and demoted the domain lord to a shogunal bannerman *(hatamoto)*. The day the headmen went to present their appeal in Edo, the steps they followed, and the month the ruling authorities handed down their verdict are identical to the dates and course of action given in stories about Sōgorō. Aoki Kōji argues that the details of this incident may have been assimilated to the Sōgorō story to lend it verisimilitude, but it is equally possible that the process worked in reverse.[5] These similarities may have also arisen out of a common store of traditions, myths, and aspirations handed down orally from one generation to another.

By the nineteenth century, the legend of Sōgorō had taken on new meanings. Some peasants who led their own protests against the government in the decades around the Meiji Restoration of 1868 called on his spirit to aid their endeavors. During the great uprising of 1867 which swept across Musashi, now part of greater Tokyo, peasants performed snatches of a play entitled *Sakura Sōgorō den*, and a puppet theater in Hachiōji used mechanical dolls to portray a scene where the ferryman Jinbei defies the authorities to break the lock and carry Sōgorō home to say farewell to his family. The leader of a peasant uprising in 1871 in Mimasaka, now the northern part of Okayama prefecture, wrote his own puppet play praising Sōgorō. As late as 1878 the leader of a riot in Hiratsuka city built a shrine for the worship of Sōgorō. In other instances as well, peasants intent on expressing their grievances to the authorities called on Sōgorō for protection.[6] Sōgorō had become the patron saint of protest.

In another environment, the Sōgorō story was dramatized on the Kabuki stage in 1851. The bookseller Fujiokaya Yūzō noted in his diary that it achieved tremendous popularity, drawing in audiences from neighboring provinces, encouraging theaters and halls all over town to put on their own imitations, sparking a Sōgorō boom in novelizations and posters, and forcing even the high-class professional storytellers *(kōshakushi)*, who ordinarily despised the Kabuki actors as little better than beggars, to incorporate the Sōgorō story into their repertoire. According to rumor, one member of the audience from Shimōsa was so moved by the difference between Sōgorō's sacrifice for his fellows and the way his contemporaries pusillanimously bought off trouble that he went back to his inn and committed suicide. Peasants dropped their hoes in the fields to run off to the theater. They shamed anyone who did not go by expelling them from their youth groups because such types did not understand the obligations owed the country *(kokuon)*. Some claimed that the actor playing Sōgorō represented the second coming of Sōgorō as a great august deity *(dai-myōjin)*. Whereas these public performances set the scene in the medieval period to satisfy government censors, in the several versions of the story copied into his diary, Yūzō gave dates for the seventeenth century, and he included the petition that Sōgorō was supposed to have presented to the shōgun.[7] From midsummer to the end of the year, this peasant martyr preempted the space usually reserved for urban heroes.

One of many plays that fed the appetite of urban audiences for cruelty, suffering, and bloodshed, the Sōgorō story was revived in 1861 and quickly found its way into popular novels. According to the playbills and scripts preserved in the Tsubouchi Memorial Theater Museum at Waseda University, the play continued to be performed through the 1870s and sporadically thereafter to 1900. Although it is generally lumped with scripts about thieves and murderers, it constitutes one of the few examples of what might be called social-protest drama, and it is one of only two Kabuki plays where the central character is a peasant.[8] This history puts it well: with Sōgorō we have "the first time that a common peasant left a name for future generations."

The widespread legends about Sōgorō and their unusual transformation into the Kabuki theater suggest that here was an authentic Japanese hero. He has, however, largely been ignored in books about Japanese history, particularly in the West, except in works by scholars of peasant protest. Neither Ivan Morris's *Nobility of Failure*, which relates the tragic legends of men beloved in song and story, nor the more staid and historically factual *Personality in Japanese History* and *Great Historical Figures of Japan* include his biography.[9] Throughout the sweep of Japanese history, and in movies like *Seven Samurai*, the peasants passively endure while the warriors win glory.

Stories about Sōgorō and other peasant martyrs have also been ignored by folklorists. Perhaps because they are based on actual or might-have-been events, these legends have been excluded from the compilations and dictionaries of folklore motifs. In the postwar period, only in *Tales of Old Japan*, a miscellany of exotic stories first published in 1871 by A. B. Mitford, and in *As the Japanese See It*, a reader for college students, have full-blown depictions of Sōgorō appeared in English.[10] Yet, as Barbara Ruch has pointed out, heroes are important. They feed "the emotional and ethical life" of their people, and they allow outsiders "to tap the sources of the nation's most enduring ideals, myths, aspirations, and historical griefs."[11]

Ruch was talking about Japan's national epic, *The Tale of the Heike*, the story of the struggle that ended in the defeat of the Taira in 1185, but on a much smaller scale she could have been talking about the Sōgorō story. The transmission and conceptualization of the Sōgorō story and classic military sagas suggest deep-seated patterns in the way the Japanese remember heroes. To speak in certain ways and tell stories about personages in the past were thought to have prophylactic or invocative properties. The Japanese called the beneficent but perilous witchery of words *kotodama,* or "the spirit of words," and through ritual incantations *(norito)* they called the spirit into life. In medieval Europe as well, people believed in the magic of the word. Mention the devil and he appears.[12] Most versions of the Sōgorō legend summoned the power of words to recount how a shrine came into existence. Like many folktales known as *jisha engi,* which related how some miraculous event took place on the spot where a temple or shrine was eventually built, these versions explained the origin of a place.[13] They ended with a prayer that with a shrine established for worshiping Sōgorō, everyone from the rulers to the common peasants would enjoy happiness. Telling tales about Sōgorō bestowed a deeply religious significance on his deeds and transformed him into a god.

The power of the voice had other properties as well. In a society in which the oral tradition existed side by side with written literature, the spoken word was the only way for illiterate men to remember where they came from. The version of the Sōgorō story presented here perpetuates Sōgorō's geneology by claiming as his ancestor Taira no Masakado (?–940), who rebelled against heaven itself in trying to wrest the Kanto provinces from imperial control. This noble descent is one indication that Sōgorō had become assimilated to the mythical model of the tragic hero whose extraordinary deeds made him an appropriate bearer of the community's impurities and sins.[14]

Recounting the deeds of the dead also helped expiate their inner agonies. As late as 1977, an innkeeper in Yamanashi prefecture published a book about his ancestors executed after uprisings in 1750 and 1872, "to placate their angry spirits."[15] *The Tale of the Heike* and other warrior sagas were recited not merely to tell a good story but to soothe and comfort the tormented souls of men who died with blood on their hands. Focused on the perils of pride and power, these tales also concentrated the thoughts of the listeners on their own salvation.[16] Legends surrounding *The Tale of the Heike,* furthermore, suggested that relating the exploits of certain warriors would cause them to appear again, bemoaning their fate. In one version of the Sōgorō legend, a monk visited a small shrine dedicated to Jizō, a bodhisattva thought to show special compassion to children. During an all-night vigil, he and the hermit who tended the shrine traded stories of the Heike heroes and Taira no Masakado, whose feats were immortalized in the earliest war tale told to placate the soul of a failed hero, the *Shōmonki*.[17] Then the monk asked about the history of a local shrine. After the hermit told the story of how Sōgorō was punished for trying to help the peasants, the ghosts of a man and a woman appeared before the monk, complained of the injustice they had suffered, and abused the Hotta family.[18] At the premier of the Kabuki play *Higashiyama Sakura Sōshi*, in 1851, it was said that the ghosts of Sōgorō and his family came to the theater carrying beams on their backs.[19]

The centrality of angry spirits in the Sōgorō story comes from an ancient strain of Japanese beliefs. The spirit of anyone who died in "unnatural" circumstances continued to roam recklessly around until it had exacted its own revenge or yielded to the appeasements of the living. The most potent unnatural circumstances were unfulfilled political emotions, jealousy or grudge, death away from home, and mistreatment of a corpse. Any victim of an unjust, premature, or violent death produced a potentially angry spirit, and Sōgorō fit most of these categories. Placating angry spirits was serious business, for as the monk Jien (1155–1225) wrote, "since ancient times there has been the Principle that vengeful souls ruin the state and destroy man."[20] Besides telling tales about the dead, one of the best ways to appease an unquiet spirit was to offer it enshrinement. Several Japanese shrines are dedicated to angry spirits in an attempt to put them to rest, and the shrine to Sōgorō erected by the Hotta family must be included in their number.[21]

Strong emotion was identified with the gods and was thought, indeed, to show their power. In Japanese folklore, many are the tales of a woman's love so strong that it lived on as her spirit after her death, awaiting only the return of the beloved to whom it could relate the sad tale of unrequited desire and terrible death before disappearing. Medieval literature includes stories of jealous women whose rage, transformed into serpents, destroyed their rivals or faithless lovers.[22] In contrast to these unselfconscious emotions felt by women, Sōgorō deliberately fed his wrath so that it would be certain to survive his death. One woodblock print based on the Kabuki plays of the late Tokugawa period shows the scene where he returned to haunt Lord Hotta as he disported himself with his maids-in-waiting. Sōgorō and his wife fly through the air, hair streaming wildly around their mournful faces, their robes ending in nothingness because Japanese ghosts have no feet. The maids have been transformed into demons underneath their colorful kimonos, and snakes rise from the floorboards to entrap Lord Hotta in their coils.[23] Good theater, perhaps, but also a reminder of the mysterious powers that ranged beyond humanity's ken.

The belief in the power of angry spirits informs even the way the Sōgorō story was presented on the urban stage. Before the first performance in 1851, the actor who played Sōgorō, Ichikawa Kodanji, made a pilgrimage to the Sōgorō shrine, which he presented with the tidy sum of 950 *ryō*. In his prayers Kodanji related how he had been casting about for a worthy vehicle for his talents when one night Taira no Masakado appeared to him in a dream and commanded him to visit the grave of his descendant Sōgorō, where he would find what he needed. Like other actors who visited the graves of their subjects, Kodanji wanted to avoid unnecessarily arousing Sōgorō's spirit, but he also sought Sōgorō's help in putting on a successful run. The play opened during the Bon season, still a popular time for ghost plays when the souls of the dead are supposed to return to the world of the living and the audience needs to be reminded to worship them. Unlike the medieval Noh drama, which focused on salvation regardless of whether the angry spirit satisfied its passion for revenge, on the Kabuki stage, salvation came as an afterthought. As in the story translated here, the emphasis was on vengeance. H. E. Plutschow argues that the Kabuki theater was a place of both placation and catharsis, a way to appease angry spirits and to empathize with their revenge on their tormenters.[24]

In the Sōgorō story, the native belief in the power of angry spirits was uneasily joined to Buddhist notions concerning retribution, magic, and language. Unlike the simple and austere Zen Buddhism so well known in the West, which taught reliance on the self and remained deeply skeptical of speech, or the popular Buddhism which promised salvation through faith in the Lotus sutra or the grace of the bodhisattva Amida, these notions harked back to the early Buddhist teachings on the ways of fate and the pull of karma.[25] Doing wrong was always punished. The first line of the text translated here evoked the theme to follow: an attachment to material pleasures ends in damnation, or pride comes before fall, a statement that foreshadowed Hotta's ruin. To exorcise Lord Hotta's pregnant consort of the angry spirits who tormented her, Buddhist priests offered prayers and the lord himself chanted the Daihannya sutra, believed to have a magical potency against evil spirits. These rites of purification expressed through language were supposed to gain Buddhahood for the spirits, thereby relieving them of their negative karma.[26] Despite the protestations of Buddhist practitioners, however, sutra readings and mysterious prayers were no more effective against the ghosts of Sōgorō and his wife than they were against the Rokujo Lady in the *Tale of Genji*.[27] In tales about Sōgorō, the Buddhist teaching on inevitable retribution for wrongdoing simply reinforced beliefs in the revenge of angry spirits; it provided a public and more universal justification for private spite.

The strongly religious cast given the Sōgorō story in the Tokugawa period gradually became attenuated over time and as the story moved from its rural origins into urban areas. In her study of Semimaru, the blind musician of Japan, Susan Matisoff pointed out that frameworks tying a story to a particular place, for example, those that explained the origin of a shrine, were dropped in texts recorded for urban audiences.[28] Kabuki librettos set the Sōgorō story in the fifteenth century in part to evade prohibitions against depicting contemporary events on stage, but this device also made it possible to omit the untheatrical emphasis on worship as a means of remembering the dead. Instead the dramatists added a new twist to the plot: having resolved to sacrifice himself by petitioning the shōgun, Sōgorō sneaked back to his village to bid farewell to his children. In some versions, he also wanted to divorce his wife because otherwise she would be judged equally guilty with him. To prevent the peasants in Edo from communicating with those in the domain, however, the officials locked up all the boats at the Inba swamp. Out of sympathy with the peasants, the ferryman Jinbei bravely broke the locks and carried Sōgorō home. In modern versions, even the angry spirits of Sōgorō and his wife have disappeared. In their place we find Jinbei.[29]

Lacking angry spirits, retribution, and magic, modern versions of the Sōgorō story have almost completely lost touch with the tradition from which they sprang. In their Tokugawa form, however, they reveal the legacy of what Barbara Ruch has called vocal literature. Unlike oral stories, which usually imply "illiteracy on the part of the producer of a story, on the part of the audience, or both," vocal literature is based on written texts. But each time a story is told, the teller either memorizes it or composes it more or less anew according to the principles of extemporizing on a basic theme. The art is in the telling, and the magic is in the voice projection. For this reason, "vocal literature, even when secular in content, cannot be easily separated from magico-religious qualities that imbued the environment in which it developed."[30] Or, as Clarke Garrett has put it, in a predominantly oral culture, "language is really sound and texts must be recycled back through sound to have meaning."[31] Ruch claims that the vocal literary tradition coexisted with the written tradition before expiring in the seventeenth century, but the Sōgorō story suggests that in rural Japan, this particular literary tradition, which sought to affect listeners in the spiritual and the real world, continued both to produce new texts and to reproduce old ones.

The manner in which the Sōgorō story spread from villages near Narita to other parts of Japan must be deduced from what we know of early modern communications. The itinerant storytellers, *sekkyōshi* or jongleurs, who roamed the Japanese countryside during the medieval period found their freedom of movement severely restricted during the first two centuries of Tokugawa rule.[32] To a certain extent, their place was taken by licensed traveling proselytizers *(oshi)* who made regular trips around Japan, drumming up business for their shrines and temples. According to various accounts, monks from a local temple wrote the petition Sōgorō presented to the shōgun and appealed the verdict to execute his entire family, episodes insinuating that the monks may also have helped disseminate stories about Sōgorō and write them down.

The establishment of a shrine to Sōgorō by the Hotta family in 1746 may have played a crucial role in propagating stories about him, most of which date from the second half of the eighteenth century or later. Once the shrine became a pilgrimage site, visitors could carry his story back to their homes, to be turned into songs and poems as well.[33] In the nineteenth-century text translated here, monks were criticized for having passively accepted the dictates of the ruling class. In two texts from the 1860s preserved in Aoki village high in the mountains of Nagano prefecture, the monks played no part at all. By this time, the ruling authorities were no longer able to enforce prohibitions against traveling entertainers, and religious proselytizers had lost their monopoly over the dissemination of news in the countryside.

The different modes of dissemination for the Sōgorō story have left a number of extant versions. The thirty-some manuscripts that remain from the Tokugawa period are few compared to the one hundred versions of *The Tale of the Heike,* but the issue of textual evolution is similar.[34] Ono Masaji, who made a close study of some twenty texts located in and around the old Sakura domain, tried to determine which was the oldest and which provided the most historically accurate account of Sōgorō's life. He based his published edition, the only printed version of the Sōgorō story in Japanese that unquestionably comes from Tokugawa-period texts, on a manuscript that was well organized under title headings, but he interpolated parts of other documents to produce a composite to suit his taste.[35] My approach follows Alfred B. Lord, who criticized the folly of viewing variant texts of the same story as derived from a hypothetical urtext. They should instead be seen as separate stories in their own right, each valid unto itself.[36] In this approach, every text stands on its own merits as an authentic rendering of the story.

The text translated here was found by a leading scholar of Japanese peasant martyrs, Hosaka Satoru, in a used bookstore far from Sakura in Aizu-Wakamatsu. Although it is undated, it was probably written before the Kabuki dramatizations of the story became widely known. Its vocabulary is much simpler than that found in the composite edited by Ono or in the story recorded by Mitford in *Tales of Old Japan,* nor does it replicate the style of Noh chanting that distinguishes parts of the Ono text. Even the religious terms would have been familiar to the common people. The political terminology is drawn directly from the documents that passed between peasants and rulers. The handwriting is clear and relatively easy to read. Less erudite than village headmen, the producer of this text was probably a low-ranking village official or simply a landholding peasant.

This Aizu-Wakamatsu version is remarkably similar to both the Mitford and the Ono texts. All three call Hotta Masanobu by the title Kōzuke no suke, the name by which he was publicly known, but also the title for Lord Kira, villain in *Chūshingura* (A treasury of loyal retainers). Also the same are the title for Masanobu's father, Kaga no kami (his true title was Dewa no kami), the positions held by father and son at the shōgun's court, the names of their chief followers, and the name of the senior councillor to the shōgun *(rojū).* Sōgorō's illness, which prevented him from joining the other village headmen in Edo, serves in all three texts to retard the forward movement of the story.[37] Although each text puts the peasants' petition at a different place in the story, the grievances it contains are similar. Like the careful attention to proper and place-names, it lends verisimilitude to an otherwise improbable tale. The central episodes of the story—from Sōgorō's appeal to the shōgun to the decision to execute Sōgorō, his wife, and children—follow the same pattern in all three texts. They even repeat the pathetic story of the boil on the second son's neck, a scene certain to wring the emotions of the audience. Common to all is how Sōgorō took revenge on the house of Hotta, including Masanobu's quarrel with a fellow noble in the shōgun's palace, an event that also resonates with echoes from *Chūshingura*. All three texts explain that a shrine has been erected in memory of Sōgorō.

The texts show the most differences where they purport to be the most precise. Was Sōgorō the headman of Kōzu village as Ono's text would have it, or was he from Iwabashi? Was he executed in 1653 (Ono), or in 1645 (Aizu-Wakamatsu, Mitford) before Masanobu became the domain lord, or at some other time in between? Was he forty-three (Aizu-Wakamatsu), or forty-eight (Ono) years old? What about the names and ages of his children, which in the Mitford text differ slightly from the other two. How many villages and what areas did Sōgorō represent when he appealed to the shōgun? On this point, the Aizu-Wakamatsu version is not even internally consistent. It also puts the curse on the Hotta family in the mouth of Sōgorō's wife, a realistic touch exposing a mother's anguish at her childrens' death, whereas in the other two texts she is resigned to her fate. Each text names a different horse that Masanobu took for his mad ride back to Sakura. Was Masanobu (Mitford) or his son (Aizu-Wakamatsu) allowed to move to Utsunomiya, and did his title then become Hida no kami (Mitford) or Chikuzen no kami (Aizu-Wakamatsu)?[38] Then there are the documents incorporated in the text, the verdict for Sōgorō and the other headmen (Aizu-Wakamatsu, Ono), and the verdict for Masanobu (Mitford). Diverse as they are, these details lend each text a spurious air of authenticity.

Aside from the episodes that constitute the essential structure of the story, each text includes sections unique to itself. The Ono text describes the siege of Odawara in 1590 and the 1615 attack on Osaka castle. The Mitford version includes a petition presented by village officials to the domain office in Edo asking that Sōgorō's children be pardoned. In the Aizu-Wakamatsu version is a long diatribe against monks, an anticlericalism absent from the other two texts, and a fantastic tale of vengeance against a domanial official, Fuchiwatari Shukei, that must have been satisfying to the peasants who heard it. Near the end of the text is a quotation on the imperative of acting loyally, from *Hagakure,* a textbook for samurai written in 1716. Sōgorō was the hero of the story, but if only the ruling class would act as they should, there would be no need for the disruptive deeds of peasants.

The Sakura Sōgorō Story

CONTENTS

1. The Origin of the Great August Deity Sōgo of Kami Iwabashi, Inba District in the Province of Shimōsa

2. Arrival of the Village Officials at the Funabashi Post Station
   A messenger is dispatched because Sōgorō is late.

3. Arrival of the Peasants' Representatives in Edo
   Sōgorō sets out for the capital.

4. An Appeal to the Senior Councillor Lord Kuse Yamato no Kami as He Rides in His Palanquin
   Lord Kuse returns the petition.

5. The Resolution to Act Together by Sōgorō and Five Others
   Sōgorō makes an appeal directly to the Shōgun in front of the black gate at Ueno.

6. A Verdict on the Crimes of Sōgorō, His Wife, and Children
   Officials decide what to do with the other five.

7. Announcement of Sōgorō's Crimes at the Sakura Government Office
   The other five are ordered into exile.

8. The Crucifixion of Sōgorō and His Wife
   His sons are also executed.

9. The Death of Lord Hotta Kōzuke no Suke's Consort
   Sōgorō and his wife transform themselves into monsters.

10. A Quarrel in the Palace
    Lord Hotta barricades himself at the Sakura castle.

11. The Death of Lord Sakai Iwami no Kami
    The shōgun sends a punitive force against the Hotta family.

12. The Succession to the Sakai and Hotta Families

13. The Worship of Sōgorō's Spirit as the God of a Shrine

The Origin of the Great August Deity Sōgorō, Headman of Kami Iwabashi, the Sakura Domain, Inba District, Shimōsa

Indulging your desires and becoming overbearing and arrogant really means that you will sacrifice everything with a slip of the tongue.

Here lived a peasant called Sōgorō, headman of Kami Iwabashi, Inba district in the Sakura domain of Shimōsa. Because he was a man of innate virtue who resolved to sacrifice himself to save the people, everyone revered and respected him as the August Deity of a shrine. Worship is truly the means through which popular sayings and proverbs transmit stories of such earth-shattering spiritual power. This was the first time, nonetheless, that a common peasant left a name for future generations.

Were you to inquire about Sōgorō's ancestors, you would find that he was a descendant of the imperial prince Taira no Masakado, who even today enjoys high repute in Kami Iwabashi.

During the Kan'ei era [1624–43], Lord Kōzuke no suke, the legitimate son of Hotta Kaga no kami Masamori, lord of Sakura castle, Inba district, Shimōsa, succeeded his father as the second lord of the castle. His father Masamori had been appointed a senior councillor because his ancestors excelled in valor, sincerity, and loyalty. After Masamori died, the succession was conferred on Lord Kōzuke no suke, and he was also appointed to a position among the senior councillors. It was only because his father had governed

47

without any irregularities at all that Lord Kōzuke no suke was allowed to serve as a senior councillor. He had reason to be extremely grateful for the shōgun's favor.

During the Shōhō era [1644–47], Lord Kōzuke no suke changed things from the way they were before and ordered that the taxes paid by the peasants of his domain be increased. He also had levied a variety of excess duties. The tax collectors became exceedingly strict. As a result, the peasants in the domain suffered extreme hardships and fell into uncommon poverty.

In desperation, the peasants presented a petition begging for the lord's mercy, but the local officials refused to accept it. The peasants thus had no choice but to plot together in small groups. Many of them ran away from their villages. Finally the village headmen and officials of 230 villages representing peasants on land worth over twenty thousand *koku* gathered to discuss what to do. After much debate, they agreed to present a petition which everyone would have to sign. At first they took their petition to the local Sakura government office, but the officials refused to accept any of it, so they went to appeal to the house elder Lord Fuchiwatari Shukei. They crowded in front of his gate carrying their petition, but once again the officials refused to accept it.

Then the headmen and village officials returned home and debated what to do. Several times they had gone to the government office. They had even petitioned one of the house elders, but the officials had always refused to accept their appeals. Now there was no one left to try. But if they just let the matter drop, the vast majority of peasants would be unable to survive. Besides, what about the poor peasants who would grumble and abuse them, saying that the officials were heartless? They were losing face. They really had no choice but to go to Edo and make their appeal at the mansion of their lord. If the officials refused to accept it even then, they would have to agree to find some way of reaching the ear of high shogunal officials, appeal to have the merits of their case investigated, and ask that the bakufu be the judge. It would be best, they decided, if the 243 headmen and village officials went together to Edo to make the appeal.

They had just reached this decision when Sōgorō, then forty-three, the headman of Kami Iwabashi, shrewd, clever with words, and more intelligent than most, came forward and asked: "What you have just decided to do, to go to our lord's mansion in Edo and make an appeal, is completely out of the ordinary and very dangerous indeed. What can you be thinking of?"

The headmen and officials all spoke together. "You're right. We think it is a dangerous thing to do." Then there was a silence while no one said anything at all. Finally Sōgorō spoke:

"Up to this point we have made a number of appeals to the local government offices, and we have even crowded in front of the gate of a house elder to make our appeal, but the officials have refused to accept any of them. Going to Edo where the lord is in residence may appear to be a good idea, but our petition is not likely to be approved very readily.

"If we go to Edo without having received permission from local government officials," he continued, "our actions will undoubtedly be judged to have been an appeal made en masse directly to the authorities, and we will be punished for our insolence. Each and every one of us will be thrown in prison and put in chains. Some of us will even be executed for being the ringleaders of a riot. Even suffering such hardships, however, will not solve our problem. We must commit ourselves to petition high shogunal officials, come what may.

"I know that we will be taking an extremely grave and dangerous step, but what do you think? If we make an appeal to the bakufu, we will never see our families again. Now are each of you convinced in your own heart that you are determined to carry through with this petition? Do any of you want to put a stop to this before the situation gets more serious? Please let me know how you feel."

Steeling his own resolve, Sōgorō ascertained everyone's views down to the very bottom of his heart. It was apparent to all that he excelled even the most splendid warrior in bravery, not to mention indomitable determination. After everyone had listened to what he had to say, they replied:

"You're right. Were we to continue to make appeals as we have been doing up to now and were the officials to continue to refuse to accept them, we would be forced to go as high as shogunal officials even if it meant running the risk of making enemies of the officials serving our own lord. Nevertheless, we don't see how we can stop petitioning to relieve the sufferings of all the peasants in a twenty thousand *koku* area, no matter how severely we are punished."

"Everyone who has made up his mind to steel himself not to return to our homeland again should now bid his parents, siblings,

49

wives, children, and kinsfolk a fond farewell and prepare for his departure," Sōgorō announced.

Everyone agreed to this, and they decided to leave for Edo on the thirteenth day of the eleventh month. Then each went back to his own home.

Around this time some people appeared in the castle town accompanied by their parents, siblings, wives, and children. In all about 734 people from eighty-five families fled to other areas, abandoning land worth over six hundred *koku* and deserting eleven temples and shrines.

According to another report, peasants in the countryside heard a rumor that a few dozen headmen from the 236 villages in Lord Kōzuke no suke's domain had gone to his mansion in Edo where they made an appeal en masse directly to the authorities, forcing them to accept the petition to remit the excess levies and taxes. The peasants assumed that punishments would follow, and so they conspired together, captured the house elder Fuchiwatari Shukei, dragged him out to a forest in the mountains, stripped him naked, and wrote the names of the 236 villages on his bare body. There they crucified him and stabbed him with bamboo spears, each aiming at the name of his own village. People have slanderously accused the house elder in Edo, Kojima Shikibu, of having insisted on Sōgorō being severely punished and even his relatives chastised for this crime committed owing to a misunderstanding, but that is not true.

Also it has been said that the priest from Tōkō-ji begged for the lives of Sōgorō and his children. That is simply an embellishment added to the main story, and it is false.

The Assembly of the Village Officials at the Funabashi Post Station

A messenger is dispatched because Sōgorō is late.

The village officials each made their farewells and finished their preparations. As they had promised, they arrived at Funabashi on the appointed day and gathered at three inns, spending a night there in a rendezvous before the departure set for the thirteenth. But Sōgorō from Kami Iwabashi did not show up. In growing apprehension, the village officials discussed whether they ought to send an envoy to find out what had happened while they remained at Funabashi through the night of the fourteenth. Finally they chose Rokurōzaemon of Takezawa, Inba district, and Jūzaemon of Katsuda, Sōma district, to be sent to Kami Iwabashi.

Sōgorō was at home, taking his ease before a fire. The two men asked, "In keeping with the pledge made a few days ago, all of the village officials left home on the thirteenth, and they have already arrived at Funabashi where they are waiting for you. But then you did not show up. Everyone agreed that your intentions were unmistakable, so what could have caused you to be so late? This has made us all very anxious. The rest have remained at Funabashi while the two of us were sent here to see you. What is the matter?"

"How kind of you to come," Sogoro replied. "Thank you for your trouble. I am indeed grateful to everyone for the effort they are making in going to Edo. I too planned to set out yesterday morning. I had already finished my preparations when last night I suffered severe abdominal pains. I am forced to stay here, unable to leave, until I recover. You two should return at once to Funabashi, accompany the officials there to Edo, crowd in at the lord's mansion in Edo to present the appeal, and then camp before his gate day and night." Thus he gave them secret and detailed instructions.

The two men left the next morning, arriving at Funabashi about four in the afternoon. There they told how Sōgorō's illness had recurred and passed on his secret and detailed instructions. On the sixteenth everyone left Funabashi, each in his own way.

The Arrival of the Peasants' Representatives in Edo
Sōgorō sets out for the capital.

Some of the petitioners took the Ichikawa road, some took the Gyō-toku road, and they all made their various ways to Edo. Upon their arrival, at least thirty of them stayed in the Koami area, whereas the others sought lodging as they pleased in Yanagiwara, Muramatsu-chō, Iida-chō, and other places.

On the seventeenth day of the eleventh month, 157 peasants and headmen crowded in front of Lord Hotta's gate below the western enceinte of the shōgun's castle. The sight of them gathered there carrying their petition astonished the foot soldiers on guard, who bustled about in great confusion.

"Who are you to create such disorder?" they scolded, defending themselves with their staffs. Then the official on duty, who had been informed of what was happening, appeared to inquire into the particulars. The village officials all shouted that they had a petition to present.

"In any case, this is the front gate, and you are blocking the public way. Go around to the back gate, all of you."

He repeated this several times, forcing the headmen to go around to the back gate, where as before they crowded in front of it. Finally an official appeared.

"Come inside the gate," he urged, but not one person obeyed.[39] Then he informed them that since the lord was busy attending the shōgun, they should go to the lower mansion at Aoyama Hyakunin-chō on the morrow. That was it for the day, and everyone returned to his inn.

Following their instructions, the headmen went to the lower mansion in Aoyama on the eighteenth. Once they had crowded in front of the gate, an official appeared and said: "Local matters are handled by officials in the domain itself. You have acted outrageously in coming to us here when you should have made your statement to the district magistrate, the intendant, or the superintendant there. In retaliation, we will not accept your petition." He drove them outside away from the gate, withdrew behind it with his men, and slammed it shut.

The headmen returned to their inns at dusk. On the nineteenth, they gathered at a teahouse in front of the Asakusa Kannon,[40] where everyone gave his ideas on what to do. Before they did anything else, they agreed that they needed to know what Sōgorō thought. The next morning, Rokurōzaemon and Jūzaemon were thus once again asked to go to Kami Iwabashi with instructions to bring Sōgorō back with them without fail. The two men left immediately and reached Funabashi in the evening of the same day.

Just at that time Sōgorō had himself set out. That night he stayed at the inn of Kikyōya Gorōemon in Funabashi, where he ran into the two envoys. Overjoyed and excited, they discussed at great length everything that had happened in Edo.

"We came this far again because we were sent to meet you. We are delighted that you too intend to go to Edo. All of us are eager to hear what you think."

"The officials in the domain and those in Edo are not colluding in their dealings over our affair," Sōgorō replied. "Nevertheless, I doubt that those in Edo will accept our petition. Therefore we will have no choice but to appeal to shogunal officials regardless of propriety. Tomorrow in Edo we will debate again with the others on what to do about our petition."

Early the next morning they left Funabashi and went in the direction of Edo.

An Appeal to the Senior Councillor Lord Kuse Yamato no Kami as He Rides in His Palanquin
Lord Kuse returns the petition.

Once Sōgorō from Kami Iwabashi had arrived in Edo, all of the peasants who had come to make the appeal went again to meet at the teahouse in front of the Asakusa Kannon, but they could not agree on what they should do. Then Sōgorō spoke: "Everything that each of you has said makes sense, but having already taken a petition to our lord's mansion and had it rejected means that we have severed relations with him. Therefore we have no choice but to wait for a day when Lord Kuse Yamato no kami goes by palanquin to the shōgun's castle, when we can then entreat him to accept our appeal. Each of you must make up your minds to do it. Now is not a time to remain silent, don't you agree?"

Sitting in serried rows, the peasants all said together, "That's it, let's do it." A decision having been reached, everyone returned to his lodgings.

Five men, Sōgorō, Jūzaemon, Rokurōzaemon, Hanjūrō, and Chūzō, then met to write a petition. On the twenty-sixth, Kuse Yamato no kami, whose visit to the castle the peasants had agreed to wait for, was seen leaving his mansion below the western enceinte in a palanquin. Everyone ran pell-mell to catch up with him. Among them was Sōgorō, who strode straight to the fore, clung to the palanquin, and cried, "I have a petition." Knowing that no one would take the petition from him, he flung it into the litter to force Lord Kuse to accept it.

"We are grateful that you have shown yourself to be benevolent," Sōgorō shouted. All the peasants withdrew.

After that Sōgorō had everyone gather at a teahouse in Ryōgokubashi, where he spoke to them once again.

"Well, we have managed to present our appeal to Lord Kuse. Officials will probably consider it within the next few days."

Then everyone spoke at once, "Goodness Sōgorō, what a relief that things worked out as you expected. As you said, all we have to do now is wait for some sort of announcement."

"Now I did say that we have managed to present our appeal to Lord Kuse, and officials will probably consider it within the next few days, but even if that is indeed what happens, we will not be summoned any time soon," Sōgorō replied. "Even in the shōgun's castle our petition will be considered only after much deliberation. No matter how hard we push, we will not speed up getting an answer, either yes or no.

"It's going to get too expensive for us to remain all jammed up here," he pointed out. "It would be best if Rokurōzaemon, Hanjūrō, Chūzō, Saburōbei, and four or five others stayed behind while the rest of you return to your villages back home. That way these six or seven men and I can be the ringleaders in making our appeal. If we get in trouble or if we are accused of wrongdoing, we are relying on you to work together in finishing things up for us. Of course I don't have to say this, but we do need money and so forth for our expenses while we are lodged in Edo to take care of this business.

"We must petition albeit at the risk of our own lives. Even if the heads of all the representatives from 236 villages who signed their names to our petition are exposed at the prison gate,[41] it will be worth it if we have saved the peasants. But now it is time for us to part."

The peasants stayed up all night over a farewell banquet. Each of them wept over Sōgorō's words as they reluctantly bid him good-bye. Finally they finished making their formal bows and returned to their villages.

The six men had already made up their minds to do what they had to do, so how could they be depressed over anything that happened now? Saying good-bye, they returned to the inn at Yanagiwara. Everyone knew in their hearts that the six were truly splendid headmen.

On the second day of the twelfth month, a summons came from Lord Kuse saying that Sōgorō should present himself at nine in the morning. Those who went to Lord Kuse's mansion were Sōgorō, Rokurōzaemon, Jūzaemon, Hanjūrō, Chūzō, and Saburōbei. Upon their arrival in court, Lord Kuse's officials, Sase Gidayū and Yamazaki Ishiki, raised their voices:

"You have acted absolutely outrageously in petitioning our master while he was going to the castle in his palanquin on the morning of the twenty-sixth. You should be severely punished for having overstepped your bounds by throwing a petition into the palanquin of a senior councillor to the shōgun, but our lord has mercifully agreed to ignore what you did. If you continue with your disorderly conduct, you will most certainly be judged in the wrong. No matter what kind of petition you have to make you must always present it to your own government office according to the regulations for petitions."

After they had made this announcement, Sōgorō came forward and spoke, "I make these remarks humbling myself before you. We have not acted simply on the spur of the moment. Every year we have repeatedly presented petitions, but not a single one of them has ever been accepted. The peasants are all having a hard time surviving, and as a result, we have been forced to overcome our habitual deference to authority. It was in fear and trembling that we overstepped the bounds by throwing a petition into the lord's palanquin. Please be merciful and accept our petition. Were you to make it possible for the peasants to survive, we would be grateful and happy."

"No, no, this we cannot do." Lord Kuse's officials returned the petition after they had written down the names of each of the six headmen. The headmen had no choice but to take back their petition and return to their lodgings.

The Resolve to Act Together by Sōgorō and Five Others

Sōgorō makes an appeal directly to the shōgun in front of the black gate at Ueno.

After that Sōgorō carefully pondered what had happened before he decided on a new plan. Turning to the five men, he said:

"What a regrettable turn of events. Since the petition we had just presented has already been returned by Lord Kuse, how shameful it would be for us to return home right now. Besides, if we simply leave things like this, there will be no end to the villagers' hardships.

Therefore I have made up my mind to find out when the shōgun appears in public and use that opportunity to make an appeal directly to him. Regardless of the merits of our case, I know that in making a direct appeal I will have thrown away my life. Nevertheless, even if I lose my life, I alone must make a direct appeal as the representative of the headmen for the peasants who produce twenty thousand *koku*. What do you think of that?"

Rokurōzaemon and Jūzaemon replied, "That's a good idea. From the very beginning we have been in complete agreement with you, and no matter what kind of wrongdoing we are forced to commit, we cannot hesitate now. Wherever you go, we will go with you."

Chūzō, Saburōbei, and Hanjūrō also moved forward to speak. "We are not surprised at what you have said. From the start, our resolve has been as hard as steel, and we have remained unwavering in our firm determination to act together."

Sōgorō nodded. "I absolutely approve of your determination to act. I have, however, thought over what we should do very carefully. The bigger the crowd that presents a direct appeal, the more likely we are to be punished and the petition rejected. Besides, if we arouse suspicion in how we appear before the shōgun, we will be unable to appeal directly to him at all. Even if he accepts our petition and does what we ask him to do, the crime of having betrayed our own lord in making an appeal directly to the shōgun will certainly be judged a serious one. Surely it will mean the death penalty, so I have resolved to take the responsibility by sacrificing myself. If each of you insists on acting with me, we will not achieve our long cherished desires because there is no way that we can avoid being accused of having committed the crime of acting en masse. In any case, you should leave everything to me. My last request of you while I am still alive is that after I have been executed, each of you should perform memorial services for me. You who have stood firm in your determination to make the appeal of a lifetime shall accompany me in spirit."

Seeing the resignation written on his face, the five men surrendered to his arguments. "Well, my lord, we are all aware of your superior talents. We have reached the point where we can do nothing, but please take us into your confidence and we will do whatever you ask."

The five men wept bitter tears in anticipation of how hard it would be to part from him. Sōgorō was deeply moved. Now that he had resolved to make a direct appeal, all he had to do was wait for a day when the shōgun would appear in public.

News that the shōgun would make a visit to Kan'ei-ji at Tōeizan in Ueno[42] on the twentieth day of the twelfth month came like a gift from heaven. Having written a petition and then hidden himself all alone under the east section of the threefold bridge in front of the black gate at Ueno, Sōgorō waited impatiently for the hour of the shōgun's arrival. His heart contained only the thought that by sacrificing his own life, he would take upon himself the entire responsibility for the peasants' sufferings and save the masses from their hardships. How firmly resolved was he to act, and how incomparable was his courage!

At eight in the morning of the twentieth, the shōgun proceeded straight toward the exact center of the bridge. At that instant, Sōgorō suddenly appeared from underneath, startling the attendants and throwing them all into confusion.

"What kind of person is this who belittles the passage of our lord the shōgun by hiding himself here?" The warriors bustled about trying to protect the shōgun in his palanquin, but Sōgorō showed not the slightest discomfiture. Instead he inserted his petition in the tip of a six-foot-long bamboo pole that he had readied beforehand and shouted, "In fear and trembling I appeal directly to you." Then he tried to thrust his petition into the palanquin.

"Get out of here," the attendants scolded him, but they grabbed the petition.

Delighted that his gamble had paid off, Sōgorō shouted, "Thank you very much for your gracious mercy," as he withdrew.

Immediately the order went out for him to be tied up with ropes, thrown in jail, and interrogated at once. The contents of the appeal that he presented are as follows:

In fear and trembling we respectfully present our statement in writing.

The domain of Hotta Kōzuke no suke

The officials from 87 villages in Inba district Shimōsa
The officials from 28 villages in Chiba district Shimōsa
The officials from 21 villages in Sōma district Shimōsa
The total yield from the above area is over 23,531.31 *koku*.

The headmen and general village representatives are:

Sōgorō of Kami Iwabashi, Inba district, Shimōsa
Heijūrō of Shimo Iwabashi, Inba district, Shimōsa
Rokurōbei of Shimo Tachizawa, Inba district, Shimōsa
Jūzaemon of Katsuda, Inba district, Shimōsa
Hanjūrō of Koizumi, Inba district, Shimōsa
Chūzō of Iwabashi, Sōma district, Shimōsa

Together these six men make this appeal as the general
representatives of all the peasants, headmen, and group
leaders[43] in the 136 villages listed above.

Between the reign of Doi Toshikatsu,[44] the first lord of the
Sakura domain in Inba district, Shimōsa, and the reign of
Matsudaira Yasunobu,[45] the ruling family changed a number
of times. Until recently, however, there has been no increase in
taxes or excess duties. After our present lord Hotta Kōzuke no
suke began his rule in 1632, he began to collect more for the
land tax starting in 1640, and the tax rates have risen
enormously. The peasants from the villages listed above are
suffering extreme hardships. In fear and trembling we have
recorded for your perusal these outrageous increases.

Respectfully we appeal to you to examine this list:

He has ordered an additional tax of .122 *koku* of rice for
every *koku* harvested.

He has also assessed various types of excess duties aside
from the land tax.

From the reign of Doi Toshikatsu down through the ages to
the reign of the previous lord, we were required to make
presents to the lord of soy beans, red beans, and sesame seeds,
but we were allowed to use the exchange rate for grain in
substituting rice in place of these excess duties. The present
lord has arbitrarily refused to accept any rice substitutes for the
excess duties.

Not being allowed to substitute rice for excess duties, the
destitute peasants who managed to scrape together enough to
pay their land taxes in full ended up without a single bit of
grain in their storehouses. Knowing that they still had to pay
the excess duties, they appealed for an extension of the
deadline for payments so they could go to other domains in

search of work, but they were allowed not a single day of grace. Besides, all of the village officials were ordered to come to be handcuffed and placed in prison for over one hundred days. We suffered extreme hardships.

Owing to these circumstances, the peasants in the villages have suffered many years of privations. Right now they are on the brink of starvation, and they are unable to survive. Even peasants who with the utmost diligence and care cultivate the fields their families have held for generations find that their estimated yields are so high that they cannot raise enough on their paddies to pay the large amounts they are assessed in taxes, and they are forced to sell the crops on dry fields to supplement their tax payments. Since the dry-field crops are used to supplement these tax payments, many peasants in the villages have almost nothing to eat, and they have fallen into deeper and deeper misery. They have lost the strength to cultivate their fields, they are unable to pay the land tax, and in the natural course of events, they end up going bankrupt and being forced to turn their land and household possessions over to the officials. Many people, old and young, men and women, a total of 737, have starved to death by the roadside or have become beggars. Furthermore, in the years since 1630, 135 farm families have gone bankrupt, and eleven temples have collapsed because their parishoners among the peasants are so destitute that they are unable to send in their contributions. Even the monks have been forced into penury; they have had to evacuate their dwellings, and they have become homeless.

Recently we appealed to the government office in Sakura along the lines given above stating that if the increased taxes and excess duties were reduced, we would not be suffering extreme hardships, and we would not be presenting petitions or doing anything else. If orders had been given to make these tax increases and excess duties conform to the tax assessments levied by previous lords, we would have petitioned expressing our gratitude, but the officials have not listened to us at all. They have refused to accept our petition, letting us know that even if the peasants were to go bankrupt and leave their homes, there is no way that they themselves can manage things any differently.

Might it not happen that some of the people who fled to
other provinces, both men and women alike, would be driven
by starvation to become robbers? If they were then arrested
and interrogated by bakufu authorities, we humbly think that
it might reflect badly upon our lord. This concern too we
reported to the provincial officials, but they refused to listen to
us. We really had no choice but to gather the village officials
together and discuss what to do. As a result, we presented a
petition to Lord Kuse Yamato no kami as he went to the castle
in his palanquin, but he refused to accept it. He returned it to
us without doing anything at all.

Not the least falsehood is contained in the statements we
have offered to your august ears. Since the peasant masses are
suffering extreme hardships, we have been forced to overcome
our fear of presenting a petition to you directly. Please deign to
be compassionate and accept our petition. No matter how
severely we six representatives are ordered to be punished, we
will not harbor any grudge against you at all. If you would be
pleased to save the peasant masses in the villages from the
pangs of hunger, from starvation and loss of life, we will be
exceedingly grateful for your compassionate mercy.

The twelfth month of 1644

A Verdict on the Crimes of Sōgorō, His Wife, and Children

Officials decide what to do with the other five.

The shōgun did not even deign to glance at the petition presented by
Sōgorō. Instead he ordered that it be turned over to Hotta Kōzuke
no suke just as it was. In accordance with his wishes, it was passed
to Inoue Kawachi no kami, who immediately thereafter, and in the
palace itself, gave it to Lord Kōzuke no suke. Lord Kōzuke no suke
received it, returned to his mansion, and read it there. Then he summoned the house elder Kojima Shikibu and said:

"The provincial officials have really blundered badly. Recently
the peasants crowded in front of the castle gate with an appeal, but
their complaints were ignored so now this petition has come to
pass. Nothing could be more outrageous. For me to have received

this information within the confines of the palace itself is a disgrace not merely for me but for my family's reputation as well. Nevertheless, I have no choice but to announce that we will remit the excess duties and lower taxes to the levels they were under Doi Toshikatsu.

"Sōgorō was not the only ringleader involved in organizing the peasants," Kōzuke no suke continued, "but he alone pushed himself forward to make this direct appeal, showing that he treats public authority lightly and despises his lord. His conduct is absolutely inexcusable. Out of all those who signed the appeal, he was the one who presented it, making his crime the most serious. For this reason, once the bakufu has transferred him to us, he and his wife will be crucified, and all of his children will be executed. His family must remain extinguished forever. Jūzaemon, Chūzō, Rokurōbei, Saburōbei, and Hanjūrō will be exiled. Their wives and children are to be made their successors."

After he had issued all of his commands, Kojima Shikibu replied respectfully: "Everything you have said makes sense, but I do not understand why Sōgorō's wife and children should be executed for his crime."

"Is it not the law that wives are punished together with their husbands? How could we mitigate his punishment?"

"Nevertheless, young children are not punished for the crimes of their fathers. It would not go well for us at all if it reached other ears that they had been executed as you have suggested. Would you mind thinking this matter over again once more very carefully?" Losing his habitual deference, he boldly spoke his mind, but Kōzuke no suke shook his head.

"No, no, that's not so. They may be young, but since their father has committed a serious crime, that won't help them."

Shikibu found himself forced to go along with what Kōzuke no suke had announced as his decision because he realized that no matter how much he argued, he would not change his lord's mind.

Once the bakufu had handed Sōgorō over, he was sent to Sakura in a basket covered with nets and thrown in prison. There the provincial officials met to pass sentence on him.

Chapter One

Announcement of Sōgorō's Crimes at the Sakura Government Office
The other five are ordered into exile.

The officials decided that Sōgorō would be crucified on the eleventh day of the second month of 1645, and they disseminated this decision to the villages in writing. Then they summoned the village officials of the 136 villages, plus Sōgorō of Kami Iwabashi, his wife, and children to the Sakura government office. There the house elder Kojima Shikibu, the inspector general Shinagawa Jōzaemon, and the investigator Machino Gennojō all from Edo were joined by the house elder, the inspectors, and magistrates from the domain plus intendants and other officials—forty-five men in all, who issued the following announcement:

"All of you village officials must understand this. We decree that the various excess duties and the land tax will conform to the assessments from the Kan'ei era [1624–43] as you previously requested in your petition."

"Thank you very much," the village officials replied in acknowledgment.

Then Sōgorō, his wife, and children were brought out. "Sōgorō, of all the petitioners from the villages, you alone made light of the shōgun by presenting an appeal directly to him. That is your first crime. Your second is that of slighting and despising your lord. Your third is that of making an appeal en masse directly to the authorities when you disrupted the way of the senior councillor Lord Kuse Yamato no kami with an appeal to him as he was riding in his palanquin. This too is a very serious matter. You are to be punished by crucifixion. Your wife will suffer the same. Your four sons will be decapitated. Your heirs will be disinherited. As for your daughters, well, we don't care what happens to them. Accept this judgment for these are the words relayed to you by your superiors." The date was the ninth day of the second month of 1645.

The verdict handed down to the peasants was as follows:

Kami Iwabashi, village

headman	Sōgorō	age 43
wife	San	age 39
heir	Sōbei	age 11

62

second son	Gennosuke	age 9
third son	Kihachi	age 6
fourth son	Sannosuke	age 3

Sōgorō's daughter Yuki, age 21, is the wife of Jirōzaemon of Kaba village, Hitachi, in the domain of Lord Araki Shima no kami.[46] His daughter Hatsu, age 16, is the wife of Genba's heir Tōshirō of Ono village, Hitachi, in the domain of Lord Naitō Geki. These two women are to be spared.

Takizawa village	Rokurōzaemon
Katsuda village	Jūzaemon
Chiba village	Chūzō
Takazawa village	Saburōbei
Ono village	Hanjūrō

These men acted outrageously in joining with Sōgorō in making a disorderly petition to Lord Kuse, but they were absent when he made his appeal directly to the shōgun. Therefore their lives are to be spared, but they will be banished, being ordered to keep at least twenty-five miles in all directions from Edo and twenty-five miles in all directions from their homes. The succession to their houses will be conferred on their wives and children. Acknowledge this announcement. It is to be followed to the letter.

The Crucifixion of Sōgorō and His Wife

His sons are also executed.

It soon became known that Sōgorō and his wife and children were to be executed at the Ebara plateau in Shimōsa province on the eleventh day of the second month, 1645. From far and near, people living in the vicinity and in the domain, or even in other domains, lamented their fate, took pity on them, and grieved as though for their own parents or brothers. Crowds gathered at Ebara. They strained on tiptoe to see the final moments while they chanted prayers to the Buddha in a last farewell. That was not all. The officials and peasants from the villages listed in the petition mourned as though they were losing their own fathers or mothers, and they too

63

came running, their sleeves soaked with tears. The people swarmed to Ebara. The bamboo fence enclosing the execution ground was so weakened by the horde pushing against it that it almost fell down.

Oh misery. Sōgorō and his wife were tied to two crosses which were then set upright. To the spectators, this ghastly sight appeared to be worse than the worst hell for criminals. Unable to bear looking at it, the people who had gathered there shut their eyes and shed many tears. They tried to chant prayers to Buddha, but they choked with tears as they repeated the stanzas, moving them to feel even greater pity.

At midmorning the four children tied with ropes were seated upon coarse mats of straw placed before their parents' eyes. Seeing this the multitude suddenly understood how the parents felt. They drenched their sleeves with tears as though their hearts would burst. The officials within the enclosure seated themselves on camp-stools and glared in all directions to restrain the crowd. The executioner advanced to the fore. Guards pulled out the eldest son, Sōbei, tied in rough ropes.

"You are a mere youth, but in accordance with the law, you are to be executed for the crimes of your father." In an instant, Sōbei's slender neck was severed from his body. Seeing this as they hung on their crosses, his parents changed color. Their eyes filled with blood. They ground their teeth in rage. Large teardrops of blood fell like the rain blown by the wind splashing against a rock. The spectators gasped. The terror and the pity of this painful spectacle were beyond description.

Next the second son, Gennosuke, was cruelly dragged out. The innocent nine-year-old said: "I have such a boil on my left shoulder that I request you to cut from the right." Even the heartless executioner appeared to hesitate slightly. The officials assembled there to witness the execution found themselves choked with tears and forced to cough. Trying not to enter into the parents' feelings, the executioner summoned his courage. With a flourish of his sword, Gennosuke's head fell forward.

His mother opened her eyes wide. "How cruel is this punishment. What crimes have my children committed to deserve it? Will their deaths be avenged?" To see her turning up the whites of her eyes, her hair standing on end, was a frightening sight, yet pathetic and pitiful as well.

Out of sympathy for the parents, the executioner hastily pulled out the third son, set him down, and cut off his head with his naked sword.

The fourth son, Sannosuke, saw some candy wrapped in paper that had been thrown into the enclosure from outside. Being a mere babe of three, he did not know he was about to die, so he stretched out his hand to take it. He had just about put it in his mouth when his head left his body. What his parents felt was indescribable. The spectators were overwhelmed with grief. Their eyes swelled with weeping.

The resident priest from Tōkō-ji in Kami Iwabashi came forward to claim the children's bodies. He put them in coffins, covered them with clothing, and took them back to the temple.

A comment: It was fine for the priest from Tōkō-ji to appear at this juncture and accept the children's remains, but it would have been even better had he busied himself before the children were killed, so as not to have had to have taken care of them. As a priest he could have written a petition stating that no matter how serious the crimes of the father, such young children would have had no knowledge of them. Why couldn't he have taken the responsibility of making an entreaty before they were to be executed? Although the lord naturally felt angry at the humiliation suffered by his family's reputation in the shōgun's own palace because Sōgorō's direct appeal, a crime which showed disrespect for his superiors, reached the ears of his fellow officials, had the priest begged him forcibly enough, might he not have shown clemency to the children? Even if he did not receive a pardon, for someone who has decided on a life of celibacy not to petition at all does not become a priest. Besides it was not as though his temple was in another domain or anything. "What is the purpose of priests putting on dyed robes and rolling the Buddha's name around in their mouths?" people muttered to each other. Sōgorō was a mere layperson, but for the sake of the peasants he took a crime upon himself, even though he could not have foreseen that he would see his wife and children executed before his eyes and depart this life ahead of him. Why didn't the priest sympathize with him? There are lots of priests in the important temples of the Sakura domain besides the one from Tōkō-ji, but they value their lives, keep their mouths shut from one year to the next, and it is asking too much of them to turn to the Buddha even when they are sick. How these bonzes stink of meat!

65

Opening his eyes wide, Sōgorō cried bitterly, "Should this kind of cruel punishment have been visited upon us? My resentment has increased beyond measure. How can it ever be dispelled?" He ground his teeth in unbridled rage and showed the whites of his eyes—a truly frightful sight. Seeing him do this, one of Danzaemon's[47] servants, Shigaemon, lowered the point of his spear and prepared to run him through.

His wife O-San raised her voice: "Wait a minute. My dear husband Sōgorō, we must now agree on what to do hereafter. My body may be left to hang on this cross, but my resolve is unshakable. Even if I am reborn five hundred years hence, I will still seek retribution for the resentment I feel now. No matter how many times I live and die, my wrath will never be dispelled. I will not take advantage of the Buddha's pledge to get myself into paradise.[48] My body has been hanged on this tree for the sake of all people, and I do not have an evil heart, but my wrath will become demons and devils. I warn you that I will kill to avenge my children. Aah, was that a kind punishment?" She rolled her eyes in a frenzy. Her disheveled hair flew out wildly. What a frightening promise of revenge.

Sōgorō heard her, spread his lips, and laughed loudly. "Well spoken. You are a woman, but the words you have just expressed are those that any superior being would be proud to utter. I agree with you completely. Our bodies are no longer of any use in this world, but our wrath will live on. Go ahead, strike."

As he spoke, Shigaemon brandished his spear and whirled to the right. "Ugh," he grunted, thrusting deep into Sōgorō's armpit. Blood spurted like a waterfall. Shigaemon pulled out his spear, wiped off the blood, turned around facing to the left of the woman in front of him, and pierced her in the side so as to hit all of her vital organs. Her breath rushed out like a flame before the startled eyes of the spectators.

"Aah, what a fine feeling," Sōgorō sneered. "Before three years have passed, heaven will punish Kōzuke no suke without his realizing it. Hurry up, strike my left side," he said impatiently. The spear point pierced him through to his right.

Then O-San opened her eyes and shouted loudly enough to be heard beyond the bamboo fence. "Farewell everyone. This is our last meeting." As she spoke, Shigaemon thrust deep into her right side and pierced her through to the left.

Sōgorō also opened his eyes. "I bid farewell to everyone who was kind enough to come here today." Having said their good-byes, the couple closed their eyes and took their last breaths as though they were falling asleep.

The assembled multitude chanted prayers to Buddha through their tears. Their voices ceaselessly proclaimed the evanescence of this life.

On the same day, the domanial officials summoned the village officials of Kami Iwabashi to give them orders saying that since Sōgorō was to have no successor, his paddies, fields, and house were to be sold at auction. His personal belongings were to be given to his married daughters to do with as they pleased, and the villagers were not to steal any of them. Jirōzaemon had requested that the two forest plots be donated to Tōkō-ji, Sōgorō's family temple, and so it would be done.

After that, an investigation was made into accusations of negligence on the part of officials in the Edo mansion and in the domain itself. As a result, over twenty men in Edo and Sakura were exiled, sent to distant islands, or dispossessed. Lucky to have escaped with their lives, the officials left Edo and Sakura, each going his own way.

The Death of Kōzuke no Suke's Consort

At the Edo mansion, Sōgorō and his wife transform themselves into monsters.

Just at that time, Lord Hotta Kōzuke no suke's consort was pregnant. In the course of her pregnancy, she took slightly ill, a condition that gradually became more serious. When it began to look as though her condition were hopeless, prayers were naturally offered in various temples and famous doctors did their best, but to no avail.

Once in the dead of night toward the end of the seventh month, the consort's birth chamber suddenly became brilliantly lit. The shrieks of a man and woman could be heard coming out of nowhere. It was indescribably dreadful. Everyone from the maids-in-waiting down to the servants tumbled about in surprise and confusion, as frightened as though a nameless criminal from hell had appeared.

On some nights a ball of fire came rolling out. Shaped like a monkey, it circled the consort with a ring of flames. The maids who worked in the women's quarters screamed in fear and surprise when they saw it.

At the beginning of the eleventh month, a man and a woman of frightening aspect, all covered with blood, entered the room, and they tried to pull the tormented consort away with them. This happened every night, making her illness worse and worse. She was much to be pitied. Despite the attempts in the middle of the eleventh month to drive the angry spirits away, they refused to leave.

Sōgorō and his wife appeared in Lord Kōzuke no suke's palace with spears sticking out of their sides. Looking like they had when they were still alive, they had ghastly pale faces, their eyes glittered like mirrors, and their disheveled hair stood wildly on end. Their angry shouts rolled like thunder.

"Aah, how regrettable, how mortifying. Now, especially, we cannot dispel the memory of how cruelly we were punished." They roamed wildly around the palace, now flying through the air, now shouting, now laughing.

Seeing the angry spirits of this couple was enough to make one's hair stand straight out. The warriors on guard duty trembled; their courage deserted them. Many who saw the apparitions fainted. No one could look them straight in the face.

Then the angry spirits caught sight of Lord Kōzuke no suke. "Ah ha, it was the cruel punishment performed by your administration that aroused our resentment." They flew about, glaring at him with the whites of their eyes.

Lord Kōzuke no suke was a brave man. Without showing the slightest hesitation, he pulled his sword from beneath a pillow and slashed with both hands. Overawed by this display of force, the apparitions instantly vanished in surprise, only to reappear behind him.

In quavering yet penetrating tones they cried, "What sufferings we endure. Can our anger be dispelled so easily?" Their shrieks pierced Kōzuke no suke to the core.

These things happened every night. Then the angry spirits of a man and wife with spears sticking out of their sides began to show themselves even at midday. Regardless of whether it was day or night, they screamed and flew madly about.

Thereafter high-ranking priests in the domain and neighboring provinces were ordered to rotate recitations of the great and secret Buddhist laws that subdue and disperse demons. The mountain shamans made strenuous and wholehearted efforts in offering their prayers. Lord Kōzuke no suke himself burned incense on a table set up in the great hall and intoned the Daihannya sutra. Nevertheless, the couple's angry spirits continued to haunt the palace. The retainers went fearfully about their duties. They guarded their master, wondering what sort of monster or enemy would next appear.

With the passage of that year, the era name was changed to Keian [1648–51]. The angry spirits of Sōgorō and his wife caused more and more trouble. Weird events continued to happen. The Hotta family suffered a number of calamities, its misfortunes increased, and turmoil erupted frequently. The retainers felt as if they were treading on thin ice, but they could do nothing except wait in breathless suspense for the next disaster.

A Quarrel in the Palace

Lord Hotta barricades himself at Sakura Castle.

On the eleventh day of the tenth month, 1649, all of the lords proceeded to the shōgun's palace as they did every year for the Gencho rites, a ceremony at which rice cakes made from new grain were eaten in thanksgiving for the harvest. Those who participated wore formal dress and trailed their long pants after them, a splendid sight like the twinkling of stars, showing that this system of government will last forever.

On that day, however, because of some trifling reason or perhaps because of a grudge, Lord Hotta Kōzuke no suke and Lord Sakai Iwami no kami quarreled in the very palace itself. Lord Sakai was forty-three. Lord Hotta, a senior councillor, showed not the slightest deference to his surroundings, but drew the sword he carried at his side and slashed at Lord Sakai. The uproar in the palace was tremendous. Lord Sakai died of his wounds the next day. He had been lord of Matsuyama in Dewa, a domain with an estimated yield of twenty thousand *koku*.[49]

This incident caused tremendous strife between the two families, but what happened is omitted here because it would take too long to describe.

At six in the evening of that same day, Lord Kōzuke no suke took advantage of the confusion reigning in the palace to creep stealthily through the disordered hall. Still dismounted, he pushed through the retainers encamped outside to return to his own home. With his own hands, he took out the horse named Harasumi, leaped nimbly on its back, and clapped the stirrups against its sides without waiting for any attendants. Seated in the saddle, he raced down Senju Avenue.

His retainers, who were still on foot, were amazed at what he had done. "How rash of him; our master has really done it now. We can do nothing here, so let's go back to the mansion and report on the crisis that has overtaken him."

The more sagacious of Hotta's brave warriors tried to prevent their fellows from jumping on their horses to follow their master and cut their way into the Sakai mansion. In the midst of all the confusion which reigned high and low, they finally managed to get everyone to dismount once more.

Lord Kōzuke no suke whipped up his horse and rode at breakneck speed for Sakura in Shimōsa. In just three hours, he covered the distance of over thirty miles. Riding up to the city gate of the castle, he shouted: "Hurry up, open the gate."

The foot soldiers on watch were amazed. "Who are you to come riding up to our gate and treat us so rudely?" they complained. "If you have business with us, come here and be polite about it."

"No, no. I am the lord of this castle, Kōzuke no suke. Open up, I tell you."

"Would the lord of this castle ever come riding up here all alone in the middle of the night? Do you have any idea how ridiculous you sound?" Grumbling, they refused to open the gate. Then they took a closer look and realized that they had before them a guest of noble appearance. Thinking uneasily that something funny must be going on, they reported everything that had happened to the house elder, Fuchiwatari Shukei. Shukei had no idea of what was happening either, but there was something about the situation that perturbed him. He got up immediately and peered through an opening in the peephole.

"Goodness gracious, it is undoubtedly our Lord Kōzuke no suke." Turning quickly, he gave orders to the guards to open the castle gate part way, then he sank to his knees. Lord Kōzuke no suke deigned to look down on him from his horse.

Shukei lifted his face. "Your unexpected arrival here on horseback all alone in the middle of the night is most surprising. There must be some good reason for this, but in the meantime, please don't hesitate to come on inside. Your attendants will be delighted to see you."

Accompanied by the warriors on guard duty and some foot soldiers, Kōzuke no suke paraded directly into the main enceinte. Suddenly there was a tremendous commotion among the retainers as they realized, each and every one of them, that something extraordinary had happened. Not yet having heard one word from their master concerning what was going on, they merely stared mutely at one another, wringing their hands in consternation.

The Death of Lord Sakai Iwami no Kami

Lord Kōzuke no suke fortifies himself in Sakura castle. It is decided to send a punitive force against him.

Rumors flew thick and fast that there had been a quarrel in the shōgun's palace in which Lord Kōzuke no suke had inflicted a serious wound on Lord Iwami no kami. In the end no medical treatment had proved effective, and he had passed away. Furthermore, Lord Kōzuke no suke had gone immediately to shut himself up in his castle of Sakura. No one knew what his intentions were. In the great hall of the shōgun's palace, the officials, the lords both great and small, and even the shōgun's relatives and brothers all held their separate councils on what to do. Everyone agreed in their reports to the shōgun that since Kōzuke no suke had unmistakably committed treason, they would have to raise an army and send a punitive force against him.

Mizuno Settsu no kami and Gotō Yamato no kami were Kōzuke no suke's close relatives. They appeared before the shōgun and pleaded earnestly, "Please order the two of us to lead the punitive force against Kōzuke no suke."

Having received their orders to lead the punitive force, the two men left that very day. By nightfall they had reached the Usui post station. From there they sent a messenger to Lord Kōzuke no suke in his castle at Sakura, telling him the following:

"Recently you wounded Sakai Iwami no kami in the shōgun's palace, then, without receiving permission from the shōgun, you secretly sneaked out of the palace and fortified yourself in your own castle. These are the deeds of a traitor. Words cannot express how

71

criminally you have behaved. Therefore the government has ordered that an army be sent against you. Just because the two of us are your close relatives, we have been forced to go so far as to ask for command of the punitive forces. If it becomes necessary, we will attack you to wipe out our family's dishonor in the heat of battle."

At the same time they secretly sent a private message to the house elder urging that the lord commit suicide.

Back in Edo, the debate continued over what to do. The officials all wondered what was going on while they waited impatiently for news from Sakura. Doubts arose over whether Mizuno and Gotō would remain loyal to the shōgun. Finally orders were issued to the lords to ready their own troops for the attack on Sakura. Lord Ogasawara Iki no kami, worth fifty thousand *koku,* and Lord Nagai Hida no kami, worth fifteen thousand *koku,* were put in charge of this force. They departed for Sakura in Shimōsa with orders given them in the shōgun's palace to take the castle and to report immediately if a rebellion was imminent. That these two men had to make such preparations demonstrated a true state of emergency.

At noon on the fourteenth day of the tenth month, a fast courier arrived with news from Sakura in Shimōsa. He reported the following:

"We have carefully evaluated Hotta Kōzuke no suke's recent illness, and we have concluded that he was insane. Having been treated with a variety of remedies, he has returned to his senses. For the first time, he realizes how badly he behaved in this affair. Now he is seriously concerned, and he admits his mistakes. We have placed him under arrest while we await further instructions."

This message was sent from Mizuno and Gotō to the senior councillors, who immediately passed it along to the shōgun. As a result, conditions in Edo quieted down.

The shōgun issued an order that Lord Kōzuke no suke be tied up in fishnets and carried back to the capital in an enclosed palanquin under strict guard, accompanied by Gotō Yamato no kami's troops. There he was transferred for safekeeping to Akimoto Tajima no kami until the entire affair had been settled. Having been ordered to make sure that all of the Hotta retainers dispersed peacefully, Mizuno Settsu no kami stayed behind in Sakura for a little while.

On the fifteenth, an announcement came from Edo. "Settsu no kami is to protect the castle while the retainers of Kōzuke no suke, who should now be dispersing, evacuate it as soon as possible.

Whoever ultimately takes charge of the castle will be announced at a later date."

With this strict order from the shōgun in hand, Mizuno Settsu no kami summoned the chief officials among the retainers to explain it to them. Then he instructed them to evacuate the castle at once. In return they presented him with a pledge of compliance. The retainers suddenly found themselves scattering in whatever direction they pleased, pulling along their old and young, women and children. The sick hobbled on sticks or had to be carried in litters. How pitiful to see their tears as they left the castle! The Edo mansion was also vacated on the same day, leaving it looking like a fire had hit it.

How fortunate that the government had such supreme authority that the lords had their troops guard against emergencies by patrolling the streets during these troubled times. When Lord Kōzuke no suke became the head of the Hotta family, a family which had endured for generations, the retainers behaved selfishly, causing the peasants of the realm great suffering, but then to have punished Sōgorō so cruelly! Aah, was it perhaps decreed by fate? What injustice for a punishment that should have been visited on Sōgorō alone to have fallen even on his wife and children.

The retainers lamented their grievous error that had polluted the family reputations bequeathed to them by their ancestors. Even if the lord had not acted as a lord should, if the retainers had acted loyally in serving him,[50] this disaster would not have befallen them. But when the lord acts not as a lord and the retainers act not as retainers, then there is nothing more to be said. What a pity that had Kojima Shikibu but thrown away his life in remonstrating with his lord, the Hotta family would not have become extinct.

Summons for the Two Families to Appear at Court

On the twentieth day of the fourth month of 1651, the shōgun Iemitsu set off on his journey for the next world at the age of forty-eight. He was given the posthumous name of Daiyu-in. Imposing Buddhist services were held for the dead. A general amnesty was granted. Descendants of Sakai Iwami no kami, whose family name had previously been made extinct, were summoned to the palace and given back their old twenty thousand *koku* domain of Matsuyama in the province of Dewa, just as they had held it before. At the same time Kōzuke no suke's uncle succeeded to the family name of Hotta. His relatives were summoned to appear at court, where they were given a domain of eighty thousand *koku* attached to Utsunomiya castle in Shimotsuke. Kōzuke no suke was ordered to retire so that his heir, known as Chikuzen no kami, could become the head of the family.

The Worship of Sōgorō's Spirit as the God of a Shrine

The leagues of villages whose petition was responsible for the extinction of the Hotta family are as follows:

Shimōsa province	Sōba district	39 villages
Shimōsa province	Chiba district	77 villages
Shimōsa province	Inba district	87 villages
Kazusa province	Musha district	7 villages

Sōgorō's great merit for future generations was that in having sacrificed his own life in making an appeal for the sake of peasants in over two hundred villages, he had forced the government to remit the high taxes and excess duties. In order to repay their tremendous debt of gratitude, the peasants wanted to worship him as the deity of a shrine and they so petitioned the Hotta family, thinking the occasion auspicious since the family was happy at having Kōzuke no suke's crimes forgiven. Nevertheless, Chikuzen no kami replied that since his castle was at Utsunomiya, it would not do for him to meddle in Sakura affairs, and the peasants would have to wait a while longer. Though it was against their will, the peasants refrained from doing anything. Then when Lord Doi Shōshō[51] exchanged domains with Hotta Chikuzen no kami in Utsunomiya, they petitioned again.

Now the peasants respect him as the god of their shrine, and they worship him as the Great August Deity Sōgo. Truly he left a great name for posterity. His body was left to hang on a cross, but his fame as a magnificent hero will shine for a thousand years. To express their devotion, everyone makes their way to the shrine, where he fulfills all their long-cherished desires. His special forte is public lawsuits wherein by distinguishing right from wrong according to morality and faith, he easily demonstrates the unreason of wrong and the strength of right. The miracles and remarkable happenings attributed to his divine spirit are utterly innumerable.

This incident shows that when a house has disloyal retainers, they inevitably torment the peasants. Once the peasants are driven into poverty, the lord's family will become extinct. Many examples of this may be found in other countries as well as in Japan. Truly if you are a warrior, you ought to leave behind a glorious reputation because your name is written down in the records for all posterity. But if you are a peasant, even if you sacrifice your life to rescue the domain and the people from their afflictions, no one is likely to eulogize your long journey. For that reason, this true account has been prepared without any fictional embellishments being added. Even today, everyone knows of the homage paid to the Great August Deity Sōgo.

The End

A Record of How the Four Orders of People in Mimasaka Ran Riot

U NLIKE THE SAKURA SŌGORŌ STORY, written nearly two hundred years after its hero died, "A Record of How the Four Orders of People [samurai, peasants, artisans, and merchants] in Mimasaka Ran Riot" *(Mikoku shimin ranbōki)* was written just a few months after the peasants in the Tsuyama domain of Mimasaka province in western Japan rose in 1727 to protest changes in the domanial taxation policies.[1] One of some twenty documents created outside the ruling class and unearthed by postwar scholars about this event, called the Sanchū uprising after the western mountainous section of the Tsuyama domain where it occurred, it is now considered a landmark in commoner literary history.[2] The author identified himself only with a pen name, Shinpū Kenchiku-ō, literally "the old man of the divine wind, eaves, and bamboo." As Herbert Bix has pointed out, this was the sort of title used by the tellers of military tales.[3] He gave his address as Takata, a post station on the road to the great shrine of Izumo, the terminus of a river traffic route and the marketing center for many of the peasants who took part in the uprising. He could not have been better placed to collect gossip.

Shinpū Kenchiku-ō wrote not in the flowing "grass" style favored by copyists of official documents, but in square *katakana* (Japanese syllabary) intermingled with Chinese phrases and antiquated Buddhist characters. From the red markings contained in the text, it appears that it was meant to be read aloud, possibly at a memorial service for those who had been executed by the state. Like some of the most representative works of classical literature, it was created to be heard.[4] Shinpū Kenchiku-ō was educated enough to have read the Chinese classics, though he did not always quote

77

correctly from them, and even with Buddhist terms he was maladroit, suggesting that his education remained incomplete. But he was well versed in the Japanese historical tradition. Nagamitsu Norikazu, who prepared this text for publication, believed the author was probably a masterless samurai, a doctor, an itinerant priest, or perhaps a traveling player who recounted stories from the *Taiheiki*, the classic military saga of the fourteenth century.[5] In any case, he probably had more learning than money. Living on the margin of society, he exhibited a ready respect for heroes who challenged the status quo and an ambivalent sympathy for peasant protesters.

Like other histories of peasant uprisings, this one opens with a platitude that sets the theme of the work to follow. In this case, the theme is ambiguity. Summed up in the Buddhist view that one cannot tell the difference between right and wrong in a complex world, it warns of the sometimes ludicrous results of taking a heroic stance. Shinpū Kenchiku-ō wrestles with the problem of disorder. He sympathizes with the peasants' plight, but he fears anarchy. He is angry at the officials for mistreating the peasants, yet he still needs them to be exemplars of moral rectitude. To answer the question of where virtue lies, he summons all of his literary and historical knowledge. Once having taken the metaphysical view that everything in experience can be simultaneously true and false, he is uncertain in the end as to whether he has written history or fiction. Thus his seemingly vague introductory remarks encapsulate a skepticism directed at his own knowledge of events.

The introduction also evokes the Japanese literary tradition. It repeats word for word the opening line of "A Tale of Mikawa" *(Mikawa monogatari)*, written in 1622 by Ōkubo Hikozaemon (1560–1639), a loyal retainer to the first three Tokugawa shōguns. Through "A Tale of Mikawa," it may also appropriate a somewhat similar passage in *The Story of the Sōga Brothers*, a thirteenth-century tale of revenge.[6] "A Tale of Mikawa" records the rise of the Tokugawa family, emphasizing the exploits of Ieyasu and his ancestors, and praising the benevolent rule he established in Japan.[7] From the confusion of right and wrong, Ieyasu plucked right; "A Tale of Mikawa" ends in triumph. From that same confusion, the peasants' leaders plucked wrong; "A Record of How the Four Orders of People in Mimasaka Ran Riot" ends not with the restoration of benevolent rule, but with the curse of a dying leader.

Shinpū Kenchiku-ō constructed this text by assembling fragments from the Japanese literary classics. He appropriated metaphors that resonate with war tales and the philosophical systems of the elites, but he displaced their meanings onto peasant action. The chronological narrative style of *The Tale of the Heike* in which events are introduced by the year, month, and day finds an echo here.[8] Like their enemies the samurai, the peasants have their army, their commanders, and their troops, but the character used for troops, *ki,* comes from the compound *ikki* or "rebellion," in contrast to the character *ki* found in the war tales, which means "cavalry." Scattered throughout the "Record" are phrases identifiable in other texts. A "jumble of rice, hemp, bamboo, and reeds" *(tōma chikuo)* explains, by using an expression found in the Lotus sutra, how two hundred thousand soldiers surrounded a castle in the *Taiheiki. The Tale of the Heike* is summoned in *tada hito momi ni,* translated here as "swept all before them," another expression used to signify troops going into battle. Shinpū Kenchiku-ō twice refers to the tedium induced by the soft rains of spring in the fifth month, an expression straight out of the *Tale of Genji,* Japan's classic novel of aristocratic love written in the eleventh century.[9] Little could be done during the rainy season, except read, write, fornicate, and talk. Walter J. Ong has pointed out that manuscript culture takes intertextuality for granted. This "Record" was deliberately created out of other texts, "borrowing, adapting, sharing the common, originally oral, formulas and themes, even though it worked them up into fresh literary forms impossible without writing."[10]

In legends and folklore, no detail is ever irrelevant, and so it is with this "Record" as well. A long episode at the beginning, for example, serves to disguise the leadership of the uprising. Descended from one of the heroes in *The Tale of the Heike,* extraordinary in his abilities and accomplishments, and a native of Tsuyama, Maki Tōsuke is a pseudonym for Maki Tokuemon, the person identified in historical documents as the instigator of the riot. The protagonist of the narrative, however, is a masterless warrior or *rōnin,* also called Tokuemon, who in a tale within the tale explains that he is the descendant of Amakusa Shirō Tokisada, leader of the Christian rebellion in Kyushu in 1637. Thus the Tokuemon who led the riot is concealed behind a double blind, Tōsuke and the *rōnin* Tokuemon, and assimilated through them to the heroes of Japan's national epic and to the most serious insurrection ever faced by the Tokugawa rulers. The double blind serves other purposes as well. If the author of this history were himself a *rōnin,* making his protagonist a *rōnin* serves to bind this class of men on the margin to the peasants and preserves a faint echo of the day when peasants and warriors fought together against a centralizing state, a fight that climaxed and ended in 1637. Besides, how else would Tokuemon have acquired his knowledge of military strategy and his famous short sword? Endowed with a noble lineage and worldly attainments, he becomes an outsider to peasant society, the "other" who achieves the stature to tie together a jumble of only slightly coordinated events.[11] When he overreaches himself to plot rebellion, action unthinkable in a peasant, his ambitions have already been explained by his lineage.

What Shinpū Kenchiku-ō chose as the causes for the riot were determined by what he needed to explain: human greed. Whereas the historian with a modern agenda of historical change would point to a tightening of administrative control and the diffusion of markets and commercial production, the first sign of trouble in the "Record" occurred when the Tsuyama lord died suddenly without a designated heir.[12] His retainers were terrified that the shōgun would claim the domain and throw them out. Peasants in western Tsuyama learned that their lands would be transferred to the bakufu, with its lower tax rates and more lenient administration. Both sides wondered what would happen to the rice collected in tax payments that had been stored in district warehouses. Exacerbating the perpetual struggle over tax revenues were government reforms instituted in 1723 to promote frugality, minimize fluctuations in the basic land tax rates, and uncover new items to be taxed. Especially resented by the peasants were the intermediaries between commoners and rulers, the country samurai *(gōshi),* who acquired economic advantages in return for their surveillance of the countryside.[13] Shinpū Kenchiku-ō brought all of these causes into play to unravel the complicated plot that traced the course of the uprising itself. The way he explained disorder determined what he saw as its antecedents.

In a manner typical of peasant-uprising literature, the antecedents for disorder wore a human if villainous face in the "Record." Out of all the domanial administrators, one man, accused of being an unqualified parvenu, was blamed for increasing taxes, corrupting his subordinates, and causing the riot. Although he became evil personified, he was never attacked directly. Instead the peasants turned their wrath against his minions nearer to hand, the country samurai who had permission to wear swords, ride horses, and use public surnames. Unlike the Sakura Sōgorō story, where a single, clearly defined villain sustained the plot from beginning to end, this "Record" included a cast of villains, many of whom appeared in only one episode. Their common characteristics were their social privileges, their commerical opportunities, and their greed. Herbert Bix has read this refusal to recognize oppressive economic and political relations as a lack of class consciousness. But Peter Burke has argued that seeing injustice as a human failing, not a fault with the social structure, what he calls a "fatalistic or moralistic stance," has its advantages, for it allows action against villains whenever it is possible.[14] The effort to humanize relations with the state, to make sense of events that were beyond the control of the ruled, and to establish a place for commoners in terms of things within their comprehension can also be seen as an attempt to hold onto humanity and goodness.[15]

This "Record" is structured much more loosely than the Sōgorō story in ways uncomfortable for modern, Western readers. In the initial incident, unidentified peasants attack one of the privileged intermediaries for removing rice from a district warehouse. He claims the rice is his own personal property, but the peasants suspect that some of it is tax rice he is holding for the government. Peasants in other districts soon try to prevent the transfer of rice from their warehouses, actions given a spurious air of coordination in the "Record" through the appearance of Tokuemon, who changes his name to Amakusa Tokisada, the doomed leader of the Christian rebellion. Soon the peasants begin to vent their wrath on the country samurai by smashing property. Domanial officials sent to quell the riot cave in completely to the peasants' demands. Except for a brief flurry of activity quickly suppressed in the eastern half of the domain, the uprising appears to be over.

At this point, the "Record" clearly contradicts itself. The peasants and their allies previously displayed in a positive light suddenly become villains. Accused of planning to overthrow the government as Taira no Masakado had tried to do in 940, the leaders, among them the *rōnin*, marshal their troops for a full-out assault on the domanial army at the end of 1726. One leader even acquires an ancestor in the person of Ōmori Hikoshichi, maligned in Japanese history for forcing the heroic Kusunoki Masashige (1294–1336) to commit suicide after the battle of Minatogawa. Juxtaposed with the standard scenes of peasants smashing property are others, disconcertingly unrealistic, in which the leaders plot strategy, stage ambushes, and resolve to fight to the finish in an exaggeration of numbers often found in the accounts of riots. After the Christian rebellion, peasants never again took up arms against government officials, nor did they ally themselves with the samurai until the Ōshio Heihachirō rebellion in Osaka in 1837, but the use of military action dominates literary conventions to embue stories of peasant protest with the martial hues of a bygone era. The peasants even wear emblems to distinguish friend from foe, whereas in reality the difference between warriors and peasants was as clear as that between heaven and earth.

Aided by several strokes of luck, the domanial officials capture the ringleaders apart from their fellows, and the peasant armies conveniently evaporate. In describing the course of these events, Shinpū Kenchiku-ō weaves in debates between officials urging caution and those who want to attack immediately. While the author could not have had any direct knowledge of these debates, they contribute to his text's narrative veracity. Episode again follows episode as the officials hunt down the troublemakers. At the end, Amakusa Shirō is still unrepentant. At his crucifixion, he curses the officials and promises to return as an angry spirit, a bitter ending that leaves the peasants unreconciled to the authorities and the contradictions in the plot unresolved. Unlike the classic realist narrative familiar to Western readers, which dissolves conflict through the reestablishment of order, closure in this text remains imperfect.

Another characteristic of the "Record," one unfamiliar and irritating to Western readers, is the flood of names. Each episode involves different people, many of whom never appear in the text again. There are lists—the names of villages implicated in the uprising and the names of men arrested and punished for their part in it. Instead of reciting the events that happened on the other side of the domain, too far away for news and rumors to have found their way back to Takata, the author simply presents the names of the villages in that region. Even the accuracy of the tally is questionable owing to the similarity of names with those in his own area. Recording constitutes one way to remember those who had sacrificed their lives, but the names of the men executed on the Doi River plain differ slightly from official records.

The effort to be precise, to name names, serves to make this history concrete and credible. These details guarantee that the uprising really did happen, what Roland Barthes called the "reality effect."[16] The author's careful attempt to remember exactly who was involved, however, ultimately contradicts his efforts to disguise the identity of the ringleaders, an ambiguity of fact and fiction that mirrors the tale itself. For the modern reader, names are less important than patterns of interactions to which they bring specificity; the convention of naming particulars, individuals, and places roots this text in the past. This convention, like the episodic structure of the story itself, reminds the reader that "we are not of that period, and we cannot experience the text as it was experienced then."[17]

This "Record" is one of many documents that bear on the Sanchū uprising of 1726. In *Peasant Protest in Japan,* Bix interpolates approximately one-fifth of the text, wringing from it those passages he felt are colorful yet close to the historical record and comparing them to a text created by domanial officials.[18] His interpretation of the text helped me prepare this translation, but the gap between English and Japanese provides ample latitude for differences of emphasis and nuance. I have also broken the text into sections and added headings to assist the reader through the welter of incidents that constitute the narrative. Omitted by Bix are many episodes that describe the heroes and their relationship to earlier rebels against the established order. Bix states that the author "had no political ideology, only a moral creed."[19] A closer look at this moral creed in the context of the "Record" taken as a whole suggests that the text resonates with the Tokugawa ruling-class ideology while containing the seeds of a social discourse not entirely congruent with it.

The samurai disguised and legitimized their domination in the seventeenth century, Herman Ooms argues, by positing the concept of the "way of heaven" *(tendō)* as the central construct that defined the place of rulers and commoners alike in a sacred order. In contrast to Bix, who offers a narrowly defined role for heaven as a "punitive concept," a "synonym for justice," Ooms sees the way of heaven as a unifying principle that encompasses both the natural and the human world.[20] At several points in the "Record" and in "A Thousand Spears at Kitsunezuka," the subject for the next chapter, this concept accounts for human nature and affairs of state. People who do good by showing compassion for their fellow men are blessed by heaven; they are not attacked even though they may be wealthy. This concept also explains why the peasants were defeated so easily, despite their preponderance of numbers. A series of unfortunate accidents demonstrates the workings of fate, of karmic forces that inevitably overwhelm anyone who steps out of his or her proper place in the social order. Finally, the way of heaven encompasses the mishmash of philosophical and belief systems—Confucianism, Buddhism, and Shintō—on which the "Record" draws to explain the arrangement of reality.

The way of heaven in the world of humans was manifested through the five relationships (ruler-subject, parent-child, husband-wife, elder brother–younger brother, friend-friend) often associated with Confucianism. Of these, the most important for a peasant was the relationship between parent and child. In the last chapter, "A Tale Told in a Dream of a Eulogy to Filial Piety," this relationship constitutes the crux of the story. Twice in the "Record," uprising leaders remembered the obligations they had incurred to their mothers for the sacrifices these women made in raising them (kōon). The emphasis on filial piety served two purposes. On a general level, it reminded the reader that parents always took precedence over their children in accordance with the norms of order established by the way of heaven. For this reason, Higuchi Yajirō (Jirō in the text) could not allow his mother to be punished, even though she wanted him to forget her and continue the fight. Incidentally, this particular episode is but one version of how Yajirō was captured. According to other legends, he was found when someone spotted his faithful dog bringing him food, and today visitors to the Tsuyama region can visit a small monument erected in its honor.[21] Shinpū Kenchiku-ō was not interested in dogged devotion. His second purpose was to demonstrate that the leaders of the uprising were upright, virtuous men who understood propriety.

To make sense of disorder, Shinpū Kenchiku-ō drew on the syncretic mixture of Buddhist and Shintō concepts found in popular religion. All the villains had one thing in common: they were greedy, covetous, and full of desire (yoku), the enemy of benevolence and Buddhist notions of compassion (jihi).[22] Since it was through compassion that one's humanity became apparent, to seek material gain at the expense of others was to deny the principle that connects people with society. Buddhism also provided metaphors for disaster and an explanatory language for retribution, reminding the reader of how difficult it was to escape from karmic pain. Even the peasants who had acted in accordance with the principle of heaven in punishing wrongdoers found that once their pride had led them to ignore the sacred teachings of the gods and Buddhas, their defeat was only a matter of time.

Shintō practices and beliefs ironically gave meaning to killing. For the vanquished, death liberated their leaders from habitual deference to the ruling class. The leaders vented their bitterness at misgovernment by promising to be reborn as angry spirits in the mode of Sakura Sōgorō. Calling on the Shintō gods also bestowed significance on the deeds of the victors. With the exception of the Shimabara Christian rebellion in which thousands of people were slaughtered, peasant protests in the Tokugawa period generally ended with relatively few deaths. No matter how many ringleaders were executed in public, their deaths were considered exemplary punishments to teach those who had gone astray respect for authority. The Sanchū uprising was unusual in the number of peasants who died—fifty-one according to the "Record," more according to other sources. There had to be a better reason than issuing a warning to those who might be tempted to protest in the future. Thus the executions were overblown into a blood festival *(chimatsuri)* to the gods of war, a celebration of bloodshed inflated by the same language used in Hideyoshi's Korean campaigns in the 1590s, when the ears of the slain were pickled and shipped to his headquarters in Kyushu. In Shintō cosmology, blood was a pollution, but as Ooms has indicated, under the pressure of overwhelming political events, even that which was most offensive to the gods paradoxically became an offering on their behalf.[23]

In reconstructing the ideology of this text it is necessary to juxtapose references to the way of heaven with other elements the text appropriates from Japanese history. It then becomes clear that the concept allows more room for deviant discourse than the Ooms interpretation of Tokugawa ideology would lead the reader to expect. By claiming that the Tokugawa polity faithfully conformed to the natural order and by rewriting the power struggles during the years of conquest before 1600 as a process of pacification, proponents of the system had tried to deny its historicity. Censorship ensured that certain topics, including peasant uprisings, were never mentioned publicly, yet among the mixed messages conveyed by the "Record" was praise for Yui Shōsetsu (1605–51), who tried to destroy the bakufu, and other historically recognized warrior rebels. This praise for rebels helped expose the contingent nature of bakufu authority. Even more subversive was the identity of the peasant leader with Amakusa Shirō. In this text, the leaders in the Sanchū uprising took noble names—Tokisada, Tokiuji, Tokimitsu—that distinguished them from ordinary peasants and everyday life, names analogous to the posthumous titles that mark the divide between life and death. By changing Tokuemon's name to one identified with a rebellion that rejected not just the Tokugawa rulers but their ideology as well, Shinpū Kenchiku-ō magnified a local confrontation to national significance and challenged the political order itself.[24] Thus in the "Record," components of a historical event were cut to fit the cloth of a heterodox ideology, one that emphasized the failings of the rulers, but also the impossibility of change. Glorified were those heroes who opposed the state, but with the recognition that their efforts were as futile as a monkey trying to reach the moon.

A Record of How the Four Orders of People in Mimasaka Ran Riot

When right and wrong are confused, both right and wrong become wrong. In dreams, both reality and nothing become nothing.

Only because they had wholeheartedly committed themselves did the mantis try to crush the wheel of a cart and did the monkey reach for the moon reflected in the water.[25]

In a remote corner of Mimasaka there lived a man called Maki Tōsuke. He was the twenty-fifth generation to be descended from Higuchi Jirō,[26] but for some trifling reason, he went by his mother's name. As might be expected of a Higuchi descendant, he was strong and extremely handsome. Knowing that an excess of emotion had brought down his house, he collected old books on war and sought to learn military strategy. For many years he served as a rear vassal to study the ways of the warriors. He became a man of the world, completely familiar with Edo and well versed in the customs of the daimyō.

After a long time had passed, Tōsuke returned home. There his relatives and his neighbors, Higuchi Yajirō, Hinata Hanroku, Ōmori

Shichizaemon, and Yamane Gorōemon, came to visit him. They ate and drank and found ways to amuse themselves. To celebrate the end of the year, Tōsuke led off with a poem:

> This is the season to drink and sing, giving no thought for
> tomorrow.
> In my tattered clothing is nothing but a clipped coin.

> —*Maki Tokuemon*

Everyone was impressed. Then Tōsuke sat up straight to say solemnly:

"I was in Edo for many years where I learned much. It is said that a lion's cub is able to leap stone walls as soon as it is born. When Amakusa Shirō of Kyushu was just eighteen, he killed bureaucrats and fortified a castle. He answered to the entire country of Japan, he defeated great generals, and his name is praised throughout the world. In more recent times, Yui Shōsetsu provoked a rebellion by raising his flag in Edo. Although he managed to shake Japan, the times were not right. In Suruga, he lost his life. The white bones of his corpse may lie unburied, but his name is extolled in Japan, China, and India." Once he had told these stories, everyone joined in the fun.

At the banquet was a masterless warrior of bold appearance named Tokuemon. He listened attentively to these ancient tales, his tears streaming. Those present said, "How peculiar," and asked him why he cried. He replied:

"My ancestors were from Hizen in Kyushu. For some reason my father became a masterless warrior, and by chance I have ended up here. Let me tell you what happened. My grandfather was Shirō no Taifu Tokisada.[27] He had set his mind on doing great things, he had a taste for the secret military arts of K'ung Ming,[28] everyone obeyed him, and once he had announced his intentions, he attracted disciples hither and thither in the neighborhood.

"One of my grandfather's close friends regretted leaving his wife a widow and encouraged her to form a new connection somewhere, but this was not what she wanted. Instead she lived alone without bothering anyone. Then, to get through one cold snowy night, she invited some men to visit and entrusted herself to them, plying them with several cups of sake and amusing them with stories. Ill at ease, Tokisada proposed the following verse:

Farewell, all is changed. Watching the snow a couple makes love.

'That is an interesting verse. Farewell indeed,' the other guests all said. They exchanged short verses until they had sobered up, then they went to the red light district nearby, where they dropped in for a moment and had just one more drink to amuse themselves.

"In this way Tokisada and the widow became intimate. There were signs that he occasionally sought diversion with her. Sometime after they had gotten to know each other, the woman wrote the following:

Hoping to see you, how painful it is to awaken from sleep.
Have I learned nothing from experience
Or will I seek to dream again?

She read it and sent it off. Then, cold-blooded though he was, his heart melted. He let the years slip by in visits to her village. Once during the tedium induced by the soft rains of spring, he went to her village and spoke more seriously to her than he ever had before.

"'I have but one great desire,' he told her. 'No matter what happens to me, I have made no plans for living past tomorrow, nor do I intend to survive to a ripe old age or die of sickness. Given that my life will not be an ordinary one, should I die and should you have a boy after my death, he must keep constantly next to his person this book telling the three secrets of Chinese military strategy and this short sword made by Seki Sonroku[29] that he inherits from his father. Please make sure that he gets them,' he repeated over and over. Knowing in her heart that this was farewell, the woman wrung her sleeves and made no reply except her tears.

"By this time, Tokisada had already made up his mind to take vengeance, but having waited too long, he ended up destroying himself. My father never forgot these words. He told me never to disgrace the name of my grandfather. Then my mother sought more congenial surroundings at Murotsu in Harima because she had been expelled from a place where she found it difficult to continue living anyway. She made a living by spinning thread to support me through the months and years until I was fifteen. But after a while, somehow or other, she seemed not quite herself. In the end, she melted away with the morning frost on the fifth day of the tenth month. Having found work as a servant to a samurai, I went to Edo where I wandered here and there seeking my relatives. At one point I met Mr. Maki, and we soon became friends. Through an unintended act of kindness on his part, I have been able to get through some hard times by staying for awhile at Maki in Mimasaka.

"I have never forgotten the debt of gratitude I owe my ancestors. Upon hearing the story which you just related, I was moved to tears, feeling as happy as though I were meeting my grandfather. It must be true what they say that one's innermost thoughts will sooner or later be betrayed by one's face. Now you have heard the story of my life."

"Well, so you are from Hizen," those present said, looking at each other in astonishment. "It's perfectly natural that you should long for your old home."

[Death Comes to the Lord of Tsuyama while Greedy Retainers Flourish]

In the middle of the autumn of 1726 came reports that the lord of Mimasaka had unexpectedly fallen ill and now lay near death. Some said he had already passed on. He had neglected to provide himself with a formally designated heir in this uncertain world, a fact that worried his retainers not a little. Those in the capital met to discuss what to do, but the results were kept strangely secret from Tsuyama.

Among the lower vassals in Mimasaka was a man named Kubo something-or-other Chikahira. He had started his career as a tea server in the bakufu, but at some point someone had managed to get him a position serving the lord of Mimasaka. He had permission to carry a sword and ride a horse. Through trickery he was able to get his stipend increased to three hundred bags. He had intimate acquaintance with Kyoto and Osaka. Pretending to be clever, he promoted frugality in all things in order to rob the public purse. Because the lord was young, he never asked any questions or investigated Chikahira, treating him instead as a loyal retainer.

By making loans, confiscating money in town and country, and levying special taxes, all of which enabled him to advance money to the higher retainers in Mimasaka, those important enough to be counted on the fingers of one hand, Chikahira distracted them from their official business of serving the lord in Kyoto and Osaka. He himself arbitrarily enforced standards of frugality right down to reducing the fires under the kettles in the kitchen. Regardless of the misery he caused those below him, he swindled the people, all because he was greedy.

What an evil man Chikahira was. The famous vicissitudes of Oguri and Ogita[30] in the past should be a lesson to us all, but now wise retainers are nowhere to be found. In their stead have risen the foolish destroyers of houses. Once those below are allowed to do as they please and favoritism becomes the way of the world, gossip runs rampant. Is it not true that just as the shape of water conforms to its containers, so people do good or evil according to the character of their friends? To a man, the retainers valued Chikahira highly. Those below did what those above taught them. Even the lowest servants took him as a model. They forgot themselves in their selfish pursuits; they betrayed their calling and disrupted the social order. This was the real reason why the peasants ran riot.

On the seventeenth day of the eleventh month of 1727, a courier came from Edo to announce, "The Lord is dead."

"Without a successor having been chosen for him, the domain is in danger," everyone whispered to each other. "It's like walking on thin ice." Out of nowhere came a rumor rampant throughout the countryside that all loans and debts and even the obligation to repay rice borrowed from the domanial authorities would be cancelled.

[The Riot Begins]

Here let me introduce a man called Kondō Chūzaemon Masatsune, a deputy district headman who lived in the Katahara section of Kōchi village, Ōba district. He made a comfortable living, plus he had permission from the domanial authorities to carry a sword and ride a horse. In the adjacent district called Nishihara was a warehouse for storing the grain paid in taxes to the government. When the people of Kondō Masatsune's district learned that, in the middle of the night on the twenty-first day of the eleventh month, he was secretly taking almost all of the rice out of the warehouse and loading it on boats to send to a nearby district, a people's army of over one hundred immediately bore down upon him, raising their voices in war cries. They surrounded the warehouse agent and beat up Kondō. He barely managed to get away from them.

Chōzaemon, a wealthy man from Akano village who lent rice to the peasants, was also a deputy district headman. Hearing what had happened, he reported that he too had had rice stored in the Nishihara warehouse along with several others, but seeing the danger faced by the domain, he feared that he would be unable to do as he pleased with his own possessions, so he had rashly removed them in the middle of the night. It was impossible to tell whether his motives were good or bad.

The next day a courier came from Tsuyama with a summons for the two deputy district headmen. They respectfully promised to obey it, but on the way to the capital they vanished from the domain. Their fellow conspirators, Nishihara Kaemon, Akano Tōzō, and Kōchi Kiichi, scattered like baby spiders and ran off to hide. Encouraged by this turn of events, the people's army disbanded.

On the night of the fourth day of the twelfth month, an unsigned circular was sent to the Maki and Higuchi villages reporting a rumor from the Kuse district that rice was being loaded on riverboats in the middle of the night. After due deliberation, everyone agreed, "We can't do anything without a people's commander, but Tōsuke is too old." Making their choice on the basis of talent, they decided to have Tokuemon become their leader. He then changed his name to call himself Amakusa Shirō no Saemonnosuke Fujiwara Tokisada. The men who followed him were from the following villages:

Mashima District

Masayoshi	Ōtsuke	Habu	Nishi Kayabe
Kanba	Mitsue	Ōsugi	Kanayama
Miakedo	Kayabe	Higashi Kayabe	Takebara
Otani	Awatani	Kuroda	Hoshiyama
Mukōyubara	Shimomi	Maga	Yasui
Kuwase	Taguchi	Nishihatake	Yabu
Hijiya	Mikamo	Kamikishi	Tane
Bessho	Shibara	Meji	Kurokui
Shinjō	Suga	Tamada	Hon Kayabe
Oka	Ishiuchi	Fujimori	Fumoto
Mio	Doi		

42 villages, 3,000 rebels

91

Chapter Two

Ōba District

Shimomi	Daikanaya	Misaka	Makago
Komi	Yamakuse	Hisami	Tomiyamane
Meki	Kuginukiogawa	Hatsuwa	Tawara
Kuse	Tahane	Nagata	Hiramatsu
Tsugitaru	Bessho	Nishihara	Nakashima
Miseshichihara	Tokuyama	Ōba	Yono
Yoshida	Akano	Nabeya	Shimoyubara
Fukuda	Kōchi	Kōkami	Shitawa
Hōkaiji	Tada	Yashiro	Kaketa
Nogawa			

37 villages, 5,000 rebels

This force numbered over eight thousand rebels, over one hundred of them armed with hunting guns or pop guns used to frighten birds, the rest armed with boar hunting spears, bamboo spears, hatchets, and axes. Each vying to be first, they advanced like a landslide. They pursued and captured the boats being loaded at the Kuse district warehouse and confiscated the rice. (It was commonly claimed that no one knew who the rebels were.) Then they took the rice to the town of Kuse, where they set a guard over it.

Thereafter they marched on the Kuse warehouse agents, where they sent a message to the sake brewer, Tsukadaniya Tarōemon, telling him to hand over his government rice.[31] Before he could finish replying that "for me, on my own, to hand over the rice I hold in trust for the government would be unthinkable," several hundred men had smashed up his front door and lattices with their axes and hatchets. Unable to withstand them, Tarōemon fled.

The rebels sent a similar message to the warehouse agent Yamaguchiya Kaneda Rokurōzaemon living in the same town. Mr. Kaneda was a mere townsman, but he understood the logic of what the peasants were doing so he handed them the keys to the warehouse.

"There is nothing in there but my own property," he said as he got out of their way.

After that, the people's commander Amakusa Tokisada ran around giving these orders to his forces: "Do not cast covetous eyes

92

upon the accumulated wealth of this district. Our enemies are the country samurai. Do not confuse them with our wealthy neighbors." That same night the peasant forces divided at Ōdankōge. One troop of over a thousand rebels led by men from Doi, Yamane, Ōmori, Hinata, and Maga marched on the home of the country samurai in Meki, Fukushima Zenbei. With their axes and hatchets they shattered his front door to smithereens. They hauled out and smashed up his coffers, chests, tools, dishes, household utensils, weapons, and harnesses.

In the midst of this, one peasant said, "Here we have a helmet. Well now, would it be so difficult to smash that up?" All the other peasants laughed.

Fukushima was a country samurai experienced in the ways of the world. Not being one to underestimate a situation, he secretly opened his back gate and hid himself in a mountain forest. His entire family, including his wife and children, also escaped.

"We have realized our long cherished desires," the peasants shouted. Having set their minds at ease, they withdrew.

Rumors ran rampant that Fukushima had been really greedy, wrongfully charging 30 to 50 percent interest on loans of rice and grain. Besides, he had taken great pride in being a country samurai.

Another troop of over one thousand led by men from Higuchi, Shinjō, Taguchi, Mikamo, Kuroda, Kanayama, and Fumoto swept all before them in marching on the home of the deputy district headman Chūjirō, who lived in the same district. With their axes and hatchets they shattered and smashed his front door and the doors inside. Chūjirō valued his life. He flew through the back door to vanish no one knew where. The troops broke into the house. They put a match to his furnishings, sliding doors, buckets and bowls, and old clothes for a bonfire to ward off the cold of the night. This was so everyone would later remember how he had been punished by heaven.

Another people's army of six or seven hundred rebels from Meki, Kōchi, Kashi, Kayabe, Akano, Tahara, and Komi marched on the deputy district headmen of Misaki village, Magozaemon. "We have been informed that a clerk from Tsuyama is here. Is that true?" Magozaemon apologized profusely. He opened for their inspection all of his rooms, including the one for official audiences. Satisfied, the people's army went home. Magozaemon always put honesty first; he was sincere and benevolent. Everyone exclaimed over and over that he had received the blessings of heaven.

[A Confrontation between Peasants and Officials]

Thereafter the three troops of the people's army gathered at Kuse. The plains, mountains, paddies, and fields were filled with people brought together like a jumble of rice, hemp, bamboo, and reeds. Travelers passing by occasionally had to stop as they would have had a new inspection station been put in their way.

At dusk on the fifth, two intendants, Yamada Bunhachi and Miki Jinzaemon, arrived in Kuse and summoned the people's army. Afraid that they might be taken hostage, no one appeared. Instead they sent a message saying, "If you have business with us, go to Ōdankōge, where the peasants will outline their position." It being beyond their power to do otherwise, the two magistrates went to Ōdankōge, where the peasants surrounded them on all sides.

The leaders, Amakusa Tokisada and men from Maki, Higuchi, Ōmori, Hinata, Yamane, Kuroda, Kanba, and Maga, lined up on all four sides. The situation was fraught with danger. Everyone spoke together in making a statement:

"First, we do not understand why you tacked a supplementary notice onto this year's tax bill, raising taxes 4 percent, or why we have to pay our taxes in full by the end of the year. When the previous ruler was still alive, his benevolence was so widely known in other provinces that even people from the shōgun's domains aspired to live in Tsuyama. Nevertheless, after Kubo got himself put in charge, he did much wrong. It is because of Chikahira and his allies among the country samurai that the first sowing of wheat in autumn was suspended and seals were attached to ox and horse plows.[32]

"It is unlikely that the central administration ordered us to pay the land tax as soon as possible. Rather it was the district and deputy district headmen who issued these instructions. They threatened those who paid late with manacles, and the way they have made the peasants suffer through their ordeals is indescribable.

"The townspeople of Tsuyama colluded with Chikahira to print up thousands of rice certificates which they then sold at whatever price they could get. The money they received was stolen by Chikahira, who used it to buy a house in Osaka. Rumors have been flying thick and fast that he is preparing to flee because he knows Tsuyama is in danger.

"In all truth, the peasants rely chiefly on the wheat crop to stave off hunger in the spring. We do not understand why we have not been allowed to plant it.

"It was as wrong as wrong can be to have pretended that the lord had received a new official rank and levied money for his expenses on town and country. Our lord's great uncle living in Tsuyama was amazed when an emissary came from Harima bearing that lord's condolences. He acted as a sincere and virtuous lord should by insisting that all the money collected in such an outrageously lawless fashion had to be returned to its owners immediately.

"Are the authorities really unaware of how the district headmen show their contempt for the peasants by subtracting the loans owed them from the tax rice, then deceiving the authorities by pretending the peasants have not paid their taxes? Herein lies the source of peasants' accumulated frustrations," they argued as shrewdly as they could.

The two magistrates listened to them. "You're absolutely right. As you have requested, we will retract the supplementary notice raising taxes, and we will allow you to pay 86 percent of the regular taxes demanded in this year's tax bill. We will abolish the district and deputy district headmen, replace the village headmen, and leave it up to you to choose whomever you please for messenger service. Debtors and creditors will negotiate their terms face to face. We will cancel your obligation to repay the rice you borrowed from the domanial authorities. Right now we will distribute to every peasant present a day's ration of rice. The former village headmen are to let us know how many there are." Since they were talking about over thirteen thousand peasants who would each receive five *go*, they realized that even 120 bales of rice would not be enough.

The poor peasants each returned to his own district, leaving behind those ordinary peasants who had become the new messengers and those who had taken the lead in being the spokesmen. The spokesmen and the magistrates then exchanged written promises, but this was all a plot on the part of the magistrates to learn the names of the leaders for the future.

Chapter Two

[Unrest in the Eastern Districts]

That same day an official courier came from Tsuyama with a report that peasants in the eastern districts had an appeal to make. Those who gathered at Kawanabe were

Tōnanjō District

Kawasaki	No	Shitobe	Katsube
Hongō	Momiyama	Higashi Ichinomiya	Oshiire
Shiboi	Ōta	Takano	Numa
Noketa			

13 villages, over 1600 rebels

Tōhokujō District

Yokono	Saiya	Takakura	Sange
Ofuchi	Haragō	Kawai	Kuwahara
Toga	Shimohara	Kugō	Uno
Ōsasa	Chiwa	Dōdōdani	Muroo
Yashiro	Shimotsugawa	Aoyagi	Yoshimi
Aoyama	Konakahara	Yukishige	Ayabe
Naruyasu	Kurogi	Kusakabe	Monomi
Tatchū	Haragō shimo		

30 villages, over 1,800 rebels

Seihokujō District

Kotanaka	Yutani	Okitsu	Terawada
Nishi Ichinomiya	Shimotanomura	Tōya	Ōmachi
Kita	Naka	Sanetsune	Kohara
Ichiba	Teradani	Kanayama	Hirada
I	Koshibatake	Kamikawara	Sawada
Iwaya	Sōja	Miuchi	Toshinobu
Yamakita	Tanabe	Kuhōden	Munushige

28 villages, over 2,000 rebels

Seiseijō District

Ninomiya	Magabe	Tsukatani	Onabara
Nunohara	Wada	Kusunoki	Okutsu

Hara	Baba	Nagatochi	Furukawa
Enjūji	Tominakama	Sugi	Kawamoto
Oza	Kuda	Hade	Takeda
Nakatani	Nishiya	Toshima	Seto
Habu	Shikōno	Takayama	Yamashiro
Hako	Saibara	Teramoto	Tomi
Yōno	Kōbe	Doi	Kuroki
Nagatō	Morihara	Ire	Izaka
Innoshō	Muneda	Dai	Kawanishi
Shimohara	Teeji	Kōchi	

47 villages, over 22,000 rebels

The total number of rebels was 27,400.

An immense horde advanced from the four corners of Tsuyama. Since contact had already been made with the peasants in the western districts, a written text of the demands was prepared without delay. I heard that the magistrates went to meet the rebels at the entrances to their districts, and, having managed to pacify them by ascertaining what they wanted, matters were concluded as they had been in the west. The details are unknown.

Once the riot in Kuse district had been concluded on the eleventh, the people's army withdrew from town and country. Out of all that number, only Amakusa Tokisada and Higuchi Jirō went to Tsuyama, where they stayed for one or two days. Then they returned home with the certificates for eight hundred bales of rice that they had received from the magistrates.

Before they divided these certificates among the people, they rested for awhile at the home of a townsman in Kuse called Odaniya Heibei. From the beginning of the riot, Odaniya had served as the communications center between east and west. On dispatch boxes sent east, for example, he had affixed his own seal. He had bribed the magistrates' retainers and servants, employed spies, and made his home a secret meeting place for Amakusa Tokisada and Higuchi Jirō. Everyone knows he did this; how could it remain a secret in his neighborhood? Evil such as this is beyond the power of words to describe. Besides, Amakusa Tokisada sent him twenty bales out of the two hundred that had been confiscated off the boats. "How foolish of him not to know what calamities he was storing up for the

97

future," the idle gossips in the capital sneered, and they clapped their hands. But it ought to offend their ears simply to repeat rumors that they don't know the truth of for themselves.

[The Turning Point]

From the tenth on, town and country became quiet. According to an old saying, People who become proud will be punished by heaven; to betray the laws of heaven is to bring destruction on oneself. Truly whereas it might be agreed that up to this point the peasants were in the right, were they now to bring ruin upon themselves because, not knowing the evil that lurked in their hearts, they abandoned the treasured teachings of the gods and Buddhas, and they made light of Tsuyama?

Amakusa Tokisada paid heed to no one. "Next year will begin with an intercalary month. Let's make it the dawn of a new age," he said. He planned to drink the four seas at a single gulp. He stirred up memories of the past as though he were a local Taira no Masakado.

"If the Tsuyama domain is divided in half, the western districts will surely become part of the shōgun's domain. In that case, the intendants will decide on new laws, and it will be difficult to borrow money as we need it," he pointed out. "Before that happens," he announced, "let's take back the rice that has been exchanged for certificates."

On the twenty-eighth, the insurrection which began deep in the interior spread to Sakanaya Jinroku's house in Takatanoshō in Mashima district. This merchant traded in sake and oil and bought up different kinds of grains in the countryside. To get him to exchange the rice certificates for rice, over a thousand men led by Higuchi Jirō marched on his house shouting fierce war cries. But then someone or other among his neighbors was able to intervene on his behalf to bring matters to a peaceful conclusion. Everyone knows what happened here, and since there is no point in wasting paper on people who might be considered ordinary, I will omit the details.

Although the warehouse agent in Takata, Tsukataniya Ichirōemon, was a mere townsman, he enjoyed the use of a two-character surname, Kaneda. When the peasants sent him a message on the same day demanding, "Exchange the certificates for soy beans," he did so gladly, and the peasants took charge of them. Everyone praised him, saying, "Isn't Mr. Kaneda skilled in the ways of the world. Rather than regretting what he had to do, he demonstrated that he is truly compassionate by showing how sorry he felt for the peasants' plight."

Also on the twenty-eighth, two thousand peasant rebels with Amakusa Tokisada as their general suddenly revolted. With tremendous force, they bore down on the home of the village headman called Fukushimaya Zenbei, in the town of Shinjō, who had collected much rice in exchange for certificates. Faced with a barrage of demands to exchange the rice for the certificates, Zenbei got angry.

"What you're saying is completely out of the question. It can't be done at all." He railed against them, shouting, "It's unprecedented. You're being absolutely outrageous."

Getting angry in turn, the people's army smashed his furnishings and utensils to smithereens. Then they got up on his mats with their sandals on.

"You're always so proud of being a headman, but you put the squeeze on the peasants, you're greedy, and no one can calculate the evil you have done," they reviled him. "That's why we're doing what we're doing."

"I won't put up with you any more," Zenbei shouted, grabbing his short sword. The situation was fraught with danger. Some people from the neighborhood tried to mediate, but he refused to listen to them.

"Just let me kill them," he went so far as to say. With boar spears and bamboo spears in their hands, the peasants resolutely forced him into a rout until, overpowered at last, he beat a retreat. "It is truly something to be thankful for that heaven takes retribution for greed and evil," people commented.

The transport office in Mikamo, which traded in sake and served as a moneylender besides storing rice exchanged for certificates, was a branch of the store owned by Tsukataniya Ichirōemon in Takata. On the evening of the twenty-ninth, the clerk was faced with a barrage of demands to hand over the rice he had previously exchanged for the certificates, but he refused: "I can't do that on my own authority." The peasants ignored him. They scrambled to remove over three thousand kilograms of iron ore and 150 bales of rice. These they put in the careful custody of Yabei and Heiemon, two peasants who lived nearby.

Someone thought they heard the peasants say, "We're going to burn down the town." Everyone struggled to flee, pulling along their wives and children and entire households. One after another, couriers raced from Mikamo to Tsuyama. The capricious deeds committed by the peasants were simply indescribable.

The next day everyone rushed around preparing for the new year. How unfortunate that while the taste of the sticky rice cakes boiled with vegetables for the first day of 1727 still lingered in the throat, every atrocity committed on the flesh and every torment endured by human beings appeared before the eyes.

As soon as the intendants Miki Jinzaemon and Yamada Bunhachi plus the inspector Yamada Hyōnai arrived in the Kuse district on the sixth, they announced, "We have urgent business with one Odaniya Heibei. Have him come here right now."

Shaking in his sandals at the thought of what he had done wrong, Heibei flew through his back door and let his feet carry him off. Then he had his neighbor Kamikaichi Jirōbei find him sanctuary in Gyoku'unzan Keshō-ji, a temple in Takata, Mashima district, that received donations in rice directly from the shōgun. The chief priest of this temple wondered at what was going on, but he dressed Heibei in the costume of an itinerant monk and that took care of him. In his place his son-in-law, Kibei, was tied up tight with his arms behind his back. The villagers were told to keep him under strict guard.

On the seventh the officials left Kuse for Taguchi. Over thirty soldiers dressed in leather jackets pressed forward in two columns. The two magistrates were each on horseback. From their spears fluttered the battle flag of Tsuyama, strips of paper inscribed with the character for *great*. Following them were over 280 soldiers carrying weapons. Upon their arrival at Taguchi, they carefully surveyed the surroundings.

"Hey, someone. We have urgent business with a person called Chōemon from this district. Show us where he lives."

A man of at least fifty who happened to be present led the way for them. As they were passing in front of a house, they saw that ten large pines had been cut down. "Who is the author of this mischief?" they asked. Even though the old man replied, "These are trees from my own forest," they remained unsatisfied. They struck him a blow on the forehead with their iron swords and tied him up. Thereafter they hunted down Chōemon, beat him about the head with their iron swords, and tied him up as well. Both men they dragged along with them.

At Mikamo the officials visited houses looking for Saburō-zaemon of Hirashima, Yamaji Jin'emon, and Matsusue Tarōemon, but these men had run off as soon as they heard the soldiers were after them, so the officials immediately hurried on to Shinjō.

On the eighth, the officials who searched the homes in Shinjō arrested Kutarō, Yosanbei, and Rokuhachi.

On the ninth, Ōhara Tōjirō of Shinjō secretly sent a courier to Amakusa Tokisada, with the following message: "Three magistrates have come from Tsuyama. They have already arrested five to seven men. I have written you this letter so that you will be aware of what has happened." Tokisada, Maki, and Higuchi were astonished to hear this news.

"What had been a mere trifle has suddenly become serious. The high and mighty who have come from Tsuyama are different from the commoners in that they are warriors who care about their repu-tation and value their honor. But on the other hand, I've heard something to the effect that in Tsuyama, Kubo Chikahira had tried to economize by firing the foot soldiers. Now he has had to make up for their lack by hiring whomever he could scrape together from among the townspeople. Not to worry. As long as I am around with my knowledge of the secret arts of Wu Tzu and Sun Tzu,[33] it will be as easy as shooting fish in a barrel," Tokisada boasted.

Thereafter he divided up the responsibility for collecting troops: "Yamane Gorōemon, Ōmori Shichizaemon, and Ogawa Onigobei, you assemble the forces from the mountains and head for the Hisami River plain. Upon your arrival, you should display your family names. Higuchi Jirō is to raise troops from Yamakuse, Shibara, Masayoshi, Kanba, and Hoshiyama and have them gather at the Hisami River plain too. We will have a letter sent to the flatlands through Odaniya Heibei to raise the forces from the thirty-seven villages around Yono, Kashi, Ōba, Meki, Kōchi, and Akano. Have them go to Jūkoku Pass. In order to assess the situation, I will raise troops from Kanayama and Kuroda to advance immediately on Mikamo where it borders on Shinjō. If things go well, I will attack the magistrates and take back the prisoners." In making this firm promise, he appeared to be as gallant as Kusunoki before the final battle at Minatogawa.

Once it had been decided who would go where to raise troops, four or five men from Doi and Maga were dispatched as far as Kuroda to spy out the situation. Without a moment's delay, over five hundred rebels gathered together.

Accompanied by eight or nine stalwart henchmen, Tokisada went with deliberate stealth to ask what was going on of Jihachi, the new message receiver for Mikamo. Jihachi deceived the people by taking his responsibilities to the government overly seriously, and four or five days earlier he had absented himself to Shinjō. Fearlessly Tokisada entered Jihachi's house to request a drink. Then, pillowing his head in his arms, he took a nap.

Resentful that the people of Mikamo did not join him, Amakusa Tokisada furiously decided to burn down the town. Faced with this threat, the inhabitants fled, carrying their children upside down on their backs and concealing the aged in nearby temples. The wretched village truly appeared to be confronted by the eight disasters feared by Buddhists and by the evils accumulated on the three paths of the dead.

General Amakusa Tokisada tried to gather his forces, but when no one showed up, he lacked the strength to advance. He withdrew first to Kuroda to assess the situation, but his troops gradually decreased so he pulled back to his home base of Maki, where he tried again to raise troops.

Meanwhile the three domanial commanders staying at Shinjō said, "It is already too late for us to stand up to the peasants' insurrection." They entrusted Yamada Hyōnai with returning to Tsuyama by fast horse to ask for help in pacification while they drove on to a place called Kamigōchi.

Having already received a number of couriers from Shinjō, Tsuyama put Yamada Sannojō with his son Hachirō in charge of over 350 troops, including over ninety foot soldiers equiped with ten muskets and forty cannon. They all appeared dressed for battle with refurbished armor boxes, arms, and harnesses. They even remembered to bring along the field curtains and the lanterns carried on long poles. On their way they ran into Yamada Hyōnai. After a brief greeting he told them everything that had happened in Shinjō.

"Don't bother going all the way to Tsuyama. Come back with us to Shinjō," the leaders decided. Soon they had arrived in the Kuse district.

Before dawn on the eleventh, the domanial troops all hurried to converge on Shinjō. The leaders met face to face to learn the details of what was going on in Tsuyama and to talk informally about what to do regarding the local people.

Later that morning, the two new message receivers, Jihachi from Mikamo and Ribei from Shinjō, were sent as emissaries to Amakusa Tokisada. "Hand over the remaining certificates that you received for the eight hundred bales of rice," they demanded. He gave the two men the remaining 370 certificates. Sending the two men to Maki on this errand may have been a ruse to learn whether Tokisada was home or not.

Tokisada gave his forces their orders: "One troop will be led by Maki Sōemon, Higashi Kayabe Shichizaemon, and Yamane Gorōemon. This force of over a thousand rebels will advance on the home of the country samurai for Yumoto, Saburōzaemon of Mikamo." His own camp he set up at Shimo Yubara. No secret was made of what he was doing.

[The Townspeople Defend Mikamo against the Peasants]

In the town of Mikamo, fifty-six men unanimously agreed to circulate a pledge sealed with their own blood. Their steadfast promise was, "In this emergency, let us value our lives less than dust blown by the wind, make our resolve stronger than steel, and raise our reputations to the heavens."

Opening his fan, Jūrōzaemon gave his forces their orders: "We will be outnumbered when the enemy attacks. Therefore we must use strategy. Place bags of ash on top of the gates so that when we see the enemy enter, we can quickly throw the ash into their eyes. Once they panic, then we should unsheathe our swords and come out fighting. Don't be cowardly for fear of losing your lives. Your reputations are all you have to worry about."

Everyone agreed respectfully. Pulling their spears and long swords from their scabbards, they resolved to make this their last day. Confronted by this menace, the people's army shrank back. No one dared approach the town.

A constant stream of couriers hurried from Yumoto to Shinjō. The situation was truly fraught with danger.

[The Peasants Try an Ambush]

One of the peasant forces heard that a column of over 350 soldiers armed with fifty guns was advancing up the river from Takata led by the two rifle-company commanders Kitagō Monzaemon and Wada Ninzaemon from Tsuyama. The following orders were given: "Under the command of general Higuchi Jirō, over eight hundred rebels from Maga, Kanba, and other places are to head for the Kuzushita Anji slope on the road between Maga and Kanba. There they are to fire guns and roll boulders from the mountains down on the government troops, throwing them into enough confusion for us to capture them."

Another peasant force numbered twenty-five hundred men was led by Maki Tōsuke, Ogawa Onigobei, and Ōmori Shichizaemon. It advanced, with the men from Kuroda and Kanayama vying for the lead. On the evening of the twelfth, this peasant force secretly crossed from Shinjō to the Hisami River plain. At a place called Dadoko, where mountain walls of deep valleys, steep precipices, towering peaks, and narrow crevices spread before them, the men divided into five troops. Some hid themselves in the shadows of rocks, others in bamboo thickets. They lined up the muzzles of their guns and settled down to wait. If the enemy soldiers were to pass by, they would be wiped out.

To waste time in deliberations is a piece of good luck for the enemy.

The three magistrates conferred privately at Shinjō. "We really ought to get to work right away," Yamada Bunhachi urged. "Let's crush those wretched peasants with a single blow."

Miki pondered for awhile. "It would be humiliating to lose to the peasants simply because we underrated them. Besides, the generals leading the two troops which went through Takata and Misaka have promised to meet us at the Hisami River plain tomorrow around ten o'clock. If we change these plans, what will happen then?"

Right in the middle of their deliberations, the couriers from Yumoto came piling in. On top of everything else, the country samurai from Mitsue, Shingozaemon, had been hanging around since early that morning hoping to greet them.

"In any case, why don't you do me the honor of paying me a visit right now. We can send out a reconnaissance party to assess the situation and then get to work sweeping all before us," he urged them, and they all agreed.

According to the gossip spread by the people's army coming from Hisami, "over 5,000 men have gathered on the river plain. Over 3,800 rebels from the mountains and 3,500 from Ōba district have filled the road from Jūkoku Pass to the area around Misaka. A force of 3,200 rebels has come from Seiseijō, over 5,000 from Yono and Kashi, and a total of 30,000 or 40,000 rebels are coming from Doi. There are hordes of people," their tongues wagged. "If you make haste to advance on Hisami by going past Dadoko under the cover of darkness, you can get there while the people's forces are still scattered," others mentioned as they passed by. This was all a plot by Amakusa Tokisada to have the domanial troops captured by the rebels lying in wait.

After much deliberation, the domanial officials decided, "Let's advance while their forces are still scattered." They sent out a warning, "Take care to guard the prisoners already captured at Mikamo"; then they debated what to do about the men caught alive at Taguchi and Shinjō. "If we leave them in the custody of local people, they will only attract trouble. It would be better to make a blood festival for the gods of war."

On the twelfth, at the river plain by Shinjō, five men—Saburōemon and Chōemon from Taguchi, and Kutarō, Yosanbei, and Rokuhachi from Shinjō—were beheaded. Their heads were exposed at the gates to their respective villages.

The domanial troops set out right after that in the direction of Mikamo, but no one was told of their whereabouts. As the sun inclined toward the west, it appeared that they were hurrying to cross the Shino Pass, heading for Mitsue.

The general at Dadoko, Tōsuke, issued his orders: "It worries me that the enemy might go over Shino Pass," so out of his force of 800 rebels he sent 300 of them in that direction. There they discovered footprints showing that the pass had already been crossed. For them to have waited in vain was a piece of bad luck.

At the Hisami River plain, Tokisada divided his forces into three troops. "The 3,000 rebels from the flatlands are to hold the passes at

Misaka and Jukoku. The 2,500 rebels from the mountains are to stay at the Hisami River plain to confront the enemy coming from Yumoto. The 800 rebels from Mio, Maga, and Yamakuse under the command of General Higuchi Jirō are to face the enemy coming up the Takata River. The remaining men from Tane, Nishi Kayabe, Tachiki, Shimomi, and Miakedo are to gather at Doi before going to Mitsue. When they set fire to the country samurai's house there, the rising flames will be the signal to set to work quickly. Recklessly trample all underfoot without begrudging your lives, ignore everyone else, but be sure to capture the country samurai Shingozaemon with your guns." Having given these orders, he withdrew to Doi.

At the same time, Tokisada sent two stalwart henchmen to spy on the house of the country samurai in Mitsue, with detailed instructions to let him know as soon as Shingozaemon returned home. Tokisada himself had a drink or two at the home of the peasant Doi Chūemon, where he waved his command baton and sent a stream of proclamations to his army.

"Tomorrow there will most probably be a battle, but perhaps like me the enemy hopes that matters will be concluded peacefully without too much difficulty. If it should come to a fight, however, I have already given orders to all my forces. A small hut is being prepared at the Hisami River plain to which the three magistrates coming from Shinjō will be invited. There Amakusa Tokisada, Maki, Higuchi, and Ōmori will talk on and on about the people's demands. While they are thus marking time, our one hundred guns are to fire in volleys from the bamboo thickets on the mountains and the shadows of the rocks, killing all three magistrates and allowing our side to enfold the enemy using the 'birds and clouds' strategy.[34] There are to be no delays, but we must be careful not to shoot each other. To distinguish ourselves from the enemy, everyone is to cut a piece of white paper in four quarters and attach it to his sleeves."

[The Defeat of the Peasants]

In the meantime, the reconnaissance party of peasants sent to the country samurai Shingozaemon's home in Mitsue was waiting impatiently when a blizzard that night made it as cold as cold could be.

To ward off the chill, the peasants drank so much sake that they forgot what they were supposed to be doing. They had just settled down for a nap in some straw outside the gate when Shingozaemon, worried about the preparations being made to receive his guests, returned home far in advance of the magistrates. Catching sight of the scum outside his gate, he struck them two or three times across the forehead with his sword-guard. Then he tied them up securely with their hands behind their backs.

"I'll bet you are Amakusa's spies. What splendid fellows you are. Confess the truth," he shouted, pulling out his sword and waving it around. They spilled everything.

Is it not true, as the old saying has it, that when the general's schemes are exposed, his campaigns will end in defeat?

The three magistrates were impressed, thinking, "Isn't Shingozaemon a fine fellow." Then they entered his home, where they were all served with food. With the first cock's crow at dawn, they hurried off to Doi.

Amakusa Tokisada had not the slightest inkling of what had happened. Delighted that the deep snow gave him a chance to rest, he announced, "We will surely win tomorrow's battle. Up to now I have had to change beds two or three times a night, but with the blizzard this evening, I can rest easy." One cup of sake tasted good, two were even better, and soon they went down one after another.

"The reconnaissance party should be returning from Mitsue any minute now. But perhaps they are busy setting fire to Shingozaemon's house, cutting off the head of that country samurai, and sending him on his way to the realm of the dead," he murmured, laying his head on his arms.

While waiting impatiently for the reconnaissance party from Mitsue, he heard footsteps outside the gate.

"It's the men returning from Mitsue," he thought, and waited.

"Is Lord Amakusa inside?" came a politely phrased query.

Perhaps it was a courier from the eastern districts sent by Odaniya in Kuse, Tokisada thought. "It's cold, come inside quickly," he said.

Yamada Bunhachi and Yamada Hachirō launched their attack through the door to the sitting room, knocking it off its tracks. The lanterns went out. Ashes billowed from the hearth. Friend could not be told from foe. Being exceptionally accomplished and strong, Amakusa unsheathed the sword he had by his side and slashed about with it, but just at this fateful juncture, he thrust it into a near-by pillar. Try though he would to pull it out, it would not move.

"I have him," cried Hachirō and struck with his iron sword at Tokisada's forehead. Using his instincts, Tokisada was fortunate enough to parry the blow with the short sword made by Seki Sonroku which he carried at his hip.

Hachirō lifted his voice. "Bring light. This is a critical contest," he shouted. A tall lantern was brought in. Someone or other inside cut it down. Thinking that things were finally going his way, Hachirō used his iron sword to exchange blows with Tokisada. For both, the situation was fraught with danger.

At that point, dozens of soldiers rushed in pell-mell shouting, "Here now, leave them to us." They flattened the peasants under a rain of blows. Some they tied up. The two sides grappled together. They fought together. In the garden they became entangled to-gether, now one on top, now another. No one allowed himself to be caught off guard.

Catching sight of Hachirō, Amakusa Tokisada recklessly rushed him. Things were looking bad for Hachirō when Bunhachi and Jinzaemon shouted with one voice, "Who knows what will happen. Just hit him, cut him, grab him." Menaced by the unsheathed swords slashing at him, Tokisada shrank back. He retreated almost without realizing it. At a tear in the straw mat, his foot fell through the floor boards underneath. Before you could say "Praise to the Buddhas," Bunhachi had struck him two or three times with the back of his sword. Blood streaming down his forehead got in his eyes to send him reeling, whereupon Miki, Yamada, and dozens of soldiers fell all over each other to tie him up in a thousand knots.

Miki and Yamada snatched up their batons. "More of the lead-ers must be hiding next door. Go look for them. Arrest them all for they are all to be executed."

The soldiers obeyed respectfully. They ransacked houses here and there to hunt down and capture twenty-seven men, whom they then brought before their generals.

"Those captured alive are all to be taken to the home of the country samurai in Mitsue," the magistrates ordered.

Just then some silhouettes could be seen on the opposite bank. Crying "Guns," Bunhachi and Hachirō snatched up muskets firing forty-gram shot. They fired three or four times. Did they make a hit?

I heard later that two men died of their wounds. The others scattered like baby spiders, running off to hide in all directions.

Being a man of surpassing talent, Maki Sōemon had performed many services as a leader in the people's army.[35] As soon as the fray began, he had started to charge the two intendants with a boar spear when a soldier cracked him over the head with his iron sword from behind. Blows rained down on him while he was still reeling. He was promptly tied up. Words cannot describe what happened to the others.

"Don't pursue them too far," the two generals ordered. "Now that we have captured the main actors, let us each give a war cry."

"Ei, ei, wauuu." Three times the shouts rang out, resounding over the earth. With this act thus brought to a close, a bank of clouds rolled in, gleaming whitely in the night.

[The Peasants are Punished]

Early on the thirteenth, the three generals gave their orders: "First, send a courier at once to the two generals coming up the river from Takata, informing them that the ringleader and general of this affair, Amakusa Shirō no Saemonnosuke Tokisada, has been captured. Another twenty-seven men have also been taken alive. The remaining units of the people's army, numbers unknown, have scattered. Our side suffered not the slightest injury. This is for your information."

Having set off from Kuse in the middle of the night, the courier met up with the two generals at a place called Yamakuse, where he informed them of what had happened and reported that there was nothing for them to do. The two generals sat down on the grass, offered each other sake, and rested for awhile.

The three generals at Mitsue also sent a letter to Yumoto reporting the same thing. The two commanders there, the inspector from Tsuyama Oka Seiemon and the captain Oki Jūemon, each read the letter carefully. "Let's stay here for awhile, search for the ringleaders, and investigate local affairs," they decided.

"The ringleaders that we captured are all to be executed," the three generals at Mitsue commented to each other. They had the ropes rearranged to make this possible.

109

"Are we to be executed?" Amakusa Tokisada inquired, turning to the magistrates.

"You are to be taken to Tsuyama," they replied.

"I have but one desire, and it looks like it will be fulfilled," he announced joyfully.

"Amakusa is the only one who realizes what rearranging the ropes means. Truly he is a man of exceptional ability," the magistrates said admiringly.

Tokisada, Ōmori, and Doi were taken down the road under strict guard as important prisoners. Just then a country samurai on urgent business hurried by. Tokisada called out, "Shingozaemon, wait a minute." Glaring at him with angry eyes, Tokisada declared:

"Anyone who commits a sin is really disgusting. You are surely one of Kubo's gang. Ever since the extra taxes were levied, all of the country samurai in the six districts have been in league with Kubo. This business of the rice certificates was no better than robbery. In your heart you should know what I'm talking about. The members of the people's army bore not the slightest grudge against our lord and master in Tsuyama. Now is it not strange that, unworthy though I am, I was entrusted with the duty of being the people's commander-in-chief? I had resolved to dissipate the peasants' deep-seated rancor by having you taste the quality of my steel when I cut you down with one stroke of my sword, but I lost my chance in the blizzard last night. How mortifying that now I have inadvertently become a prisoner. I had resolved that we would cross swords, go together to the river between this world and the next, and hand in hand lead each other to the realm of the dead. Fate has sadly put this beyond my power. Oh my chagrin at the shame of being captured," he cried, gnashing his teeth, his body trembling.

"Though my corpse becomes a pile of bones, throughout the six worlds and four lives that I must exist, I am determined that my resentment will endure unchanged." He breathed fire and wept tears of blood. How dreadful it would be if the agonies of death were even more excruciating.

"Indeed, your resentment is all very well," the magistrates said roughly. "Nevertheless, the crimes and sins which you yourself committed are your own fault. Don't blame others for them. Besides, we still have many things to interrogate you about after we have finished with the other executions."

The twenty-five men captured alive were all taken out to the river plain at Doi. Those executed were:

Tane village	Shichibei	age 37	Saburōemon	age 41
	Tabei	age 29	Rokubei	age 21
	Chōbei	age 41	Sanzō	age 40
	Ichizō	age 41	Chō	age 25
	Ninzō	age 22	Shōtarō	age 25
	Jirō	age 19		
Shimomi	Sankurō	age 25	Heibei	age 47
	Shinbei	age 21	Ichibei	age 55
Nishikayabe	Yosuke	age 21	Kanshirō	age 20
	San'emon	age 34	Roku	age 33
	Yobei	age 48	Hyōsuke	age 27
	Chōzō	age 30	Ichi	age 19
	Itoshirō	age 60 (substitute for Sukeroku)		

The total was twenty-four decapitated heads.

These men were executed at Doi. Thirteen heads were exposed on bamboo pikes at Jūkoku Pass. The remaining eleven were similarly exposed at Kiroozaka in Yamakuse village.

Nishikayabe	Chōsuke	age 16	Ninzō	age 18

These two men had been captured together. Just as they were about to be executed, the country samurai from Hijiya, Shishido Kiemon, earnestly begged for their lives, so they were pardoned.

Kitagō Monzaemon and Wada Ninzaemon, who had been heading upriver from Takata, went directly to the town of Ogawa where they camped for a considerable stay.

On the fourteenth, according to rumor, the ringleader and general of the people's army, Makino Tōsuke Tokiuji, who had been heading for Shinjō, thought to himself: "I have heard that the commander-in-chief Amakusa Tokisada was taken alive on the night of the twelfth. Doi and Ōmori have also been captured. What an unfortunate state of affairs. That I alone could achieve our basic desire is inconceivable. Therefore, I will go to Edo and wait to see what happens," he decided. Since he already had sixty pieces of gold in his purse, he knew he need have no worries on the journey. He went far away, no one knows where, and no one knows what happened to him.

Two men: Doi village   Sōshichi   Doi village   Gobei

The country samurai from Mitsue, Shingozaemon, petitioned on their behalf. They were pardoned after they had been interrogated.

[The Capture of Higuchi Jirō]

The three magistrates staying at Mitsue deliberated among themselves. "It is strange that no one knows where Higuchi Jirō from Mio is. Since he is one of the ringleaders and generals, it is imperative that we search for him," they agreed. They issued the following announcement:

"To Hoshiyama, Suga, Takebara, Shibara, Masayoshi, Okamura, Kanba, Nishi Hatake, Nakama, Maga, Mio.

"The people of these villages are to search diligently for Higuchi Jirō. If there are any delays, one man will be taken from each village to be executed in his place."

The peasants conferred together. They combed the mountains and probed the valleys. At night they lit thousands of pine torches as they searched through his own and neighboring villages, but to no avail. They were simply dumbfounded. They put his mother in the custody of the village. They tied up his elder brother Heibei and set a guard over him.

One man from Mio thought long and hard about what to do. "In any case, there is something disquieting about the cave in that jumble of rocks over there," he said, and he sent a scout to search it. On the sand were suspicious-looking footprints. Entering the cave, the scout saw a human silhouette at the back.

"Is Yajirō in this cave?" he asked, shouting from a distance.

"Tokimitsu is here," came the reply. The muzzle of a gun pointed toward the scout. The scout ran back home to report.

In the midst of the deliberations on what to do, Yamada Bunhachi whipped the cover off his spear, saying, "Why waste time debating such a small matter?" With one accord, six stalwart soldiers joined him on either side. They recklessly rushed over the sand, but since there was, after all, a gun in the cave, they appeared to be unconsciously holding back.

Miki pondered for awhile. Then he had Higuchi's mother bound with ropes and paraded around where she could be seen below. Spotting her from afar, Higuchi tearfully dropped his sword.

"I had resolved to fight one last time, but even that hope will not be realized. What a disappointing state of affairs. I lost my father long ago while I was still young. Only through my mother's sacrifices did I grow to manhood. If I let my mother die before my very eyes, I will deserve the punishment of heaven for having strayed from the path of filial piety. If you would please spare my mother, I will become your prisoner," he cried.

Hearing this, his mother gnashed her teeth and soaked her sleeve in tears. "You were one of the most important leaders. What a regrettable state of affairs for you to become a prisoner because of your feelings for me. Abandon me, fight the generals from Tsuyama, and have your reputation praised to the skies. Everyone knows how truly mortifying it is that Amakusa allowed himself to be captured so easily."

"I am deeply grateful for your solicitude. Nonetheless, to neglect filial piety is abhorred by heaven. I would be despised for it in the future, and people would surely talk about me." Turning to the magistrates, he pleaded, "Let my mother go and take me in her place."

Feeling sorry for him, the magistrates released his mother at once. Higuchi threw his gun and short sword down upon the sand.

"Hurry up with the ropes," he beseeched them, but there the sand was too loose.

"It won't work except on level ground," he said. He went with them down to the flats, where he tied himself up with his own hands.

Is it not true that strong though evil is, filial piety is yet stronger. But when you think about things like this, words cannot express the blessings of the love between parent and child.

[More Peasants Are Captured and Punished]

On the fifteenth, Shichiemon from Higashikayabe was captured at Shimofukuda and taken to Tsuyama.

On the sixteenth, Chōjirō from Mukōyubara, Ichirōbei from Kamikishi, and Tokuemon from Miakedo were captured and put in the custody of their villages.

On the seventeenth, Yoichibei from Higashikayabe was captured and put in the custody of Yochiemon from Shimotokuyama. Itobei and Denkichi from Maga and Yoroku from Kuroda were captured at Yumoto and taken to Tsuyama.

On the eighteenth, Chūemon's son Shichibei from Doi was captured and put in the custody of Heiemon from Ogawa.

On the nineteenth, Tarōemon and Saburōzaemon from Mikamo were captured at Yumoto and taken to Tsuyama. Jiemon and Zensaburō from Nishikayabe were captured and put in manacles. Jiemon from Nakafukuda, Chōbei from Shimotokuyama, Chōsuke from Yoshida, and Gensaburō from Shitawa were captured at Yumoto. Saburōzaemon and Jirōemon from Kamifukuda, Ibei and Kabei from Shitawa, Jirōbei from Shimotokuyama, and Saburōemon from Yoshida were captured at Yumoto. Shichirōbei and Kobei from Kakeda, Zenbei from Shimofukuda, Genbei from Shimonagata, Itohachi and Heibei from Yoshida, and Chōbei from Bessho were captured at Yumoto.

On the twentieth, Shōbei from Habu, Ichibei from Tamada, and Jiemon and Chōkichi from Doi were arrested. They were placed in the custody of their villages.

On the twenty-first, Sōemon from Kanba and Gorōemon from Yamane were arrested at Yumoto and taken to Tsuyama. Itoshirō from Hoshiyama, Kutarō, Heishichi, Jiryōsaburō, and Tarōbei from Mikamo, and Tōemon from Kaminagata were arrested. They were placed in the custody of their villages.

On the twenty-second, Jin'emon from Mikamo, Tarōemon from Ogawa, and Gobei and Rokubei from Miseshichibara were arrested at Yumoto and taken to Tsuyama.

On the twenty-fifth, the seven men listed below were beheaded at Yumoto. Their heads were exposed on bamboo pikes set up in the riverbed:

Maga village	Zenbei	age 30
Kanayama village	Shichirōbei	age 38
Shitawa village	Kibei	age 50
Kayabe village	Yosuke	age 50
Nakafukuda village	Jinkurō	

Shinjō village	Chūsuke	age 57
Mikamo village	Chōsaburō	

In this wretched state of affairs, the people truly appeared to be confronted by evils worse than the eight disasters feared by Buddhists or those accumulated on the three paths of the dead. The suffering of the wives, children, and households of those executed was a sight more painful than the eyes could bear to see. Today, here, has been demonstrated their fateful destiny—to suffer the unceasing torments of the lowest circle in hell.

"Let's set out for Kuse district to enforce the law there," the magistrates agreed. What a pitiful sight to see the prisoners being dragged along. Having arrived in Kuse district, the magistrates decided that to restore order they would interrogate and arrest all the members of the people's army in Kuse. "No one will evade punishment," they announced.

On the fourth day of the intercalary first month, seven men were beheaded on the riverbed at Odani. Their heads were exposed on bamboo pikes. Who they were is listed below:

Kamikōchi village	Kiichi	Nishihara village	Kaemon
Akano village	Tōsaburō	Kashi village	Yosanbei
Kashi village	Shinbei	Ogawa village	Onigobei
Tahara village	Moshichi		

One of the men executed, Kaemon from Nishihara, had once been a warehouse agent. Eminent in rural society, he had enjoyed using the name of his locality as his surname. But then recently he had become impoverished. At the beginning of the riot, he had thought to preserve himself from danger by hiding in another province. When he learned that, as a consequence, his father of over eighty years old had been manacled and placed in the custody of his village where he was strictly guarded, he thought, "No matter how many years I have left to live, the punishment of heaven would be frightening were I to allow my father to come to grief through a lack of filial piety. I will substitute my life for his."

He returned home to bid his parents a final farewell. Then he went to Kuse district where, having tied himself up, he confessed to a false crime and surrendered to the authorities. He was beheaded on the river plain at Odani, but his fame for filial piety remains fresh.

Was it not justifiable to wonder, as everyone did, why there were no temple priests in the neighborhood who could have pleaded for his life?

On the fifth, the magistrates carefully revised the domanial regulations. They then returned to Tsuyama, dragging their prisoners along. Those arrested were harshly interrogated, even though it had already been decided that their crimes were so serious that they would have to be executed. All of a sudden, the high priests of the thirteen temples in Tsuyama used the secret arts of the gods, spirits, and Buddhas to get themselves put in charge of the condemned men. In other words, before the most virtuous priests of Tsuyama associated with Hongenji, the prisoners reluctantly took the tonsure. They must have been very much obliged. It was laughable to see everyone in the group suddenly conceal his profane desires under a shaven head.

Why bother with such willy-nilly monks? Five will get you ten that they reverted to being laymen as soon as they returned home. Some people said, "These men should not have evaded execution. Even though they managed to save their lives through bribery, they are unworthy to be treated as human beings. Shouldn't they be called nonhuman?"[36] Others said, "Someone with no understanding of obligations and human feelings represents the worst kind of evil. Can't a stop be put to this? But, on the other hand, the reputation of a country hick is not worth considering."

Many of those arrested after the riot were executed. Those who were unexpectedly rescued through the good graces of the high Buddhist priests in the temples of Tsuyama or saved themselves by bribing the officials to regard them with favor were ostracized by their fellows and suffered enduring infamy.

[The Curses of the Dying Leaders]

One of the generals who participated in the peasants' conspiracy was Ōmori Shichizaemon, a descendant of Ōmori Hikoshichi, who had performed many services as a leader in the people's army.[37] He had been prone to attack the magistrates and country samurai, hoping to perform feats praised by future generations.

Unable to evade the consequences of his crimes, he was beheaded in prison. His head was exposed along with that of Tokisada near the Tamoto River. His last words were, "Look at me, look at me, you officials great and small from Mitsue, Hijiya, Oka, Maga, and Shinjō. Even though I die, my spirit will appear to take your lives within three years." His final appearance was frightening yet wretched. Those with guilty consciences had better be careful.

There is an old saying that a firefly gleams for a mere twenty nights; a mayfly is as ephemeral as a single day. The early months of 1727 saw countless sorrows. The prisoner of state Amakusa Shirō Taifu Tokisada was closely confined in jail, fettered hand and foot, and constantly watched by the guards. He was tortured before various high officials, who, after having heard his confession, agreed: "He cannot evade punishment. Have him crucified two miles from Tsuyama near the Tamoto River."

In the middle of the third month, Tokisada and Higuchi Jirō were executed. The end was decent. Crowds of spectators from Tsuyama and common people from the nearby districts came to watch.

Tokisada spoke: "There is an old and true saying that when the head reaches of a river are impure, downstream becomes muddied. When the country is poorly governed, the people riot. Look at me, look at me. Before seven years have passed, the country samurai will have ruined themselves and the state. All the toadies will have been punished by the gods and Buddhas of heaven. My life may end, but my earnest desire will continue through the cycles of rebirth, though it were to become a snake or a demon. Until the Buddha returns to earth, my grudge will remain." Weeping tears of blood, he was more to be pitied than censured.

When everything was ready, Tokisada was pulled to the top of a cross. It looked like the end had come. Casting his eyes in all directions, he said, "For three weeks after my death, I will not change color, nor will my face decay. Even though I die, I will have my revenge." He bit off his tongue with his teeth and spit a mouthful of blood toward the sky. "All the gods of heaven, heed my plea. Please take the lives of all the toadies." He closed his eyelids and fell silent.

Having heard his cry, the outcasts seized their spears and callously thrust several times through his sides. Tokisada opened his eyes once more.

"My life is over. But I want you all to know that even though my soul is bound for the nether world, my spirit will remain in this one through countless reincarnations." And he meant what he said.

Higuchi had nothing to say except words for his mother back home. He appeared to go to sleep.

All of this is now an old story. As Tokisada had promised, his color strangely remained the same for a week after he died. It was said that people with guilty consciences had reason to be frightened.

Truly marvelous things have flowed from the track of my pen as I have written down what I have heard to while away the tedium of the spring rains.

People who read this should not think it contains nothing but the truth. Who is to say wherein lies the fiction in fact or the facts in fiction? Let it end. The writer does not know either.

1727, mid-June   *Mimasaka, Mashima district*
Takata

Old man Shinpū Kenchiku wrote this.

T H R E E

A Thousand Spears at Kitsunezuka

FORTY YEARS AFTER THE SANCHŪ RIOT in Tsuyama, peasants in the provinces northwest of Edo rose in a disturbance known as the Tenma (post-horse) riot. In the largest peasant uprising since the Shimabara Christian rebellion of 1637, between a hundred thousand and two hundred thousand peasants marched on the shōgun's capital at the end of 1764 to protest new demands for corvée labor to help maintain the transportation system. On the surface, the two events were remarkably alike; even the histories describing them share a common ambivalence toward the rioters and impose a similar structure on the pattern of events. In both cases, confrontations with government officials gave the peasants a chance to express their grievances and justify their actions. They thereafter smashed up houses to punish wealthy commoners who had treated them unjustly. Following the rioters' defeat by their enemies among their neighbors, government troops arrested the ringleaders in a symbolic reassertion of authority.

Despite these similarities, the two uprisings erupted in areas notably different. Tsuyama was a backwater compared to the provinces northwest of Edo. Located in a basin distant from the main highways, it took weeks for information to reach the castle town, let alone the peasants isolated in their mountain villages. In 1727, the spread of a commercial economy had not completely replaced older systems of barter. The major bone of contention was who would reap the profits from trade in rice, a food staple. In contrast, the Tenma riot centered on one of Japan's major distribution routes, the Nakasendō, which linked Edo with Kyoto through the mountains of central Japan.

The Nakasendō was one of the five strategic roads centered on

Edo, the country's major center of consumption. Supervised by the bakufu, these roads crossed both the shōgun's house lands and domains ruled by daimyō, affording, along with a standardized currency and written language, one of the few national systems that tied Japan together. Edo had an enormous population servicing the bureaucracies of state, and their food, shelter, and clothing arrived in the city carried on the backs of porters and peasants. Along the highway also passed the daimyō (who were required to spend half their time in their domain and half in Edo), the daimyō's retinues numbering in the thousands, emissaries from the Imperial Court on their way to pay their respects to the shōgun, pilgrims, traveling entertainers, and merchants. By the latter half of the eighteenth century, peasants from the mountains and valleys in the path of the Nakasendō were beginning to produce articles of clothing and adornment, regional specialties, and goods of every sort to sell for cash to the many travelers going to and from the shōgun's capital.

At regular intervals along the Nakasendō were officially designated post stations where travelers could rest, eat, and sleep. Those requiring transport for themselves or their baggage had to change porters and pack horses at each station. In his seminal novel about the Meiji Restoration of 1868, *Before the Dawn,* Shimazaki Tōson (1872–1943) described the anxieties and rewards for post station officials.[1] Responsible for greeting and sending off every important visitor, with the appropriate courtesies performed in formal dress, the men who ran the post stations also had to apportion baggage according to the rates established by the bakufu and guarantee that enough men were available to carry it. The bakufu had decreed that each station must employ fifty men and horses, but few had the fiscal resources to maintain that number. Even if they did, the enormous retinues that flooded the roads required much more. By the middle of the eighteenth century, post station officials were authorized to call on nearby villages to assist them with their duty to transport baggage.

Cumbersome in the extreme, this transportation system was often subjected to real and suspected abuses. High-ranking officials, the shōgun's tea, and anyone or anything so designated by the bakufu and its deputies traveled free. Most of the ruling class—the daimyō and their men, plus lower-ranking bakufu officials—paid a low fixed rate set by the government. Everyone else negotiated costs directly with the porters or their representatives. Managers at the post stations were supposed to call for peasant assistance with the official travelers only when the traffic was more than their own men could handle, but all porters preferred to take the more lucrative private jobs. A system already overburdened with official traffic in the seventeenth century was placed under severe strain by the increase in commercial goods beginning to be shipped a few decades later. Peasants accepted the corvée as a fact of life, but they resented the way post station officials manipulated the system. Throughout the last half of the Tokugawa period, their duty to provide transport assistance led to constant contention between them and the post stations.[2]

The beginnings of the Tenma riot may be traced to 1761, when residents of villages near the highway, who already provided transportation assistance, petitioned to have more villages included in their number. Two years later the magistrate in charge of roads agreed to make a survey of outlying villages for all the post stations from the outskirts of Edo at Itabashi to Wada in the mountains of Shinano. It took the outlying villages no time at all to realize that to be surveyed meant to become responsible for helping the post stations with their transportation problems on a regular basis. At the same time, the bakufu levied an ad hoc tax on villages in Musashi and other provinces to help defray the expenses of a Korean delegation to Edo in the spring of 1764. The villages to be subjected to this double burden thus had two quarrels—one with the villages whose proximity to the post stations could also prove to be an advantage for marketing their goods, and the other with the government officials who had insisted on an unusually heavy tax for the Korean visit and who had agreed to go along with the request to increase the number of villages serving the post stations.[3]

A number of records were composed soon after the peasants rioted; more were written or copied in the 1860s and early 1870s by local intellectuals and village officials. In 1863, a special Buddhist memorial service was held to honor Hyōnai, the sole man executed for having led the uprising. Written by Nakazawa Kidayū, a wealthy village official interested in nativism, who combined reverence for the emperor with a respect for his own position, a song and dance performed in Hyōnai's honor continued as part as the annual autumn festival through the 1970s.[4] In 1874, a member of the Takahashi family from Kawadaya which had been attacked in 1764 made a copy of a complex, convoluted, and multilayered text and entitled it *Kitsunezuka senbon yari* or "A Thousand Spears at Kitsunezuka."[5]

"A Thousand Spears at Kitsunezuka" identifies the chief villain as Takahashi Jinzaemon from Kawadaya, the man responsible for the proposal to increase the number of villages obliged to assist the post stations. Called a *chōja*, a term commonly found in Japanese folklore to signify a wealthy, important person, he lived at Kitsunezuka, or fox mound. Foxes too played a prominent role in folklore with the spread of a commercial economy. Men able to take advantage of new opportunities to set up manufacturing businesses or grow cash crops soon began to lend money to those less able or less fortunate. Foreclosures made them landlords. What an economic historian might see as the harsh necessity of proto-capitalism, people at the time saw as an extraordinary, mysterious power—the ability to use foxes to steal the property of others.[6] The unbelievably rich Jinzaemon worshiped not the gods of agriculture, significantly, but the god of wealth.[7] He is further damned by comparison with Sanshō the bailiff (Sanshō Dayū), a legendary ninth-century figure whose example of cruel and avaricious behavior has been told and retold in Buddhist sermons, literary classics, dramatic performances, traditional history, and modern cinema.

Central to the plot of "A Thousand Spears" is the corrupting power of money. The policy decision that preceded the riot is repeated ad nauseam to iterate the full infamy of what the author sees as a gratuitous effort to harm the peasants. He argues that the proposal to include outlying villages in the supply area for the post stations is made not to ease the burden of villages already providing porters and horses, but simply to line the pockets of a small gang of conspirators, who plan to have the outlying villages send money to hire substitutes, thus selfishly putting their own interests ahead of the common good. In 1764 the villages had actually protested that they lacked the opportunities to make money through trade enjoyed by peasants living nearer the road. To assist the post stations, they would have to take time away from their fields. Their grievances run counter to the logic of the text, an opposition that exposes the difference between conditions prevailing in the countryside in 1764 when the riot erupted and 1874 when the text was copied.[8]

The author's assumptions clearly color his narrative of the events preceding the uprising. For him, a political cause is an insufficient explanation for disorder. Since the peasants are excluded from politics, they would not ordinarily oppose a policy decision. Only a threat to life itself brought about by crop failures and famine—the most dire threat to a subsistence economy—explains why the peasants rioted. This perspective on why men rebel is reinforced by an anecdote concerning an earlier visit made by the Koreans when bad times drove the peasants to protest. Despite the seeming connection between the two episodes, however, this history of peasant protest does not expose the development of an oppositional political consciousness on the part of its authors. The riot is simply a kind of change in climate, to which the peasants both for and against react as best they can, pursuing community goals only when these correspond to personal goals and adjusting themselves to the circumstances when they cannot manipulate them to suit their own convenience. Given a maladroit administration, uprisings are depicted as being as inevitable as natural disasters.

Descriptions of the riot itself drew on the peasant movements of earlier times. During the civil wars of the sixteenth century, peasants banded together, on the basis of religious affiliation, in egalitarian communities known as *ikki,* a term that resonates with the subversion of the hierarchical order imposed by a centralized state. Fukaya Katsumi has argued that the same communitarian principles underlay the Christian rebellion of 1637.[9] The Tokugawa rulers so feared the word *ikki* as a sacred symbol of unity opposed to their principles of rule that they forbade its use entirely, substituting for uprisings the term *totō* or "conspiracy." But peasants continued to insist that their *ikki* was the will of the gods. In "A Record of How the Four Orders of People in Mimasaka Ran Riot," *ikki* was implied in the term I have translated as "rebels." In "A Thousand Spears," peasants covered themselves in straw raincoats and carried bamboo spears, a sure sign that they had transformed themselves into gods and demons. They gathered in a sacred forest to renew the bonds of community, and a god led them to commit acts of destruction.[10] They momentarily took themselves outside the status order by drawing on an ancient tradition of holy terror.

Like other histories of peasant uprisings, this one makes an inconsistent effort at factuality. It fabricates a theory of conspiracy to develop a causal explanation for why specific individuals were attacked in the riot, but the names do not match the official records made at the time of the riot. Denzō was from Fujigane, for example, not Igusa, and Hanzō from Kitanomachiya was really Hanbei. The story's hero, Hyōnai from Seki village, Kodama district, Musashi, is placed first in Nitta district, Kōzuke, then Haruzawa. The narrative describes only part of an uprising that swept across four provinces, but it takes this part to represent the whole.

In this history, convention sometimes substitutes for facts. The lord of Kawagoe castle, for example, demonstrates a stereotypical sympathy with the peasants. It is as unlikely that any peasant was worth two hundred thousand *ryō* as it is that thousands of men died in battle or that thirty-five generations of a peasant family would have come between the 1590s and 1764. Aron Gurevich sees imprecision with quantitative data as typical of people who receive their information orally rather than reading it exactingly and unambiguously recorded.[11] Traces of this "ordinary perception," plus the occasional mention of variant versions and the wisdom of storytellers, hint that a large part of the text builds on prior versions in oral sources. By incorporating other voices, it refuses a single point of view and resists coherence. Nevertheless, the effort to establish exact details, whether exaggerated or misplaced, also points to a desire to re-create the particularity of this event in all the ways that distinguish it from other areas and other points in time.

"A Thousand Spears" places the responsibility and the praise for taking action squarely on the shoulders of local notables, unusual cultural heroes for peasants, but perfectly appropriate for village officials. Wealthy and respected peasants supposedly organized this protest against the government and proposed to burn down the house of any peasant who refused to participate. Who but a village official would emphasize how the headman Hyōnai accepted the risk of death for himself to save the community? Despite his unlawful behavior, he acted morally because to ignore the sufferings of the peasants was to make a headman unworthy of his office.

The emphasis on a unified leadership composed of village officials denied ordinary peasants the power to act. Documents made at the time of the riot, however, suggest that young men in Seki forced Hyōnai to pen the circular that summoned the peasants to meet. So many people came to the first assembly that each village had to choose two or three representatives, who then selected further representatives for the collectivity as a whole. Only then could a decision on what to do be reached. In other areas, mountain priests played a prominent role in uniting the peasants behind sacred instruments, long poles topped with a mane of white paper streamers that symbolized the god of purification, Bonten.[12] In general, the peasants' actions were coordinated more by rumor than by a common leader. They attacked only that post station to which the ruling authorities had assigned them, and the attacks came on market days when peasants from nearby villages went to the post stations to sell their goods. After bakufu authorities agreed to rescind their decree, forces from the Kōnosu area decided to punish villages that had not joined them. Other peasants attacked men known to be habitually unjust.[13] By papering over the actual diversity of purposes, activities, and actors, the text undermined its overt project of total explicitness. The author was himself too far removed in time and space to appreciate the details of how peasants in so many different districts organized themselves, and his assumptions regarding who was qualified to act made it impossible for him to recognize the role of anyone else.

The text suffers from an internal contradiction, partly because by the 1870s, few village headmen would have put the community ahead of family and also because the author of this text took an ambivalent stance toward violence. The three notables who begin by advocating sanctions against nonparticipants end by piously denying their role in stirring up trouble. Nakazawa Kidayū, author of the song and dance performed in Hyōnai's honor in 1863, also tried to overcome the discrepancy between his appreciation of correct headman behavior and the events of 1764 by omitting from his text both the riot and the appeal made collectively by the peasants to bakufu officials.[14] Instead he too depicted Hyōnai as acting alone, as acting in the same mode as Sakura Sōgorō.

The author also imposes on his cultural heroes conventions of behavior that undercut their role as leaders of protest. Of the some three hundred men arrested by the bakufu, only two are discussed in any detail. The first, Ono Kichiemon, gives moral meaning to the story because he was filial to his aged mother. To develop this theme, the author quotes from the Chinese classic on filial piety, then describes Kichiemon in terms similar to those found in the collective biographies of virtuous individuals. As we have seen in chapter 2, incorporating a story about the parent-child relationship into a tale about social disorder is not uncommon. In political terms, it grants representations of virtue to those heretofore considered outside morality altogether. It also reveals a desire to regulate and organize the reality of social life according to well-defined categories, but in so doing, the author subverts the significance of the riot itself. Unlike Higuchi Jirō, who in 1726 Tsuyama took pride in his role as an uprising leader, Kichiemon cares only for his mother. He makes a commitment not to the standards of justice articulated through community action, but to the private world of family ties.

Hyōnai's arrest provides another opportunity to subvert representations of peasant heroism when his willingness to sacrifice himself is discordantly juxtaposed with his wife's declaration of love. Why does romance enter this history of social protest? H. D. Harootunian has pointed out that a number of rural nativists in the early nineteenth century associated sexual intercourse with the wonderous work of the creation gods. They attributed greater significance to the roles of husband and wife and the creation of descendants in society than to any other category of activity. By valorizing the union of male and female, they drew a sharp contrast with the model for social structure found in the more conventional and impersonal relationships between lord and retainer, or, I would add, the hierarchy of parent and child.[15] The pretty speeches made by Hyōnai's wife suggest that the author of "A Thousand Spears" was so anxious to comprehend this nativist position that he incorporated it into his statement on a radically different issue. To balance the demands of filial piety with the desire for conjugal affection, he even opened his text to a female voice.

Like "A Record of How the Four Orders of People in Mimasaka Ran Riot," texts about the 1764 riot were written by men who pursued their own conception of Japanese history, received a certain amount of education in the Chinese and Japanese classics, and maintained a lively interest in rural affairs. They drew on quotations from the great literary traditions of Japan and China and from elements of the past that emphasize the role of the underdog to narrate a local event. With a title that sounds more like a Kabuki play than a local gazatteer and with contents drawn explicitly from a diversity of sources, "A Thousand Spears at Kitsunezuka" exemplifies the confluence of orality and literacy. Its demonstration of how high culture flowed into peasant villages might be viewed either as a corruption of folkways or as a dilution of civilization. Nonetheless, it points to the mediating role of a rural elite who combined a high level of education with a lively concern for their communities.

In "A Thousand Spears," as in other histories of peasant uprisings, allusion is made to the legendary heroes of the Japanese tradition. A satirical poem mocked one of the conspirators by comparing him to Kumasaka Chōhan, a semimythical bandit from the tenth century famous for the risks he took at gambling. Taira no Masakado is remembered by association with the era in which he rebelled (Shōhei, 931–937). Here we also find the great general Minamoto no Yoshitsune (1159–89), whose exploits and those of his faithful follower, the powerful monk Benkei, became a model of martial prowess and poignant defeat.[16] The Shimabara Christian rebellion is evoked with mention of Itakura Naizen no kami Shigemasa (1588–1638), so humiliated at the news that his forces confronting the peasant rebels were to be reinforced that he attacked before the troops arrived and died in battle. Once again the men incorporated into the history of peasant uprisings did not lead governments; instead, they in some way opposed them.

Summoned ironically to a sordid tale of greed are literary quotations from a wide variety of sources. One is from Yoshida Kenkō (1283?–1350), a poet and hermit whose famous miscellany *Essays in Idleness* is a central work in the development of Japanese aesthetics.[17] Another is from Chuang-tze (circa 300 B.C.E.), a famous Taoist philosopher and writer whose zany anecdotes have delighted generations of students.[18] A cynical poem by the Zen monk Ikkyū (1394–1481) takes yet another swipe at the Buddhist clergy. Known as an eccentric, Ikkyū's reputation in the Tokugawa period rested on "hilarious apocrypal and scandalous tales" about his doings that suggest how little piety had to do with success.[19] In a lively description of the kind of talk that would engage men during vigils for the god of wealth, these selections taken from the works of literary giants are brought to bear on making money.

Selections from Japan's literary traditions also serve more serious purposes. The author borrowed the techniques of satirical poetry to comment on the rioters. One copy of "A Thousand Spears" includes a stanza, slightly misquoted, from a poem by Sugawara no Michizane (845–903), a Heian period courtier whose death in exile transformed him into the most famous of the angry spirits. The poem not only displays the copyist's erudition, but also heightens the appreciation for a beautiful natural setting. An early Han dynasty (206 B.C.E.–220 C.E.) collection of biographies and miscellaneous stories provides the image of a praying mantis so singlemindedly pursuing its goal that it does not watch for danger. The "Classic of Filial Piety," a text often used for beginners in Chinese language studies and a major source of inspiring admonitions for commoner behavior, provides an opportunity to reflect upon the conduct of rulers.[20] In a text often critical of bakufu officials whose lack of integrity was defined as a cause of the riot, the garbled reminder that "one who governs the state should not despise the masses" has ramifications beyond a pious plea for condescending concern. If the audience and the author for this text were village officials, it is entirely appropriate that they selected this quotation as a judgment on members of the ruling class, whom they were increasingly less likely to see as their betters.

Village officials and local notables designated themselves, not the authorities, as responsible for maintaining their communities. Like Hyōnai, the leader of the rebellion, they believed themselves to be "superior to the warriors." Given the failure of authority above, it was only natural that they should become the ones to exercise benevolence.[21] They were the leaders of intellectual life in the countryside, writing poetry, studying history, and practicing the tea ceremony and even the martial arts. By the 1850s and 1860s, they had become increasingly concerned about the rise of social disorder. In search for a solution that privileged their own role as village leaders, many turned to nativism. They were especially interested in local custom, the content of unique and particular experience. For most, a concern for the texture of local life led them to ethnographic study in an attempt to deny change over time in the real world of the peasants' everyday practice, but some local leaders also studied the histories of the family and the region.

Only wealth provided the local notables with the leisure for the study of the Japanese and Chinese classics and the time to write long histories of past events, but not all of them were comfortable with what money could do. Like rural nativist scholars, the author of "A Thousand Spears" wrestled with the problem of how to justify being rich. Harootunian has pointed out that rural nativists were acutely sensitive to those economic activities that had become divisive influences in their communities.[22] Nevertheless, because he ignores their role as the primary exploiters of the peasantry through their control of capital in the countryside, he does not deal with the contradiction between what they did and how they defined a responsible attitude toward the acquisition of property. In "A Thousand Spears," the effort to grapple with this issue is focused on Watanuki Hanbei of Irimagawa, guilty by association with

Jinzaemon, equally rich, and punished for his part in the riot by the destruction of his possessions. The difference between these two men was that, like the rural nativist Miyahiro Sadao (also read Miyaoi Yasuo, 1797–1858), Hanbei understood how wealth must not "be limited to the glory and honor of one household, . . . but must become an endowment put back into the service of the community."[23] After the riot, Hanbei prospered even more than before. By thus making a distinction between just and unjust wealth, the text tried to overcome the duality in the social roles of rich peasants exposed by the riot.

The rural nativists/local notables did not agree on how to interpret peasant uprisings. Miyahiro saw peasant revolts as examples of cheating, robbing, and deceiving, whereas Miyauchi Yoshinaga (1798–1843) saw them as omens portending the failure of leadership at the top. Like the author of "A Thousand Spears," he argued that when the lord committed violations against the people, the people would surely retaliate. Furthermore, "by knowing the basic cause of a rebellion, people would be in a position to avoid it before it happened."[24] For this reason, it became necessary to study past events of protest, and what better place to start than with one that had brought destruction close to hand.

A Thousand Spears at Kitsunezuka

CHAPTER ONE

A Tale Told at the Vigil for the God of Wealth

The popular saying that the rich are insatiable is correct. Thus it is common for even our rulers to pray for wealth.

Let us inquire into the reasons for the riot over post-horses that broke out in Musashi province. At a place called Kitsunezuka in the village of Kawadaya, Adachi district, Musashi, there lived a rich peasant named Takahashi Jinzaemon who owned many paddy fields and possessed twenty thousand *ryō* in gold. Like Sanshō the bailiff of old, he was sly, cunning, and greedy. He prayed constantly to the god of wealth.

At the same place lived a miserably poor man named Heisuke.

On the night of the vigil for the god of wealth in the eleventh month of 1761, Heisuke went to see Jinzaemon on business.

"Tonight is the vigil for the god of wealth," Jinzaemon said. "Let's talk." He hospitably set out refreshments.

"I am much obliged to you."

After the two men had chatted idly for several hours, Heisuke turned to Jinzaemon and joked, "Is it true that things turn into treasure when you strike them with the lucky mallet carried by the god of wealth? I too would like to get my hands on this lucky mallet, turn goods into gold and silver, and put an end to my poverty."

"That's not how it is," Jinzaemon replied. "The lucky mallet comes only to those who humble themselves in all things, avoid luxury, keep their eyes fixed to the ground, and don't look up. Most people just study their superiors and ignore those below them. You will not become a notable by simply wanting to wear beautiful clothes or spending money unless you take advantage of every opportunity. Even someone who can't get through another day may look like a rich man. How do you think people get rich?"

"How did you get as rich as you are right now? I get up in the morning before dawn and go home at night with the stars. Even though I work hard all the time, I still can't seem to make a day's living. Why is it that the harder I work, the poorer I become?" Heisuke fretted.

Moved to sympathy, Jinzaemon replied, "A person's lot can't be improved simply by hard work. You will find it difficult to support your family if, in addition to hard work, you do not follow the teachings of the god of wealth and exercise your ingenuity. By foolishly disobeying his teachings and pursuing luxury, you end up leading a miserable existence."

"What, do you think I am a fool?"

Jinzaemon laughed. "My dear fellow, I had no intention of ridiculing you for a fool. Look around you and pay attention. Lots of people are unable to make a living even though they are extremely talented and cultivated and even quite shrewd. The only thing that gets remembered in this world is whether you've made a success of yourself. People unable to succeed are thus fools. Why bother learning the arts? Yoshida Kenkō wrote in his *Essays in Idleness*, "The wise man is never rich." Perhaps I am a fool, but who can succeed by learning the arts? What Kenkō meant by wisdom is just a matter of calculating three in the morning and four at night."

"What is meant by three in the morning and four at night is precisely what I wanted to learn."

"I heard this from the abbot at my family's temple. A long time ago in China lived a wise man named Chuang-tzu. In his writings there is a story about a monkey trainer from the state of Ch'u. He had laid in a lot of food for his monkeys, but being a poor man, he turned to them and said, "For one day's rations will it satisfy you to eat three kernels of arrowroot in the morning and four at night?" This made the monkeys mad, so he thought up another proposal. "Well, would you be satisfied with four kernels in the morning and three at night?" The monkeys were all delighted. Anyone unable to succeed through his own shrewdness is just like those monkeys who didn't know the difference between three in the morning and four at night. A person's position ultimately depends on how clever or foolish he is.

"Being a wise man, the abbot was able to accumulate lots of money," Jinzaemon continued. "That reminds me of a poem by Ikkyū:

While encouraging everyone to abandon desire,
The high temple priests use Amida to make money.

This poem makes an important statement about Buddhist law. It shows how the bonzes mislead the people by putting their profits first. According to the abbot, even a layman can do a lot to encourage people to give him money, but if you don't hold on to even the littlest coin that comes your way, you will never succeed."

Heisuke had listened intently. "Obviously the way that people with nothing think is different from the rich. Poverty makes us stupid. We think it's great to spend whatever money comes our way, and perhaps it's for that reason that we are poor. It must have been the divine will of the god of wealth that brought me to see you on the night of this vigil to hear such marvelous things. Hereafter I will do as you have said, take advantage of every opportunity, believe in the god of wealth, and pray for riches. Dawn will soon be breaking so I will take my leave." With these final remarks, Heisuke returned home.

The Two Men Hatch a Scheme

Thereafter, the two men prayed harder and harder for riches. One night Takahashi Jinzaemon came to see Heisuke.

"If you are willing to go along with me, there is a way for us to make money. How about it?"

Heisuke listened to him and said, "I'm a poor man with no way of making money. No matter what you have in mind, I'll follow your lead. Come on, tell me."

"Let's have the regular assessment of horses and porters for official business from Adachi district that services the post stations of Ageo and Okegawa increased to include the villages that currently provide this service on a supplemental basis," Jinzaemon proposed. "Those villages which lie far from the highway will find it difficult to send the necessary men and horses, so they'll probably want to hire substitutes to do the work for them. We'll take charge of the money for the substitutes, have the people in Adachi do the official work for the post stations on a regular basis as they have been doing up to now, and for the portion of the work paid for by the hitherto supplemental villages, we'll hire other porters and horses. Even when there is no official business to be done, we'll pretend that there is, and that is how we'll make money."

Heisuke was delighted. "That way we'll certainly get as rich as the god of wealth. If just the two of us enter into this plot, however, success will be difficult. Of course I have no idea how many villages provide supplements of porters and horses, but there must be lots of them, so even if we include ten to twenty men in our scheme, that won't be too many. We need to talk to the people we know and invite them to join us."

"You're right. I'll let you know the details fairly soon," Jinzaemon replied. That night he returned to his own home.

Jinzaemon Conspires with Some People in Oki Village

In Oki village of Adachi district there lived a peasant named TomomitsuGonzaemon, a shrewd village headman and a relative of Jinzaemon. Jinzaemon secretly paid this Gonzaemon a visit to tell him the particulars of everything that had transpired.

"Through your efforts, we should easily be able to win over lots of people." Gonzaemon was basically sly and cunning, the greediest man alive, and he was ecstatic.

"Please leave everything to me. I know just how to bring lots of people into this."

Shortly thereafter, Gonzaemon tricked some rogues into letting him get close to them. First he won over Seibei from Hirakata village. During the vigil to the god of wealth in the last month of the year, the two men went to visit Jinzaemon. Delighted to see them, he summoned Heisuke and set out refreshments to entertain the three men. They spent the entire night talking at their banquet.

In the early part of the second month of 1762, Gonzaemon conspired with Kojima Kandayū from Uedaya village; then in the third month he won over Rokuzaemon from Tajima. After that, he talked to Denzō of Kumasaka. Finally in 1763, he got to Hikoshirō from Kon'ya, Kansuke from Kanō, Hanzō from Kitanomachiya, Yasōji from Hiratsuka, Kōnosuke from Takakura, and Shokuemon from Kujirai. Afterward the members of this gang met occasionally to talk through Gonzaemon's good offices.

The Conference at Jinzaemon's House

In the spring of 1764, the whole gang of over ten men met at the home of Takahashi Jinzaemon in Kawadaya for a conference. Their names were Jinzaemon, Heisuke, Tomomitsu Gonzaemon, Seibei from Hirakata, Rokuzaemon from Tajima, Yasōji from Hiratsuka, Hikoshirō from Kon'ya, Shokuemon from Kujirai, Kōnosuke from Takakura, Denzō from Kumasaka, Hanzō from Kitanomachiya, Hanbei from Irimagawa, Kandayō from Uedaya, and Kansuke from Kanō.

At the conference three men, Rokuzaemon from Tajima, Gonzaemon from Oki, and Yasōji from Hiratsuka, made a statement: "In order to get more villages added to those that already service the post stations, we should get the officially appointed inns for the daimyō at Ageo and Okegawa to act in concert with us in making our appeal. In that case the villages now providing supplemental porters and horses will most certainly be ordered to provide them on a regular basis. What do you think of that, everyone?" As they spoke, they ran their eyes over the assembly.

"That's a great idea," everyone agreed. Then Jinzaemon spoke:

"How do we get the inns for the daimyō to act in concert with us?"

"I've already become close friends with one of the masters," Gonzaemon replied. "There is not the slightest need for concern."

"Well in that case," Jinzaemon said, "once you have discussed this matter with them, we'll plan what to do next." Everyone went back home the same day.

A little while later Gonzaemon from Oki acted in concert with the masters of the two inns for daimyō in presenting a petition to the magistrate in charge of roads, Lord Andō Danjō. The text was as follows:

> Fearfully we offer up a petition in writing
> In recent years the traffic of daimyō along the Nakasendō has grown increasingly heavy. If our ruler would be pleased to exercise his compassion by ordering the villages providing supplemental porters and horses to do so on a regular basis, we would be exceedingly grateful.

This is the petition that they presented. Lord Andō was basically a cunning and crafty guy, and he reported to the senior councillors that he thought the petition was a good idea. It was said that the senior councillor Matsudaira Ukon no Zō then reported the matter to the shōgun. Thereafter Lord Ukon no Zō decreed that all of the villages previously providing supplemental porters and horses would supply them on a regular basis.

A New Land Survey, Porters and Post-Horses, and Loans to the Government

In 1764, Korean envoys came to the court at the inauguration of the new shōgun. A decree went out that the government's expenses for the visit would be divided among the peasants at a high rate. For each hundred *koku* of taxable yield, they had to provide a loan of three gold *ryō*, one *bu*, and two *shu*. At the same time, villages previously providing supplemental porters and horses had to supply them on a regular basis. To make sure that all of this happened, at the end of the eleventh month Nomura Denhachi and Hiratsuka Ichirōemon traveled around Musashi and Kōzuke making a new land survey. Their guide was Rokuzaemon from Kita Tajima.

That year the era name changed to Meiwa. During the last month, Naruse Hikotarō and Kurabashi Yoshirō made an official trip to the Okegawa post station, whence they summoned the headmen, group leaders, and peasants' representatives from the villages providing supplemental porters and horses to read to them the following announcement:

> This is to announce to you a decree from the senior councillor Matsudaira Ukon no Zō that the villages previously providing supplemental porters and horses must henceforth supply them on a regular basis. In accordance with this decision, we are telling you now that you must provide porters and horses beginning in the new year without fail.

After they made the above announcement, the two officials forced the headmen to give them a pledge that they would do what was required without fail.

> We obey with respect the particulars of the decree we just received which had been transmitted from Lord Matsudaira Ukon no Zō to the magistrate in charge of roads, Andō Danjō Shōhitsu, saying that the villages heretofore supplying porters and horses on a supplemental basis must now provide them on a regular basis. We will so inform the peasants and make sure that they perform these duties carefully.

1764/12　　　　　*Headmen*
　　　　　　　　　　Group Leaders
　　　　　　　　　　Peasants' Representatives

Lord Naruse Hikotarō and Lord Kurabashi Yoshirō deigned to receive this document. Thereafter they went to the post stations of Ageo, Okegawa, Kōnosu, and Kumagaya, where they made the same announcement.

On the fifth day of the twelfth month, Gonzaemon went to see Jinzaemon and said, "Our petition has succeeded beyond the shadow of a doubt in having the villages previously providing porters and horses on a supplemental basis ordered to supply them on a regular basis. Now we should send around a notice saying that an assembly hall will be built in Kumagaya where the villages supplying porters and horses can discharge their duty by sending to it six *ryō* per hundred *koku* of taxable yield every year."

Jinzaemon listened to him, agreed with what he had said, and made his preparations.

CHAPTER TWO

An Assembly Hall Is Built at Kumagaya

Now on the night of the twentieth in the twelfth month, over ten men, Gonzaemon, Heisuke, Jinzaemon, and the others including Seibei from Hiratsuka and Kandayū from Uedaya, met to discuss what to do. They agreed on the following statement:

"Our petition has most certainly been successful because Lord Naruse Hikotarō and Lord Kurabashi Yoshirō made an official visit to issue the decree regarding a regular supply of porters and horses. Nevertheless, if the peasants are simply informed that they have a duty to perform in supplying porters and horses without any indication that they can do so by paying fees instead, we won't have any way of making money. Therefore we think it would be a good idea to issue an announcement saying that an assembly hall will be built at Kumagaya, and the villages providing porters and horses should send there six *ryō* per hundred *koku* of taxable yield every year. In the near future some of you should hire carpenters to build the assembly hall. Others should send a circular to the villages heretofore providing a supplemental supply of porters and horses that falsifies the decree issued by Naruse Hikotarō and Kurabashi Yoshirō."

Once this agreement had been reached, the master of the inn for the daimyō at Kumagaya hired some carpenters. As early as the twenty-second, they began erecting the framework for the assembly hall. A circular was duly sent to the villages:

Recently Lord Naruse Hikoshirō and Lord Kurabashi Yoshirō sent us the following announcement: villagers who think that because they live far from the highway, they will experience hardships in providing porters and horses on a regular basis should send six *ryō* per hundred *koku* of taxable yield every year to the assembly hall being built in Kumagaya. The two officials having made this announcement, villagers whose distance from the highway will cause them hardships should send money to this assembly hall every year. We affirm that we will most certainly hire the porters and horses to provide the transportation service required by our rulers.

This announcement was written down and circulated through the villages supplying supplemental porters and horses in the provinces of Musashi and Kōzuke.

But then, on the twenty-sixth, the peasants became agitated. After the circular had gone through four or five villages, it was stopped and went no further. The assembly hall was not built; instead the peasants came en masse to smash the lumber to smithereens. The carpenters took fright and scattered in all directions.

[The Third Reason for the Riot]

Famine in a country causes strife. Let us now inquire into why there was a famine. In the latter part of the fourth month of 1761, a flood had damaged the wheat crop. Then at the beginning of the eighth month more flooding prevented the autumn harvest. The peasants were already suffering from hunger when, between the end of the fourth month and the ninth month of 1762, there were fifteen floods. There were even three floods in 1763. Conditions were unsettled everywhere; robbers and bandits plundered the weak and looted their property. Few were able to escape with their lives. The great fear for parents was that even if they abandoned their children, they would not be able to save their own lives, and children worried that even if they killed their parents, they would not survive. No one knows how many old and young lost their lives because of the famine. Many people suffered severe hardships.

[The Storyteller Tells of an Uprising in the Past]

In the Irima district of Musashi there lived a man over a hundred years old who told the following story:

"A long time ago when Lord Matsudaira Yamato no kami, the castellan of Himeji, was ordered to transfer to another domain, the former castellan of Maebashi in Kōzuke, Lord Sakai Utanokami, graciously took over Himeji castle. Lord Yamato no kami had been moved to Himeji seven years earlier. From that time on, taxes were

strictly collected, miscellaneous taxes tripled, the villages were assessed corvée labor for all sorts of things, and every year they were
ordered to make loans to the government. Because of these exac-
tions, the peasants and the townspeople suffered dire poverty. Then
one year the government ordered that the people make it loans of
fifty thousand *ryō* to be collected in full because the Korean envoys
were to pass through the domain on their way to the court. Since
taking care of the Koreans was the most important business assigned to the lord during his reign, he took great care to please the
shōgun in this matter.

"These loans were never repaid, yet preparations were made
for the Matsudaira family to leave the domain. Consequently the
peasants and townspeople from the domain and even people living
elsewhere who had loaned the government money each discussed
what to do.

"'With the Matsudaira family being transferred to a domain far
away, the loans will never be repaid. It's a lot of money to be throwing away, and most of the peasant families will starve. Besides, we
will not be able to disobey if the lord who takes over this domain
uses this precedent to exact even more from us. The people of the
domain will suffer worse and worse from hunger. What are we
going to do about it?'

"Then other people said, 'The land tax has been collected very
strictly over the years, so let the entire domain unite in signing an
agreement. Then we can fortify the frontier and petition the government to repay the loans. Given the present confusion in
government circles, we don't think that presenting just an ordinary
petition will get it accepted. For this reason, we must all risk our
lives in crowding before the main gate to the castle to ascertain what
is going on.'

"Having arrived at this decision, every man between the ages of
fifteen and sixty, a total of sixty-eight thousand, joined the conspiracy on the Jōshū Plain. Women, children, and old people were sent
away for safekeeping. After they had set up camp, the men made an
oral statement to the domain elder, Matsudaira Hyōnai: 'We have a
petition to make regarding the transfer of our lord's family. Are you
planning to repay the money you ordered us to loan the government when the Koreans came to the court in years past, or are you
thinking of overlooking this matter when you move? This is what
we wanted to ask you about. What is your reply?'

"At first Lord Hyōnai did not know what to make of this. When repayment had been delayed, the deceased lord had issued a command which stated, 'At some point the money must be repaid.' Now, the peasants who had suffered for so many years had risked their lives in uniting together to come out and talk to him. Again and again they beseeched him to act. He felt a special reason for concern because the lord was implicated in this matter, but with so many men involved, his pronouncements had no effect.

"The peasants broke down the gate, rushed inside the walls, shouted war cries, and brandished sickles and bamboo spears. They attacked the castle, fighting furiously. Just then a youth of about seventeen or eighteen of unsurpassed bearing and ability came running up out of nowhere. He scowled at the castle defenders, launched himself wholeheartedly at the mass of soldiers, and wrecked havoc in all directions. The forces fought like wild tigers. Over five thousand peasants were wounded, and some of them died. I heard that the houses of twenty-seven headmen were also destroyed.

"All of this arose from dire poverty. Right now famine has struck our province, and everyone is suffering hardships. What kind of disasters are yet to come?" Thus spoke the old man.

[In 1764, Three Wealthy and Respected Peasants Foment Protest]

The demand for porters and horses plus loans to the government had worsened the people's sorrows and afflictions. They simply wandered about in a daze at wits' end.

Now in the castle town of Serata in Kōzuke province there lived a peasant called Tokugawa Utajūrō from Tokugawa village. He owned fields and paddies worth over a thousand *koku,* and he also received a stipend of five hundred *koku* from the government. Long ago, when Serata castle held by Tokugawa Ukyōdayū Chikauji had fallen, Utajūrō's family had sheltered his forces of over thirty thousand men for three whole days. At that time the entire army had signed an agreement which the family has retained down to the present. Then when Lord Tokugawa Dainagon Minamoto Ieyasu became the shōgun of Japan, he summoned Utajūrō's ancestor to meet him and receive a stipend of five hundred *koku.* The family thus became peasants under the patronage of Ieyasu's divine spirit. The present Tokugawa Utajūrō was the thirty-fifth head of his household since that time.

In Oka village of Kōzuke there lived a peasant called Tokugawa Tokujirō. He came from the same sort of family as Utajūrō, his ancestors having been given three hundred *koku* by the government. He too was a peasant under the patronage of Ieyasu's divine spirit.

Six and a half miles in the other direction there lived a peasant called Hachirōzaemon. He owned fields and paddies worth three thousand *koku*, and he was the master of three thousand tenants. It was said that his lineage was equally distinguished.

Hachirōzaemon went to visit Tokujirō, where the two men discussed at great length the implications of the government loans and the requisitions of porters and horses. After the three men had held council, they made the following statement to Hyōnai, headman of Seki village, Nitta district, Kōzuke province:

"Lord Matsudaira Ukon no Zō recently issued an announcement. He decreed that the villages supplying porters and horses on a supplemental basis must now provide them on a regular basis, and he has had the headmen, group leaders, and peasants' representatives go to Kōnosu and Kumagaya to receive his orders. If they consent, the starving peasants will find it hard to survive. Please send around a circular, assemble the peasants of Kōzuke and Musashi, and after having held council with them, appeal to be exempted from this decree.

"The route of the Nakasendō was the one taken secretly by the divine Ieyasu whenever he wanted to go to Kyoto without dealing with the problems on the main road, but right now all of the daimyō use it going back and forth, which was not the idea at all. Besides, from what we remember of the expenses for the Koreans' visits, the loans we had to make to the government for the twenty-six times they have come to court up to now were as follows (per hundred *koku* of taxable yield):

132 *mon*	100 *mon*	32 *mon*
50	68	92
39	24	35
40	29	500
200	200	300
200	190	390

600	700	3 *kan* 500 *mon*
2 *kan*	3 *kan* 20 *mon*	530 *mon*

This is how we remember it being. Thus the current notice that we will have to pay three *ryō*, one *bu*, two *shu* per hundred *koku* is incomprehensible.

"We should hold a council to let the peasants know what we think. If even one man is left out or does not appear for the meeting, his house should be burned to the ground. Nevertheless, since the three of us are peasants with distinguished lineages under the patronage of Ieyasu's divine spirit, were we to go to Edo to make an oral statement to the authorities, many officials would then suffer. For that reason, we are relying on you. If we are to do what we can to save the multitudes from their hardships, you must do your utmost and not begrudge your life." Hyōnai respectfully indicated his assent. The three men returned to their own homes.

Here is another version. Having held council, the three men sent a notice around to the 875 villages in Kōzuke telling them that they should gather at the Adachi Plain, meet in three groups within three days to discuss the problem, and then set out for Edo. The 875 villages of Kōzuke then gathered at the plain and held council.

"Because we have received the recent announcement, we really ought to go to Edo and write a petition for exemption to be presented to the senior councillor as he rides by in his palanquin. If he does not accept our appeal, tens of thousands of peasants should go to Ina Hanzaemon's, where they should crowd in front of his gate with a petition. If he does nothing about it, we should surround his mansion to make repeated and forceful appeals for him to grant us an exemption. If he still refuses to accept our petition, we will not cultivate our fields at all for three years, and we will survive simply by eating things we have on hand like millet and grasses."

This version is incorrect. If the fields were not cultivated for three years, the starving peasants would all suffer for want of food. Besides, how can it be said that they would eat things like millet and grasses when no one could possibly have enough millet and grasses on hand to last for three years?

After Hyōnai had been arrested, the three men were summoned for interrogation, whereupon they made the following statement:

"The three of us held council and told Hyōnai that he should go appeal for an exemption, but none of us went ourselves. Even in our wildest dreams we naturally never imagined that the peasants would destroy houses and other property." It appears that they were then allowed to go home.

Following the discussions, Hyōnai sent this circular around the villages:

> Headmen, group leaders, and peasants' representatives
> were summoned to Kumagaya to receive the directive issued
> by Lord Matsudaira Ukon no Zō stating that the villages
> previously supplying porters and horses on a supplemental
> basis are henceforth to provide them on a regular basis.
> Villages that want to be exempted from its provisions should
> please have all of their men over the age of fifteen show up at
> Jūzūgahara on the twenty-fourth. There we will decide what
> to do, all of the peasants will unite together, and we will go to
> Edo to appeal for an exemption. This has been written by
> Hyōnai of Seki village, Nitta district, Kōzuke.

The Gathering of All Peasants at Jūzūgahara

By and by the peasants of Musashi and Kōzuke who saw Hyōnai's circular bid farewell to their parents, wives, and children.

"We have dedicated ourselves to going to Edo to appeal for an exemption from serving the post stations, and it is doubtful that we will ever return home again." They left their families in tears. Loath to part from them, wives, children, and brothers were overwhelmed with grief. Their lamentations resounded through the villages from north to south. How pitiful they were.

In this fashion the peasants hurried tearfully to Jūzūgahara. For his attire each wore a straw raincoat and hat and carried a bamboo spear. Everyone flocked to Jūzūgahara, where they erected flags enscribed with the symbols for their villages. The forces numbered over seventy-eight thousand men.

Turning to the multitude, Hyōnai said, "I am your humble servant, the headman from Seki called Hyōnai. For me to ignore the sufferings of the peasants would make me unworthy of being a headman. I therefore considered a variety of alternatives in trying to figure out how I could save the peasants from their hardships before, unworthy though I am, I sent around a circular. I am most profoundly grateful that each of you agreed to appear. Now, if there are no objections, let us all sign the petition together." From his purse he drew a huge ledger. Pushing forward, all of the over seventy-eight thousand men signed the petition. Delighted, Hyōnai said that they should start at once. Everyone hurried off toward Edo.

CHAPTER THREE

The Peasants Run Riot through the Post Stations

Once it became known that the peasants had resolved to go to Edo, Lord Ōno Etchū no kami placed a guard station at a place called Namakubi [lit., freshly-severed head] in the Kumagaya domain. It was defended by officials dispatched for that purpose, but the peasants destroyed it and ran riot through the Kumagaya post station.

Protected only by soldiers, the doors to the inn for daimyō were shut. The sheer size of the crowd enabled it to break down the gate in an instant and run riot inside. Even though they knew that their situation was almost hopeless, the soldiers fought valiantly. The peasants tackled them with their spears, while their opponents fought like their lives depended on it. Many peasants suffered wounds, yet they wavered not at all. The fight continued, the sparks flying. Finally, with five of their number gored to death and unable to withstand the peasants any longer, the soldiers retreated. Three peasants were wounded. Over ten were killed.

Long ago, when Minamoto no Yoshitsune led a punitive force to subjugate Kiso Yoshinaka, he happened to ask the way of an old man. The old man replied, "The quickest route would be the road that goes by the place called Decapitation Falls."

"For someone on the eve of battle, the name Decapitation is bad luck. Is there no other road, old man?" Yoshitsune asked.

The old man thought once more, then indicated a path that led by the shrine to the Utte Myōjin [lit., punitive shining deity]. This is the road that Lord Yoshitsune took. Later he defeated Yoshinaka and won renown as a great general.

This story shows that anyone about to go into battle must take

143

everything into consideration. Even though the retainers of Lord Ōno Etchū no kami were privileged to be born into the families of warriors, they did not know this old truth, so they went to Namakubi which they fortified against the peasants. Oh how foolish of them. How unfortunate that they lost their lives on the points of bamboo spears. Had the peasants been supposed to know things like that, they would have scrupled to avoid a place called Namakubi.

Thereafter the peasants utterly destroyed the inn for the daimyō. Shouting war cries, each vying to be first, they advanced boldly and ran riot. With their sickles and bamboo spears at hand, they smashed up the houses of Kumagaya. The inhabitants of the post station had never dreamed that such a thing could happen. What could be going on? Everything was turned topsy-turvey. Some tried to defend themselves, but they were few and the attackers were many. Having no choice, they ran off, scattering in all directions.

Having smashed up the Kumagaya post station, the peasants hastened on to Kōnosu. Astonished at their war cries, the inhabitants tried to flee, each and every one of them. The peasants running riot smashed up houses and shouted war cries that reverberated throughout heaven and earth. The noise was tremendous. This happened on the twenty-seventh day of the twelfth month.

The next day the peasants burst on Okegawa. War cries rang out continually. They smashed up lots of houses, but strangely enough, not even one person was there, for everything had been abandoned.

Frightened of the peasant multitude, the two officials, Naruse Hikotarō and Kurabashi Yoshirō, had fled Kumagaya on the night of the twenty-sixth. They returned to Edo, where they reported to the authorities what was happening. Even the shōgun deigned to feel astonishment.

The shōgun's three collateral houses and the senior councillors promptly held council. "Ina Hanzaemon is the Kanto intendant, and he sympathizes with the peasants, so he should be put in charge," the senior councillors announced. The three collateral houses and the shōgun agreed that would be the best thing to do. To prevent the peasants from running riot through Edo, they had all the gates to the city fortified. Then they summoned Hanzaemon to the castle to give him his orders. Hanzaemon respectfully acquiesced to their wishes, left the castle, and set out for Okegawa.

Not knowing what had happened, the peasants tried to smash up the inn for the daimyō in Okegawa. One after another they beat on the gate with their sickles. Those inside tried to defend it. Because the crowds were so large, they finally broke down the gate and killed four or five men. "Horrors, what an outrage," people shouted as they ran away.

Just at that point, two samurai came out of the interior. "Quiet!" they ordered. The peasants gradually calmed down and lined themselves up in rows. Then the particulars of the shōgun's command, brought by his special messenger Ina Hanzaemon, with a decree for exemption from post station duty, were announced to the peasants. The peasants respectfully received the document. Overjoyed, Hyōnai and the others hurried off for home.

Two Suns Appear in the Sky/Hyōnai Receives a Scroll

Just as the peasants were leaving Okegawa, a strange thing happened. Two suns appeared in the sky. Struck dumb with amazement, the peasants could say nothing.

"The appearance of two suns means either a national emergency or a natural disaster. What a mystery," Hyōnai stated. The multitude of people knit their brows and spoke in whispers. After awhile, the suns faded and disappeared.

Suddenly the skies clouded over, flashes of lightning struck all around, and thunder reverberated through heaven and earth. Needless to say, it was really something. The peasants were still pondering how mysterious it all was when a strange figure at least eight feet tall with the head of a lion and carrying a scroll abruptly became visible in the midst of the black clouds. He called himself Harada Hikobei. In the twinkling of an eye, he had handed the scroll he carried to Hyōnai and flown off. The sky cleared instantly; a white sun appeared and shone brightly.

Hyōnai opened the scroll and looked inside, where he found a complete record of how Jinzaemon and the others in his gang had plotted to have it decreed that the villages heretofore supplying porters and horses on a supplemental basis would provide them regularly. Hyōnai became enraged when he saw the list.

"Let's attack their homes and requite our rancor," he shouted.

145

"This was all their doing, was it. Now let's teach them a lesson," the seventy-eight thousand men roared in reply. First they turned toward Kitanomachiya. This all happened on the night of the twenty-eighth.

The People Whose Houses Were Destroyed

That same night the tens of thousands of men in this uprising marched on the home of Hanzō in Kitanomachiya. They shouted war cries; their lanterns glittered like stars. Layer upon layer they surrounded Hanzō's house on all sides. It was the middle of the night and their arrival was completely unexpected. What a sight to see men and women shrieking and wandering about in a daze. The multitude tore down the gate and ran riot on all sides, smashing up the house and storehouses in a flash. Thereafter they demolished Takakura Kōnosuke's house.

The next dawn brought the New Year's day of 1765. Shouting war cries, the crowd marched on Hikoshirō of Kon'ya village. Somehow the members of the household, young and old alike, managed to escape by turning everything upside down. Each carrying sickles and bamboo spears, the wretches in the uprising vyed with each other for the lead. In a flash they had crushed everything in the house underfoot. Clothing they tore up, tools they smashed, and everything they shattered to smithereens. Then they completely demolished the house and the warehouses, a cruel sight. As the person in charge of the hawking grounds for the bakufu, this Hikoshirō had recently been ordered to survey the whereabouts of birds in his vicinity. He became the subject of the following satirical poem because he was the greediest man alive:

> For the crime of extorting money (surveying the whereabouts of birds)
> Tonight (in Kon'ya), the crowd has taught him a lesson.[25]

That night the crowd marched on Denzō of Kumasaka village, shouting war cries. For some reason, a man wearing a grass belt came running out. The members of the uprising chased after him, yelling, "Don't let that suspicious character escape!"

"Help, murder, help!" he yelped in astonishment. With trembling limbs he ran off, no one knew where. Denzō was off somewhere, leaving only an old woman of at least eighty and a young one of about thirty at home. The crowd wrecked havoc. That night someone wrote another satirical poem:

Once Kumasaka (the bandit and gambler) had thrown the
    dice,
The multitude shook the house (cheated).

Later the crowd turned toward the home of Watanuki Hanbei in Irimagawa. He did not look it, but he was really wealthy, owning fields worth twenty-eight hundred *koku* and having on hand two hundred thousand *ryō*. In his household were 120 people. Even though he lacked for nothing, he had thoughtlessly allowed himself to be won over by Gonzaemon. For him to become a victim in this ordeal shows that once you have been led astray by greed, you will have to accept the decree of heaven.

According to an old saying, a kindness is never lost. Watanuki Hanbei felt deep compassion for his fellow men, and he was constantly taking pity on his neighbors. He was especially good to widows and widowers, orphans, and all those who had no one to care for them. As he said, "By chance my ancestors stored up a lot of gold and silver, but this treasure is not just for my family alone." From dawn to dusk he dispensed alms.

Hearing voices shouting that today, during this riot, the crowd was going to swarm through Hanbei's house and run rampage, one after another, everyone in the village, even women and the aged, grabbed up hoes and sickles and surrounded the house. "Now we will repay the many favors we have received in the past." Every single one of them gallantly tried to defend the house.

Master Hanbei truly appreciated their efforts: "I'm much obliged to you for all your good intentions, but I don't want any of you to get hurt."

"Say nothing of it. We have resolved to end our lives here today."

"What! You're being outrageous! As far as I'm concerned, I'm delighted at what you've said, but if you neglect your aged parents and young children, I'll have no excuse to make to my ancestors."

He tried to explain himself, but everyone shouted together. "Nothing could be worse than for this house to be destroyed. That's absolutely unthinkable. We wouldn't be able to bear it. We don't care even if we are killed." They simply refused to listen to him.

Holding his voice down as much as possible, Hanbei replied, "Even if all my possessions are smashed to smithereens, I'll be able to get new ones once order has been restored, but you can't be restored to life. Please try to understand what I'm saying."

Still they refused to listen to him.

"Now look here all of you, what sort of grudge do you hold against me that you refuse to listen?" Hanbei shouted.

The crowd finally yielded to his words. There being nothing else they could do, they started to depart for their own homes, but they felt such reluctance to leave that they could not bear to move. At last, urged on by Hanbei, they were forced to return to their own villages. In their hearts they continued to plead with him.

It is as true today as it was in the past that no matter how much conditions change, the one thing that does not is benevolence. People should be aware that this is what morality is all about.

The wretches in the uprising gave vent to war cries. In an instant they had swept all before them and destroyed everything. The members of the household now appeared here, now wandered there. The cries of men and women rent the heavens. How pitiful it was. In the meantime the wretches made quite a racket trying to break into the earthen warehouses. There were eighteen of these warehouses—seven for sake, the rest holding rice and pawned goods. Later that day the crowd set up camp on the Irima River plain to wait for dusk.

It is true what they say that virtue always brings happiness.[26] This is the kind of disaster that Hanbei experienced, one in which he lost all of his family's possessions. For countless years thereafter, however, his family prospered, his children and grandchildren flourished, and they all throve with the vigor of the rising sun. If you exert yourself for others, you will inevitably receive a return for your efforts. It is something to be thankful for, but it is also rather frightening, that if you help lots of people and store up virtue, the way of heaven will reward you with riches as it did Hanbei, right down to your children's generation and your grandchildren.

As dusk fell that day, the wretches in the uprising turned toward Rokuemon's house in Kita Tajima. It was the second night of the first month, 1765.

Rokuemon's house was located in the Kita Tajima section of the Kawagoe castle town. The castellan of Kawagoe was Lord Akimoto Tajima no kami, but he was then in Edo. That evening in the dead of night, the Kawagoe city magistrate, Tanaka Moemon, heard repeated war cries. On a fast horse he rushed to the keeper of the castle, Takayama Bunzaemon, where, heaving deep breaths, he related in some confusion: "It seems that the peasants are marching on the castle. I have heard their war cries close at hand. Please summon the warriors to defend us."

Takayama Bunzaemon was utterly astonished. Having prepared his weapons, he promptly sent a notice to the retainers, "Everyone must report for duty at the main gate." After awhile, each and every one of the warriors reported at the main gate wearing full armor.

The most intrepid among them was Mochita Kingorō, who appeared on horseback with his armor buckled up. He carried a bow of fourteen handbreadths unpullable by most men, plus prong-tipped arrows winged with hawk feathers. Marching straight up to the castle, he turned to the keeper and announced impetuously, "Even if ten or twenty thousand of the peasant rabble come charging up here, it is nothing to make a fuss over. It is unmanly of us to fortify the castle against them. I alone will attack and drive them off!"

Iwata Hikosuke admonished him sternly. "Do not despise the peasants. Lord Itakura Naisen no kami was a brave and strong man, but he was defeated by the peasants at Shimabara castle. If something like that were to happen here, it would be a lifelong disgrace. It's not worth it," he said repressively. Realizing the truth to what he had heard, Kingorō quieted down.

Guarding the main gate were Takayama Bunzaemon and Nagai Kiyodayū, supported by over 30 samurai, 300 foot soldiers, 50 riflemen, and 320 bowmen. At the south gate stood Mochita Kingorō on guard with 150 men, 15 riflemen, and 70 bowmen. Takayama Jingobei and Iwate Hikosuke guarded the main enceinte with 500 men, 350 riflemen, and 450 bowmen. In addition, there were over 50 men in the reserves.

Following the keeper of the castle's orders, the captains of the guard fortified all four gates leading to the castle town to prevent the peasants' entry. The leader of the first unit was Nagayama Ichirōzaemon, who guarded the entrance to the lower town with 50 foot soldiers, 11 riflemen, and 20 bowmen. At the entrance to Takazawa ward stood Yasui Sachūji. The city magistrate, Tanaka Moemon, patrolled the wards with 150 foot soldiers and police, ready to defend the city should the peasants break down the gates and run riot inside. Troops were to have been sent to the five villages directly outside, but the peasants had already approached to within two hundred meters of the gates.

The time was about two in the morning. The peasants carried lanterns and pine torches that shone like stars for hundreds of miles. There were so many of them that it was impossible to tell how many tens of thousands there were.

Tanaka Moemon advanced and gave the order, "Fire at will if they enter the town." The samurai and foot soldiers fitted arrows to their bows, ready to shoot. The peasants did not approach the town. They turned instead toward Kita Tajima.

Seeing this, Tanaka said, "Hey, they're not coming into town. Follow them to see what they're up to." The soldiers followed at a distance of three hundred meters to reconnoiter what the peasants were doing. It was just like the praying mantis so intent on a cricket that it did not realize it had been spotted by a bird.

Shouting war cries, the peasants attacked Rokuemon's house. In an instant they had swept through it and destroyed everything. The members of the household, young and old, men and women, all ran away and escaped. Afterward, an anonymous lampoon appeared:

Tens of thousands of men raised their voices at Kita Tajima.
Abandoning his possessions, Rokuemon got out of the way.

Once they realized what was happening, the samurai and foot soldiers all vied to be first in ripping into the masses gathered there. This way and that they threw their ropes to capture alive five hundred men. These men were completely exhausted, and since they were only peasants anyway, it was difficult for them to resist successfully. Having for some little while carried all before them with their sickles and bamboo spears, now they did not know what to do. Everyone scattered like the autumn leaves falling from the trees and disappeared without a trace. As night faded to dawn, Tanaka Mozaemon appeared before the judicial court with over five hundred peasant prisoners.

At that juncture, Takayama Magozaemon raced his horse over the twenty-five miles between Kawagoe and Edo in about three hours to report what had happened to Lord Akimoto Tajima no kami. From his lord he received the following statement:

"The peasants never intended to attack the castle. Recently that false courtier Andō Danjō curried favor with his superiors to have it decreed that henceforth villages supplying porters and horses on a supplemental basis must do so on a regular basis. He also had the peasants ordered to make loans to the government of three *ryō* per hundred *koku* for the Korean emissary's visit. These two decrees were promulgated because he claimed to be acting on the shōgun's wishes, but the peasants found it difficult to survive. A multitude had gathered to come to Edo with a petition for an exemption when Ina Hanzaemon showed his compassion by going to the Okegawa post station as the shōgun's messenger. Once he gave the peasants a letter granting them an exemption from their post station duties, the peasants expressed their gratitude by promptly quieting down. This Rokuemon was in league with Andō, and that must be the reason his house was destroyed. Before the bakufu finds out what has happened, return home and have the captured peasants released from custody."

Calling for his horse, Magozaemon flew back home. The peasants were released as Lord Tajima no kami had wished.

CHAPTER FOUR

Another Version concerning the People Whose Houses Were Destroyed

According to one version, after the courier had left for Edo, over ten thousand members of the people's army marched up to the entrance to the lower ward in Kawagoe defended by Nagayama Ichirōzaemon. There Hyōnai made this statement:

"To dispel our resentment at the demand for porters and horses, we peasants all went together to Rokuemon's house, but you arrested many of us and took us to prison. Being peasants, we naturally never intended to attack the castle. You really ought to return to us those whom you have captured. If you do not release them, we will do what little we can to break through your defenses and march on the castle. We will fight as long as life is left in us. If we fail, we will die in battle." Hyōnai was indeed superior to the warriors.

"Instead of dying of starvation, let's fight the warriors and die below the castle," the other wretches raved.

"I have to agree with what you've said," Nagayama replied.

Frightened of the spirit displayed by the wretches in the uprising, he released the prisoners. The captured peasants thus received pardons at noon on the third. Just as delighted as they could be, the other peasants took heart and hurried on to Kon'ya Kansuke's house.

Kansuke was skilled beyond all others in the martial arts. He had already realized that his house would be attacked, so he asked some three thousand of his neighbors for help. He built a dense hedge of thorns around the house, he armed himself with a short sword, and, prepared to defend his property, he awaited the crowd impatiently. The attackers shouted war cries. The three thousand defenders joined in with their own. The multitude outside broke down the gate and ran riot inside. Planning to kill them, the defenders lined up their spears to charge. Despite their efforts, the crowd attacked vigorously. The defenders had soon had enough. Off they ran, all helter-skelter. Then brandishing his long sword, Kansuke came to the fore in the attack. He stood fast despite the crowd; he cut and parried in all directions. Looking just like a flying dragon, he slaughtered thirteen men and wounded another seven.

Frightened, no one dared stand up to him. Then three men, Harada Goemon, Matsubara Kibei, and Ōno Kichiemon, attacked. They eagerly exchanged blows, thrusting forward and back, using all their secret skills in battle. His spear broken, Matsubara Kibei hesitated. Kansuke pressed forward, striking again and again with his long sword. Kichiemon knocked it down with his spear. Without a moment's delay, Kibei grappled with Kansuke. Being a master at unarmed combat, he grabbed Kansuke's left hand and threw him down. Ōno Kichiemon and Harada Goemon both clinched him tightly. They wrestled together, now one on top, now another. Kibei jumped up, seized a spear, and with all his might he thrust it into Kansuke's side. With a grunt, Kansuke dropped dead.

As day turned to dusk the crowd destroyed the house. While they were trying to decide where they would spend the night, a peasant from Demaru, Ōno Kichiemon, came forward and spoke: "In Mihonoya there is a vast forest called Nagamiya. Let's sleep there tonight. Then in the morning we can go on to Kawadaya."

Following his suggestion, the crowd spent the night at Nagamiya. Two rich men from the vicinity, Sanzaemon and Kichiemon, sent rations upon request so that everyone had something to eat. The peasants gathered dead wood, built a bonfire, and waited for dawn.

This forest was sacred to the great shining deity Kōrigawa. Pine trees veiled in green the shrine to the crown prince; the tips of the young leaves from the sakaki trees gleamed deep within its depths while the spring moon shone faintly. When Sugawara no Michizane wrote, "The moon shines as clearly as the snow," he must have had a scene such as this in mind. The fire before the de- ified manifest Buddha flickered feebly. The traveler spending the night in the open air beneath the floating clouds might wish to ponder the past and the future, but warding off the cold of the night would leave him no time to spare. Thinking of his parents, wife, and children, even the most monstrous man would feel his chest tighten and tears come to his eyes.

According to the "Classic of Filial Piety," "People originate in the fullness of time and utilize the earth to the best advantage. They should nurture their parents by restricting their personal desires and enjoyment. This is the filiality of the commoner people." Or again, "It would not do for one who governs the state to despise the masses."[27] A ruler who ignores this teaching will despise and de- vour the peasants, everyone will suffer tribulations, and the commoners will endure hardships comparable to those of the el- derly abandoned to starve.

The men in the uprising shook the villages with their war cries. The peasant forces numbering seventy-eight thousand divided into two groups and crowded forward, planning to cross the river with the coming of dawn. One group tried to cross at the Tarōemon ford. The rest turned toward the Azeyoshi ford to get across the river there.

Here, distant from any habitation, stood a small temple. Before they ran off to the ford, the members of the multitude pressed their hands together in prayer before the Buddha. In their hearts they worshiped the goddess of mercy. They prayed that through the pledge of her great compassion they would be allowed to return in good health to their home villages.

[Here follows an anecdote explaining the origin of this temple and the powers of its statue of Kannon, the goddess of mercy.[28]]

A long time ago this statue of the goddess of mercy was en- shrined in the sacred ground of a huge temple as its main object, the Holy Goddess of Mercy. In the Shōhei era [931–37], a raging fire destroyed the temple, but it was promptly rebuilt. Then a flood one night washed away the main hall. The Buddhist statues were lost.

The people lamented and grieved, but to no avail, and the site became a wasteland. Only the place-name "Goddess of Mercy" remained down through the years. At last during the Kan'ei era [1624–43], while Matsudaira Izu no kami Nobutsuna was lord of the domain, the area was reclaimed for a miscanthus field. Every year the people expected to cut the miscanthus reeds there, but just at the wrong time, drenching rainstorms would make it impossible to harvest anything. Finding this odd, the domain lord summoned diviners and people from the environs for questioning. It was discovered that the place was sacred to the goddess of mercy.

Years after the statue had been swept away by the flood in the Shōhei era, a fisherman pulled it up in his net far away on the Miyado River. Plans were made to enshrine it anew as the Asakusa goddess of mercy, so it was loaded on a ship bound for Edo. Many miracles occurred along this river. The boat going to Edo was unable to move at all. While the boatmaster was racking his brains over what to do, a strange thing happened. In the space of one night, the boat went all the way upriver to arrive, without human aid, at the statue's original location. Thereafter it became known as the place where the compassion of the goddess of mercy pulls one up. Owing to this affinity, the statue became known as the boat-pulling goddess of mercy. It has been venerated ceaselessly down to the present. Anyone who piously makes a pilgrimage to it will most certainly be blessed by the Buddha.

Those who at the time of the uprising prayed before the Buddha survived unharmed at Kawadaya. Those who passed by without worshiping the goddess of mercy were either killed or wounded.

Knowing that the crowd was going to have to cross the river, a force of over forty thousand men from Adachi planned to stop them by rolling logs and hurling boulders. This was the crucial moment for the defense. The attackers knew that the Adachi side of the river had high banks, and for their part they feared that once they had reached it, the sticks and stones would make their passage difficult.

Just then the men on the riverbanks heard war cries sounding thick and fast. "Hey, the enemy is advancing on both sides. Retreat, retreat," they shouted. Everyone withdrew. Taking advantage of this weakness, the crowd surged across the river and marched on Kawadaya.

Here was the abbot Kyōko of Jinzaemon's family temple, a bad bonze, cunning and unequalled in the martial arts. To him came Jinzaemon's son, Jiemon, who asked, "The enemy is even now advancing from the east and west. What are we going to do?"

"In this emergency, there is nothing we can do," the abbot replied. "I will take your storehouses under my protection and try to appease the crowd."

"Well, we're relying on you," Jiemon called over his shoulder as he went back home.

Jinzaemon had secretly lined up and armed with bamboo spears over forty-six thousand men from Adachi, his clients from all over, and some one hundred experts in making trouble. Tons of sand had been piled on the roof of the gate so that if the enemy tried to destroy it, the sand could be thrown in their eyes. The defenders also positioned logs and boulders besides building a dense hedge of thorns around the house. While they were waiting impatiently, they heard the sound of war cries coming closer and closer. Those inside also raised their voices. Despite these preparations, the crowd unexpectedly turned toward Heisuke's house.

Heisuke had already given the matter careful thought. Having armed several hundred men with bamboo spears, he got up on the roof to issue his orders. The attackers were at the gate, shouting war cries. The hundreds of men who were supposed to fight for the defense could not withstand them. The crowd burst through the gate and ran riot inside. Boulders rained off the roof while they were trying to smash up the house, but they finally managed to destroy it. Matsubara Kihei was killed.

With this the crowd's spirits rose yet higher. Then, for some reason, they turned back for a moment to wipe out that other household. Just then the abbot Kyōko residing at Senfuku-ji, the village temple, hurried up, riding in a palanquin. Seeing what had happened, he pressed his hands to the earth and lowered his head.

"I am your humble servant, the monk at Jinzaemon's family temple, and I find it difficult to ignore his hardships. If you would please leave just the warehouse in my keeping, nothing would make me happier. Naturally you have my permission to smash up the house and the workers' quarters. If you would thus sate your pent-up resentment and be pleased to return home, I would be most grateful."

"We will do as you request," Hyōnai replied.

Abbot Kyōko then saluted the crowd, had the gate opened, went back inside, and reported what had transpired. Since the crowd was going to attack the workers' quarters first, he had a ladder put up to the roof from outside for them. Just then, someone inside threw a stick of firewood. Riled by this, the crowd raved,

"Don't let the abbot escape."

"Kill him!"

The abbot shut the door tight, but the forces in the uprising climbed up on the roof and rained down stones. At Hyōnai's orders, they burst through a side door and recklessly ran riot inside, thrusting with their spears. The abbot retreated a little. Riding on the crest of victory, the attackers relentlessly pursued him.

"I've failed. How mortifying," Abbot Kyōko cried. Gnashing his teeth, he ran off.

The attackers smashed up the workers' quarters and two warehouses. They tore up the clothing they found in the storehouse for pawned goods; then they started to destroy the house. At that point Abbot Kyōko came prancing out of one of the interior rooms armed with a long sword that he waved about.

"Don't let him escape!" The crowd surrounded him. Despite their numbers, he drove them off just as though he were sweeping leaves in his garden. No one advanced to the fore. The Adachi forces who had returned to protect the abbot lined up the points of their spears and thrust about them. The attackers too shouted and fought.

Unequalled in the martial arts, Abbot Kyōko thrust and parried, taking on the entire crowd at once. He looked just like Benkei, the fighting monk of old. He showed himself to the left, now hid himself to the right; he rolled up his sleeves, and the sparks flew as he fought. The smoke from this battlefield scorched the heavens. The peasant forces soon had to pull back a little, but because they were constantly being assailed with rocks, they were unable to take a stand. As they pulled out toward Dōsaka, the Adachi forces scented victory and pursued them, throwing stones. The peasants shrank back, then flew from Dōsaka to Fukuda. Faced with these hardships, everyone dispersed and ran off.

The Adachi forces heaved a great sign of relief, then turned their attention to putting things back in order. They lost over five hundred men killed and wounded. Two thousand of them suffered bruises. Surveys made here and there discovered over three thousand dead among the enemy and over two thousand wounded. Hyōnai and the rest of the attackers must have been deeply grieved. Nursing their wounds, they returned to their home province.

Early on, Kojima Kandayū of Uedaya village had realized that he would probably be attacked, so he requested help from over ten thousand peasants living nearby and armed each of them with bamboo spears. He, his elder son Yōsuke, and his younger son Kinai carried short swords. Around the house he built a dense hedge of thorns. Ringing bells and beating drums, the defenders waited impatiently from the first day of the month until, at ten in the morning on the fifth, there came a report that the peasants, who had been routed the previous day at Kawadaya, had all retreated to their home province. Kandayū was delighted. He set out refreshments for every man among his ten thousand supporters, entertained them, and sent them home. That night someone or other wrote a satirical poem:

Yōsuke needlessly broke out the bells.
(When no one came) Kinai and Kojima were delighted.

At the first morning light on the fourth, Takahashi Jinzaemon of Kawadaya went to Edo to report in detail everything that had happened to the city magistrate Tsuchiya Echizen no kami. Tsuchiya Echizen no kami then had Jinzaemon stay at an inn while he went to the castle and respectfully reported these events to the shōgun. Then Lord Tsuchiya went home.

CHAPTER FIVE

**The Inquiries Made by Investigators Who
Go to Kawadaya**

Shortly thereafter, Lord Noda Yaichiemon's clerk Hashimoto Moshirō and Watanabe Hanjūrō's clerk Kōzō were dispatched to find out what had happened. Accompanied by Jinzaemon, the two men set out for Kawadaya, where they performed a thorough investigation.

In the house they found a number of wounded and fifty dead. Twenty had been pierced by bamboo spears in at least two places.

The other thirty had been struck by rocks, stabbed by spears, slashed by swords, or hit by poles. They had fallen every which way.

In the garden were three hundred men. One hundred had lost their lives when they were struck by rocks. Nineteen had been killed with sticks. The rest had been trampled to death, hit with stones, or pierced with spears.

In the gardens attached to the branch store were 150 men. Fifty had fallen in a spring or had been killed with stones. One hundred were in the formal garden with its artificial miniature hill. They had fallen all over the place; many had suffered a variety of wounds. Two hundred men had been hit with sticks, pushed into the hedge of thorns, or struck with swords. At Dōsaka were four hundred men, all of whom had been killed with spear thrusts. In front at Matsuyama were six hundred men who had lost their lives because they had suffered spear wounds or because they had been hit with sticks and other things.

Besides those listed above, here and there were clusters of three to five of the slain for a total of over one thousand dead. Corpses littered the ground for ten or fifteen acres around Jinzaemon's house. Sticks, stones, thorn trees, straw raincoats, flags, all were smeared with blood. Blood flowed like water from Dōsaka to Fukuda. Hashimoto Moshirō and Suzuki Kōzō drew detailed sketches showing the configuration of the mansion and the positions of the dead; then they went to Heisuke's to make a survey there.

Heisuke's front gate had been smashed. Sixteen men had fallen, all with spear wounds. In the garden were fifteen dead, each of whom had been wounded by spears in three or four places. One man in the garden had two bruises left by rocks on his head, three spear wounds in his chest, and one wound in his groin. This was Master Heisuke himself.

Here too the two inspectors wrote down a complete account to take back to Edo.

The Affair of Sanzaemon at Mihonoya

Afterward Gonzaemon from Oki village reported that Sanzaemon from Mihonoya had sent provisions to tens of thousands of peasants hiding out at Nagamiya, and he asked for the matter to be investigated. As a result, a message was sent to the headman of Mihonoya telling him to bring Sanzaemon to Hashimoto Moshirō and Suzuki Kōzō. The headman did as he was told. In response to their inquiry, Sanzaemon made the following statement:

An Oral Statement

At dusk on the third, a dark-skinned man of at least forty with a hood covering his head and a straw raincoat wrapped around his body came to me and said, "The peasants of Musashi and Kōzuke are hiding out at Nagamiya, but without provisions, they will starve. You are richer than it appears, so we are relying on you for help. Please send there enough rations for seventy or eighty thousand men." I replied, "The crop failures of recent years mean that I can't supply that much food." The man then said, "If you refuse, a crowd will attack you tonight and smash up your house and storehouse. If we don't get the provisions, we will beat you and every wretch in your household, and we will eat your flesh. We won't hesitate at all if we have to. Well, how about it?" He abused me outrageously and struck me with a short spear. Given his high-handed request, I had no choice but to send the provisions to save my life. I heard that they ate what I sent and hid at the shrine. Aside from having sent them provisions, I know nothing more about them.

The first month

The peasants from Adachi district were ordered to maintain a guard over the dead day and night. Placards were raised telling families and other relatives to come to the ford to make their inquiries, receive the corpses, and bury them. Over two thousand people from the villages came to make their inquiries. They identified the bodies, gave their statements, and went home. The remaining corpses were buried at Jinzaemon's mansion. A small shrine was built there which remains down to the present. Behind the house was found a verse of poetry:

The tall bridge (Takahashi) suspended over Kawadaya was
   destroyed.
The rough river (Arakawa) carried away the dead and
   wounded.

159

Having finished making a thorough investigation, Hashimoto Moshirō and Suzuki Kōzō arrived back in Edo on the fourteenth.

The Capture of the Peasants

After Hashimoto Moshirō and Suzuki Kōzō had arrived back in Edo, the person in charge of making arrests, Tsuji Gengorō's clerk Ōtake Tōichi, rode through the villages. He used over two thousand soldiers who dressed themselves inconspicuously in all sorts of different costumes. Just then the peasants were wont to gather in large groups, now at this house, now at that store, and chat carelessly about all sorts of things. Dressed as travelers, the soldiers visited them and gradually got the crowds to talking.

"We've hurried back home from far away. Is it true what we heard recently that what with loans to the government and demands for more porters and horses, everyone suffered hardships, and there was a riot? What kind of high-ranking officials could have come up with such a selfish scheme?"

Peasants who did not realize what was going on got themselves arrested by talking too freely.

Disguised as peddlers, other soldiers got the neighbors reminiscing.

"We've heard that so-and-so from this village really did a lot. So-and-so was killed, and someone else was wounded."

"Yes, so-and-so from this village really did well," the peasants foolishly responded. It seems that the soldiers disguised themselves in all sorts of ways to make arrests.

Here was a peasant from Demaru village, Hiki district, Musashi, named Ōno Kichiemon. Extraordinarily talented, he stood six feet tall, and he had the strength of ten men. During the riot he had done good work here and there. Owing to what he had accomplished one night, Sanzaemon of Mihonoya had been forced to send the peasants provisions. He had slain Kansuke. Afterward, on the seventh day of the second month, he was arrested by Ōtake Tōichi and sent to Edo.

Kichiemon had an old mother of over eighty to whom he had always been devoted. He grieved deeply in parting from her because he realized that in going to Edo, he was going to be punished, and he would never see her again. It is said that filial piety begins with not permitting any injury to be done to one's body, but now he would be tied in the shameful ropes of a prisoner and allow his soul to be released at the Edo execution ground. Sorrowing at the thought of disgracing his mother, he parted from her in tears, a truly moving sight.

In Edo, Kichiemon was interrogated by the officials Jokurō and Kiemon. The two turned to him and said, "Come on, confess. We have a report that you did a lot in the riot."

"I am a peasant like all the rest. I may have gotten involved without thinking much about it, but I did not do anything out of the ordinary," he replied.

"We have heard that you killed Kon'ya Kansuke. What about it?"

"I am not the one who killed him. The whole crowd killed him, so it is impossible to say who did it." Even under torture he confessed nothing. He was even summoned to the bakufu tribunal to be interrogated by Lord Tsuchiya Echizen no kami and Lord Yoda Izumi no kami. Still he did not confess. That day he was returned to prison. Later he was subjected to various forms of torture, but he said not one word by way of confession. Realizing its ineffectiveness, the officials had the torture stopped.

Early in the last month of the year, Kichiemon received word that his mother was ill. Prison officials told Lord Tsuchiya that day and night he wept and grieved, he was unable to eat, and he was on the verge of death. Lord Tsuchiya and Lord Yoda conferred with the inspectors, and then they reported to the senior councillors.

"Kichiemon has committed serious crimes, so he should not be sent back home just for his mother's sake," Lord Matsudaira Ukon no Zō argued.

"This affair of Kichiemon should be reported to the shōgun, and his august opinion should be sought," Lord Akimoto Tajima no kami suggested.

"That would be the best thing to do," everyone agreed. Then Lord Akimoto Tajima no kami reported to the shōgun, and the shōgun heard him.

"Since Kichiemon is a filial son, he should be sent back home to devote himself to his mother's care," the shōgun announced.

Pardoned on the twenty-eighth day of the twelfth month, Kichiemon returned home on the second day of the first month of 1765. His joy was boundless upon seeing his mother, and he devoted himself to her care. Nevertheless, on the second day of the second month, she passed away, having come to the end of the life span allotted her by heaven. Despite his grief, Kichiemon had no choice but to hold her funeral. Thereafter he shut himself up at home day after day.

Around the early part of the third month, Kichiemon recalled that owing to the shōgun's great compassion, he had seen his mother die, but now he had no worldly attachments. Rather than remain aimlessly at home, he decided to go to Edo and receive his punishment. On the tenth day of the third month, he went to Edo, where he made the following appeal to the city magistrate, Lord Tsuchiya Echizen no kami: "I feel thankful and fortunate that owing to the shōgun's great mercy I was able to see my mother again. I devoted myself to her care and searched everywhere for medicines and exotic treatments, but because she was old, she passed away at the age of eighty-two on the second day of the second month. Now I have no worldly attachments at all. I would be grateful if you would be pleased to punish me quickly."

"A little while ago your case was reported to the shōgun so I can't decide it on my own. Nevertheless, your quick arrival is truly praiseworthy. Instructions will be given later. For now you should stay at an inn," Lord Tsuchiya replied.

Later, on the sixth day of the seventh month, Kichiemon was summoned to the bakufu tribunal, where all of the officials had assembled to issue him the following decree: "You should have been condemned to death, but it is known everywhere that you devoted yourself exclusively to being filial to your mother. Were it not for your crimes, you would be given a cash award, but unfortunately we cannot go that far. Instead you will be rewarded with your life."

On that same day, twelve men were exiled. Perhaps because his life had been spared, Kichiemon became known in Edo as a filial son.

CHAPTER SIX

Hyōnai's Arrest and His Wife's Affectionate Farewell

Here is another story. Hyōnai was from the Harusawa district in Musashi. During the summer of 1765 in the sixth month, fifteen peasants were arrested in Kōzuke. Among them was one called Hyōnai from Seki. Now Tsuji Gengorō had sent men to make arrests at Seki. When they announced what they were there for, Hyōnai turned to his wife and said in tears, "Men have just come from Edo to arrest me. Tonight will be our final parting in this life, for we shall never meet again. No matter what happens now, my life is over. After I am gone, I want you to bury my body."

His wife grabbed hold of her husband's sleeve. "Last winter after you left our home, my heart pined for you. In my mind I wagered on the cries of the birds as to whether you would be killed today or live tomorrow. Anxious and troubled, I ceaselessly soaked my sleeves in tears. I valued the passing of the days and nights only because they brought your return closer. Now at last I thought I could rest easy, but again I am to suffer bitterly. If your fate is inescapable, I too will go to Edo and together we will face whatever happens." It was apparent that she had no intention of leaving him.

"I deeply appreciate your feelings," Hyōnai replied, "but what you ask is impossible. You may think like this now, but afterward everything will be yours to manage." He pondered further, then said, "I beg of you again, please stay here." He too wrung tears from his sleeves.

After a little while, his wife said simply, "It must have been the Creation Deities who brought us together toward the end of the spring of my sixteenth year, for I fell in love with you at first glance in the garden belonging to the gods. We soon became intimate. Then we became husband and wife. For twenty-four years we have been together both day and night, and we have whispered sweet words to each other until the small hours of the morning. You said that no matter what happened, we would be together to the ends of the earth, but that turns out to have been a lie. When did you start to become so unfeeling of me? I am going too." Saying this, she dissolved in tears. She could do nothing but cry as time slipped away.

Hyōnai shook off the sleeve she was clinging to; his body was cruelly fettered. The spectators were deeply moved. The officials who had made the arrest started to march him off, but his feet dragged as he walked, and his heart was torn between going and staying. How pitiful to imagine what he felt.

The Torture of the Peasants

At that time the Edo city magistrates were Lord Tsuchiya Echizen no kami and Lord Yoda Izumi no kami. The magistrates in charge of roads were Lord Ōkuma Chikuzen no kami and Lord Andō Danjō Shōhitsu. The investigators were Jokurō and Hikoemon.

[Following is the peasants' justification for having rioted.]
We would like to make a general statement in connection with the investigation to explain the circumstances under which the peasants became impoverished. We humbly beseech you to read what follows before you reach your verdict.
Between 1761 and 1763, we harvested not one year's worth of crops, and we ourselves were starving, to say nothing of food for our wives and children. Brothers, wives, and children had to leave each other to go begging in other provinces. Then in 1764, the government ordered us to make it loans. Everyone in the province gathered at Jūzūgahara where we held council and decided to unite in a joint appeal. We were just getting ready to bring it to Edo when Ina Hanzaemon came to meet us with new orders. He gave us a letter saying we would be exempted from the loans and regular post station duty and told us to be grateful. We petition the authorities to show us compassion by allowing our households to continue and not leaving the peasants to die of starvation.

Lord Tsuchiya read this statement and realized that it made sense. He thereupon launched an investigation to find out who the leaders had been.
"As we already said before," the peasants retorted, "just when everyone was worrying about how poverty-stricken and hungry we were, somebody announced that all the peasants would gather at Jūzūgahara for a council on the fourteenth, so we should all leave our villages to go there at such-and-such a time. We departed our homes to gather on the appointed day, but not one single person could be called our leader. If what we have done is illegal, you should order that all the peasants receive some sort of punishment."
Lord Tsuchiya asked more questions. "Why did a crowd of

people go to Jinzaemon's in Kawadaya village and other places to smash up warehouses and houses?"

Thus interrogated, the peasants gave him the list of names they had acquired near Okegawa and asked him to examine the evidence. "We respectfully ask for an investigation once you have perused this document," they said.

The document stated: "The reason why the villages providing porters and horses on a supplemental basis were recently ordered to supply them on a regular basis was because of Jinzaemon's plotting. Around the ninth month of 1761, this Jinzaemon held council with Heisuke in the same village. They decided to have the villages providing porters and horses substitute money for this service on a regular basis, and with this money they would then hire the necessary transport. After that they invited Gonzaemon from Oki village to join them and explained what they wanted. 'Would you please get together some other people and figure out what to do,' they said. Gonzaemon then got together some fourteen people. Among them were Seibei from Hirakata, Kandayū from Kawadaya, Rokuemon from Kita Tajima, Denzō from Igusa, Hikoshirō from Kon'ya, Hanzō from Kitanomachiya, Yasōji from Hiratsuka, Kōzō from Takakura, and Shokuemon from Kujirai. In the spring of 1764, they held council at Jinzaemon's house. Through Gonzaemon's efforts, they got the masters of the inns for daimyō in Okegawa and Ageo to speak to the magistrate in charge of roads, Lord Andō Danjō, and the senior councillor, Lord Matsudaira Ukon no Zō. Therefore Lord Ukon no Zō decreed that villages providing porters and horses on a supplemental basis should supply them on a regular basis."

This document was sent to the shōgun. The peasants were tortured for several days, but they said nothing not in the original statement. Then one man came forward and said, "Please stop torturing all these peasants. I alone led the peasants in the recent uprising [ikki]. Please have me punished in place of all the peasants, no matter what that punishment may be."

"Who on earth are you?" Lord Tsuchiya inquired.

"I am the headman of Seki village," he replied. "Most people thought that they had gathered together spontaneously, but at that time I had already decided to risk my life to save the peasants from their hardships, so I sent a circular to all of them in the eighteen districts."

The officials stopped torturing the peasants. Instead they turned to torturing the headman of Seki village, but since he had already resolved to die, he said not one word by way of confession.

The Men Ordered to Be Punished

On the seventeenth day of the first month of 1766, Hyōnai of Seki village was beheaded in place of all the peasants. Tsuji Gengorō's clerk Ōtake Tōichi took the head to Seki village in Niita district where it was exposed. That same day one man was exiled to a distant island. Two were banished from their villages. Then on the twentieth, Jinzaemon and the other fourteen were ordered banished. Their property was passed on to their wives and children. Nomura Junhachi and Ichirōzaemon from Hiratsuka were exiled to a distant island. Over two hundred peasants were banished from their villages.

The previous year Kurabashi Yoshirō and Naruse Hikotarō had fled by night from Kumagaya and returned to Edo. It became known to the authorities that they had good reason for their flight in that they had accepted bribes to exempt certain villages from post station duty. Only those villages which did not give them money were to be instructed to provide porters and horses. Ordered into prison, for several days they were tortured to the brink of leaving this ephemeral world. Hikotarō died in prison.

The next time Yoshirō was tortured, he said, "The headmen from seventy-five villages gave us two *ryō* apiece when they appealed to be exempted from providing porters and horses, but we refused to listen to them, returned the money, and told them that they had an obligation to perform post station duty. We did not take even the smallest bribe or indulge in favoritism."

"All right, we'll summon the headmen from the seventy-five villages and interrogate them." The headmen and group leaders from the seventy-five villages were summoned to the bakufu tribunal. First the headmen and group leaders from Negishi and Mizo were interrogated.

They all said, "Thinking that we might somehow receive exemption from post station duty, we presented the two officials with two *ryō* when we appealed for a change in the ruling. Nevertheless, because this was a matter of great concern to the government, we weren't able to use bribes to get the decree relaxed."

Since the other village officials all said the same thing, Kurabashi Yoshirō's statement stood, and he was pardoned. The headmen of the seventy-five villages were all dismissed from office. The group leaders were fined five *kanmon* each. In addition to Naruse Hikotarō, over twenty men died in prison. Trials continued to the fifteenth day of the eighth month.

This was truly the biggest riot of all time. It often happens that men of property plot to enrich themselves by ignoring the hardships of everyone else. Some of them are just as thoughtless as Watanuki Hanbei of Irimagawa. How dreadful. How deplorable. The riot over post station duty came to an end only because there was one man like Hyōnai of Seki. Everyone followed his instructions, for he was always conscientious. It is truly fortunate that things turned out well.

Afterword

By the early nineteenth century, the circumstances envisioned in this text had become a reality. Villages distant from the post stations had the wherewithal to raise enough cash to compensate for the porters and horses they were obligated to supply. In addition, there was a new source of labor: men forced out of their villages through ill judgment or bad luck when they were unable to repay the high interest on loans they had contracted to pay taxes or to participate in cottage industries such as silk reeling. Moralists castigated the degeneration of village society and the lure of easy living in the urban areas, and agronomists mourned the decline of agriculture. For whatever reason, the post stations found that they could hire enough day labor to fill their transportation requirements from the riffraff who floated down the roads, if supplemented by the corvée demanded of the peasants. The bakufu designated specific families in the post stations to see to the official transport needs and granted them a monopoly over all transport. Protected by the government, these freight dispatchers *(toiya)* had heavy responsibilities, but also the opportunity to make handsome profits.

Whether the *toiya* were honest or not, they were mistrusted by the peasants, whose own interests lay in avoiding as much work along the highways as possible. Already a problem in the 1750s and 1760s, the phenomenon of "resting" villages, those that alleged that their hardships made it impossible for them to spare the labor required by the post stations, had compromised the ability of some freight dispatchers to fulfill their obligations to provide free or low-cost service for government officials and retain a reasonable profit for themselves. In 1804, purveyors along the highway connecting Edo with the castle town of Mito to the north decided to act. They petitioned the authorities to require the "resting" villages to return to their duties, a move the peasants saw as a blatant attempt to shift the transportation burden back on their shoulders.[29] The ensuing struggle pitted the peasants directly against other commoners whose official patronage had aroused their ire, but that is the subject for the next chapter.

F O U R

A Tale of a Dream from the Fox Woman Plain

A T A CROSSROADS NEAR THE MITO HIGHWAY stands a three-foot-high stone monument. On its south side are carved the posthumous Buddhist names of three men and the year of their death, 1805. On the west side it is written that Iijima Jizaemon erected this marker in 1823, nineteen years later. The three men died in prison for having led six thousand peasants in a protest against a plan to incorporate their villages into the transportation system. Jizaemon (the name of his store was Asaya) was one of their victims and the man they blamed for having proposed their inclusion in the first place.[1] Why he felt called upon to erect this monument to the men responsible for destroying his property is left unstated. Perhaps his neighbors reproached him for the three deaths; perhaps he felt guilty himself; perhaps he feared vengeance by evil spirits. Even in contemporary Japan, people find it safer to worship their dead enemies.[2] Whether he erected the memorial (kuyō-hi) to placate the animosity of others or to show his remorse, he disguised it as a simple directional marker, for any reminiscence of the riot had to be kept hidden from the authorities.

Centered on the Ushiku post station, also the headquarters for the low-ranking Yamaguchi daimyō, the 1804 riot lasted less than a week, attacked only three households, and resulted in only three deaths. Even before it had run its full course, ending with the official verdict rendered on those deemed responsible, accounts of what had happened had begun to appear, embellished with folktales and local lore. Six different versions of the events, in twelve texts produced between 1805 and 1889, remain today, all located in villages from Katchi district which had participated in the riot.[3] It is possible that they once circulated widely. A note at the end of one states, "No

169

matter where this book ends up, please return it to Matazaemon's second son, Torazō, in Gōchū village."[4]

The text translated here is "Onnabake hara yume monogatari," or "A Tale of a Dream from the Fox Woman Plain," copied in 1863. The first half presents a seemingly straightforward recital of the events surrounding the riot, from the nefarious attempts by freight dispatchers *(toiya)* to increase the number of villages burdened with post station service to the deaths of the men held responsible for the riot. The author apparently did not care to know the details of how the peasants organized themselves or exactly what role was played by the leaders. Instead, disorder is depicted as spontaneous, and scenes of the uprising are presented in stereotype. An anonymous poster summons the peasants to meet and threatens retribution against those who refuse, a shadowy group of leaders organizes them into units based on village affiliation, they agree on their goals and methods, and then they march off under banners proclaiming who they are to wreak havoc on individuals designated in advance. Once the orgy of destruction has ended, the peasants return to their original meeting place, congratulate each other on their success, and go home. Government troops then move into the area to make a pretense of defending their territory (described with perhaps an underlying note of sarcasm) and to round up those suspected of being the ringleaders. Of the five men arrested, three die before their trial. Based on the incriminating evidence happily uncovered in their homes (and how can the modern reader not suspect a frame-up), these men are labeled the leaders. The villagers are forced to pay fines and return to serving the post stations. The second half of the tale contains apparently irrelevant material, folktales, and local legends.

Compared to the texts translated in chapters 2 and 3, "A Tale of a Dream" makes little effort to summon the classics of the Japanese or Chinese tradition, and it is structured much more loosely. Only the opening lines allude to earlier texts, and the references are garbled. An essay on *renga* (linked-verse poetry) written by the poet Shinkei (1406–75) stated, "lions and tigers in the mountains prevent poisonous snakes; sagacious sages prevent wicked scheming." In appropriating this phrase, however, the author twisted it in such a way that it made sense to himself. Peasants climbed mountains to gather fodder and food supplies, and they feared wild animals as well as snakes. Tokugawa-period writing is generally characterized by loose verbal constructions and phrases strung together with only the vaguest of connectives, but in this text the practice is carried to an extreme.[5] One "sentence" begins with the bakufu refusing to exempt the villagers from post station duty, continues through the discovery of incriminating evidence in the homes of the three dead ringleaders, and finally ends with the declaration that the other two prisoners are innocent. The artless and straightforward recitation of events found in this tale suggests that the individuals who wrote and copied it had not achieved the same high degree of erudition possessed by other peasants concerned with riots.

"A Tale of a Dream" also suggests what can happen when a text is copied repeatedly. Perhaps reading an unidentifiable original version of the riot and thinking about where it took place reminded one copyist of the legends associated with his locality. These in turn reminded another of the folktale about the fox wife, another interpolated local history, and so forth. These accretions to the story brought different points of view into an unresolved collision. To a lesser extent, the same process is clearly evident in "A Thousand Spears at Kitsunezuka," where the reference to Sugawara no Michizane's poetry is found in one but not the other extant copy of the text and several episodes that retard the forward movement of the narrative have nothing to do with the main theme. Even in "The Sakura Sōgorō Story," the curious incident of the murdered samurai must be attributed to a creative copyist. As a result, there is no single authorial authority; no copyist dared silence the incongruent voices or reduce the polyphony of the text.[6]

Owing, perhaps, to its polyvocality, "A Tale of a Dream" contains a mass of contradictions. The opening platitude in the prologue, drawn from the Chinese text *I ching* or "Book of Changes," states that peace and war follow each other in an endless ebb and flow of fate, a denial of the necessity for human intervention, but then the text goes on to enumerate specific causes for the riot, causes arising directly from the deeds done by men.[7] The peasants are depicted as acting entirely righteously; they even refuse an offer of sake for fear it would cause them to lose self-control. On the other hand, the central metaphors used to depict crowd action—thunderbolts and crumbling mountains—would seem to equate the crowd with the inexorable forces of nature, thereby undercutting the rationality of the peasants' behavior. This denial of subjectivity to the rioters is reinforced in the descriptions of destruction where extraordinarily strong men, not ordinary peasants, toss bales of rice down a well. It turns out that the peasants used to perform corvée labor at the post stations but recently stopped, making their motives suspect. Finally, the positive appraisal given the peasants' deeds at the beginning of the tale is contradicted by the resoundingly negative assessment of disorder and the men who caused it at the end. Throughout the tale, the lack of curiosity about the peasants' organization and the details of what they did undermine the intent of the text: to understand what had happened in order to prevent its recurrence.

The contradictory messages which undercut each other in the text suggest an extremely ambivalent view of social disorder. The term for uprisings that had positive connotations, *ikki,* appears repeatedly, but the conclusion refuses to valorize the rioters' deeds. It is also possible that the strong disharmony between the author as storyteller and as moralizing judge arises directly from deep roots in the Chinese tradition where the appreciation for a good story was never allowed to preclude drawing a lesson from it, even one that contradicted the content.[8] Yet the tale lacks the sets of contrasts that structure other works. The crowd does not act righteously one moment and wrongly the next. The acknowledgment that it had reason for its actions does not encompass the peasants as actors. The fact that one of the ringleaders who died in prison was a village official does not appear in this narrative at all.[9] The victims of the riot are all equally damned; no one is saved from the crowd by either a divine blessing or helpful neighbors. Even the government officials are neither particularly good or bad. Instead, like the village headmen, they act correctly. The identity of virtue between village and government officials denies virtue to the rioters. Only village officials who understood the meaning of benevolence should act on behalf of, not along with, the peasants.

The effort to define political virtue in a system that denied it to commoners is perhaps one reason why histories of peasant uprisings continued to be written and copied long after the events they purported to relate. Komuro Shinsuke (1852–85), a journalist and schoolteacher, searched Japan's past for examples of men who understood the principles of freedom and human rights. In 1883, he published an appeal in the *Jiyū shinbun* (Liberal Newspaper) for materials on men who had sacrificed themselves for their communities.[10] One response came from Komatsuzawa Kaemon (1830–

93), whose family had been the hereditary headmen in one of the villages that joined the 1804 riot at the Ushiku post station. He copied a text written in 1805, then traveled to Tokyo to deliver it into Komuro's own hands. It appeared in the third volume of "One Hundred Biographies of Oriental Advocates of People's Rights" *(Tōyō minken hyakkaden)*, with additions by Komuro that highlighted the importance of the leaders in promoting mass action. In his own comments, Komuro compared this riot with the Shimabara Christian rebellion to argue that the peasants had not rebelled against the principle of public authority; they had simply stood up for their rights. He added his own postscript as well, proclaiming that the end of the uprising brought justice, peace, and prosperity.[11]

In the books written in today's Japan about peasant uprisings, local historians give much more unqualified praise to peasant martyrs than did these Tokugawa-period texts. Documents and stories about the Ushiku post station riot have been published in local collections and nationwide surveys of peasant protest. Yet with two exceptions, both produced privately by Suzuki Hisashi, all of these publications delete the folktales and local lore that fill the second half of the earlier histories. This suggests that the meaning of this lore is opaque to modern scholars. The folktales must have been important to the people of the time, however, for they were appended to every single extant history of the riot.

The second half of "A Tale of a Dream" consists of separate segments, though not designated as such in the Japanese text, that narrate folktales and legends of the region and that are only loosely connected with the history of the riot. In the first of these, the author, casting himself in the role of a wandering ascetic who traveled for the purpose of placating unappeased angry spirits, claims to have heard the tale from an old woman, but when morning comes, she has disappeared, becoming a shadowy, mysterious presence that undermines the verisimilitude of her story. The author thus manages to place himself at a double remove from the action. He learns the story while he is asleep, and he learns it from someone who could not possibly have had any direct experience of what had happened. Like the author of "A Record of How the Four Orders of People in Mimasaka Ran Riot," he questions whether someone even a few months later could know all the ramifications of what really happened. Underlying these doubts are epistemological questions concerning how the will to knowledge can be explained

and how the truth of what is known can be verified.[12] On a super-
ficial level, simply recording a dream releases the author from the
responsibility of having disobeyed official prohibitions to discuss action taken against the state. On another level, the claim to dream
reminds the reader that social disorder is by its very nature ephemeral; even life itself is as evanescent as an illusion. Lest the dream
world of chaos undercut the seriousness of purpose that informs
this text, however, it is written down, giving a permanence denied
to the event it relates. Left unstated is the possibility that the tale is
being told and recorded to propitiate the souls of those who had
died in prison.

By describing a dream, "A Tale of a Dream" discloses its origin,
but it also has another origin to explain, that of the place-name Fox
Woman Plain, where the peasants assembled before the riot.[13] The
second sequence thus draws on folklore to answer the questions of
who the fox woman was and what she did. The notion that foxes,
and indeed other animals, can take on human shape is an old one in
Japan. Like the other creatures that people the Japanese pantheon
of spirits, they are morally ambivalent. They enjoy playing tricks,
but they are, after all, the messengers favored by Inari, the goddess
of rice, and they are capable of showing gratitude. The story of the
fox wife appears with many local variations across Japan, and they
all contrast sharply with the Western image of the vixen. One version from a district near Osaka includes a farewell poem similar to
the one found in this text; another from Aichi prefecture tells how
the wife prevented the grain from ripening until after the harvest
had been inspected.[14] These are cruel tales, but thanks to the female
fox's sacrifices, the families become prosperous.

"A Tale of a Dream" draws on elements common to the folktales
about fox wives. What gives this text specificity, however, is the
third section, which describes what happens to her descendants.
Throughout the region where the Ushiku riot took place can be
found stories about a great general, Kuribayashi Yoshinaga, whose
mother or grandmother was a fox. He appears in local legends
placed in the civil wars of the sixteenth century, before the
Tokugawa rulers imposed peace. Three war tales tell of his exploits,
his cleverness in deceiving his enemies, his victories over the Satake
family through trickery, and his death by natural causes just before
peace is imposed on the region after the defeat of the Hōjō rulers of
Odawara in 1590. His prowess derived from his ancestry, and it was

said that the spirit of his (grand)mother protected him from harm.[15] Although Yoshinaga participated in real events and fought real enemies, no records aside from legends confirm his existence. Like Sōgorō, he may well have been a figment of the popular imagination.

The incorporation of Kuribayashi Yoshinaga into the story of Chūgorō and his fox wife undermines the folktale by transforming it into a legend. To take the folkloric elements first: Chūgorō experiences no sense of fear, curiosity, or sense of "other" in dealing with his new wife, nor is it miraculous that a boy could have a fox for a mother. The ordinary is mixed with the incomprehensible in a completely effortless way; one dimension encompasses both the real and the enchanted. Although three children are born and eight years pass, neither Chūgorō nor his fox wife age; there is no indication of when the rice starts to ripen in the stalks; there is no experience of time. Chūgorō cannot make any decisions on his own; what he does is impelled by the demands of others, and his personality exists only in connection with what happens to him. Thus he has no inner life, and the story lacks depth. The external world for Chūgorō and his wife is represented abstractly. Only what is essential to the plot is mentioned. The different situations dovetail unrealistically in a manner characteristic of the folktale.

Yet on the other hand, the textual dynamics of the story lead it in a direction more often seen in legends. Chūgorō is embedded in a family structure; he has a son and grandson with their own histories, a generational continuity absent in folktales. With the mention of the famous general, we move decisively into the world of legend, where Yoshinaga is tied to a specific time and place. Implied is his relationship with the persons and objects that figure in a variety of different ways in the everyday world of the warrior. He is a heroic figure; he is transformed by the process of aging, and he eventually dies. Although the heroes of legend live and work in their native villages, whereas the protagonists of folktales wander, it is Chūgorō who stays at home and his grandson who travels as far as Kyoto before his return. "A Tale of a Dream" disregards these conventions to interweave elements from two genres: folktales and the life cycle patterns of legends.[16]

The local historian Suzuki Hisashi has his own interpretation for why folklore and legend find a place in this history of a riot. To give the origin for the shrine where the peasants gathered before the

175

riot indicates that local people believed their uprising to have been legitimized by the divine will of the goddess of rice at the Fox Woman Plain, and it demonstrates their respect for a local hero, Kuribayashi Yoshinaga.[17] But the story also speaks directly to the peasants' fantasies and experiences, to their desire to get ahead. True, the result implied in the tale—that the size of the harvest be hidden from government officials—is undercut by a pious declaration—that the rice crop ripen while still protected from damage. Whether the peasants remembered the deception or the bountiful harvest, however, it was nonetheless a benefit that would put them on the same road to prosperity traveled by Chūgorō. For the grandson of a poor peasant to become a great general could only have happened before 1600. Kuribayashi Yoshinaga reminds the reader of the flexible and egalitarian structures submerged in the rigid hierarchies of the Tokugawa period. By the nineteenth century, visions of fame and easy profits remained figments of the imagination, but they also gave a satisfying significance to local history.

The significance of the locality where the riot erupted is reinforced by another local legend. The story about Ōkubo Gorōzaemon is attributed not to the peasants' own history but to a local ruler, a *hatamoto* or shogunal bannerman who derived his income from some villages in the area. What distinguishes this family from all others is the account of a loyal dog, incorporated into the narrative in a matter-of-fact way that belies its origin in folklore. A similar story is told in Kyushu, where it is connected to the ancient hero Minamoto Tanetomo (1139–70).[18] Like the fox woman, the dog is given human virtues, but the nobility of its sacrifice is reduced at the end of the tale with the reminder that animals are inferior to humans. Nevertheless, the episode provides the flesh and blood to differentiate the Ushiku region from all others.

Important to the writers and readers of this text was the stuff of local lore. Village officials and local intellectuals of the early nineteenth century took a pride and interest in their immediate environment that went far beyond the requirements of their position.[19] For example, high in the mountains that faced the Japan Sea, in what is now Niigata prefecture, Suzuki Bokushi (1770–1842) wrote an ethnographic account of life in the snow country and had it published in Edo to explain to the rest of Japan how his people lived. His aim was to celebrate the particularity of local custom.[20] Whereas Suzuki depicted the unique features of his environment by concentrating on the present, for the same purpose the author of "A Tale of a Dream from the Fox Woman Plain" brought to his task the history of his region.

The account of the Ushiku region given at the end of the tale, however, denies and subverts the significance of peasant action. Brought to bear instead is the history of ruling families whose struggles defined the political character of the landscape. First summoned to lend dignity to the text is Oda Ujiharu, also called Ten'an (1534–75), who claimed descent from Minamoto Yoshiie (1039–1106), unparalleled for his warlike prowess and literary sophistication, and one of the most renowned heroes of his age. The Oda family was wiped out when Ujiharu was defeated by the Satake family, one example of the losers in the civil wars of the sixteenth century that fill this segment. With the exception of Takeda Shingen (1521–73), these men have largely been forgotten in history, but not in local lore. This tale stands as a monument to the rural literary spirit—proud of its particular tradition but unable to ignore events of national significance, disparaging of disorder but unable to pretend it never happened.

A Tale of a Dream from the Fox Woman Plain

Ponder this carefully. Wild animals in the mountains make it impossible to pick brambles and pulse. Loyal retainers in the state make it impossible for wickedness to arise. Peace or war is a question of fate. When peace reaches its extreme, war follows; when war reaches its extreme, peace follows just like the ebb and flow of cold and heat.

Let us inquire into the genesis of the conspiracy and insurrection at the Mito Road post stations in the Katchi district of Hitachi province at the end of the tenth month of 1804. Asaya Jizaemon, who called himself the representative of 106 villages from the eastern and western sections, petitioned for an increase in the number of villages to provide pack horses and porters on a regular basis for the two post stations of Ushiku and Arakawa in Katchi district on the Mito highway, but the petition was not accepted. Next, Gonzaemon of Ami in the same district and Watōji of Kuno in Shida district made similar appeals. This time they were successful.

Two clerks, Suzuki Iisuke and Ōta Kōkichi, were dispatched by the bakufu to survey the land and inspect conditions in the villages.

177

They had duly completed their task when, in the tenth month, men from over fifty villages from the eastern section designated in the petition fomented a conspiracy and assembled their forces at the Fox Woman Plain. What had happened?

Someone from who knows where had plastered a poster on the official notice boards in the villages. It read:

> The government recently agreed to accept a petition concerning the number of porters and horses to be supplied by the villages on a regular basis to the two post stations of Ushiku and Arakawa. If the villages designated to assist these stations do their duty in providing porters and horses, those who live nearby will naturally suffer hardships, and those who live in villages far away will experience even more difficulties. Therefore we anticipate that villages far away will most certainly be forced to make up their share with cash payments.

> The petitioners have been overcome by greed. They are outrageous, detestable, and unprincipled rascals whose wicked scheme is to embezzle lots of money from the villages by contracting for those times when official retinues pass through the post stations. Therefore we are going to smash up the houses belonging to these three men to eradicate the roots of evil from their hearts. If things are left as they are with the petitioners being allowed to have their own way, the villagers will suffer unspeakable hardships.

> The villagers must gather at the Fox Woman Plain between seven and nine o'clock on the morning of the nineteenth. Do not be late. If any villagers do not participate, their houses will be smashed up just like those of the petitioners.

This poster was plastered on the official notice boards in the villages in the middle of the night.

The Fox Woman Plain was a broad wasteland on the flat soil of Katchi district in the province of Hitachi; it stretched for seven miles in all directions. At its center was a shrine called Onnabake Inari. It was the middle of winter when the gods desert their homes to gather at the great shrine of Izumo; the weather was frigid, and the fields were desolate. Only the green pines in the shrine precincts towered over the wilderness.

On the nineteenth day of the tenth month, the villagers who had seen the posters on the official notice boards scrambled to assemble on the plain. Nevertheless, the peasants from Okubara held back out of deference to the authorities when the conspiracy for the uprising was fomented. When the ledgers listing those who had arrived were unfurled and examined, a rumor quickly spread that among the nonparticipating villages was Okubara.

"That being the case, let's send our entire force to Okubara first and smash it up before we turn to Kuno, Ushiku, and Ami," everyone said together.

While the crowd was all in an uproar, more level-headed men tried to ingratiate themselves to calm it down. "It is exasperating that Okubara village made a mistake in not joining us, but the best thing to do would be to demand an apology. Besides, we need to assess all of our expenses equally on all the villages according to our own regulations. The people in charge will decide how these are to be allocated."

Everyone was still prepared to rush forward when, for some reason or other, Chōbei of Kaminaga and Kaemon of Otsubara from the Sendai domain tried to force a stop by shouting, "Hey, wait a minute." The crowd was so big that no one could hear or understand what they were saying. Instead it started on its way to smash everything to smithereens. Some other organizers came running up. They finally forced the crowd to stop and listen to what the two men had to say.

"We just wanted to say that with such a big crowd, if we just roam around going here and there as we please, it seems to us that we run the decided risk of forgetting what it is that we are supposed to be doing and making mistakes in the confusion."

Everyone agreed with what the two men had said. First they surveyed the number of men present at the Inari shrine and counted over six thousand. Then they allocated their forces by dividing them into 120 units of fifty men each. They made paper flags that gave the place in line of each unit and whether it was the first or second from each village. So that there be no mistaking friend for foe, they agreed on passwords. Late-coming villages were forced to donate twenty barrels of sake to all the people as an apology to the united villages. At the first meeting of the peasants' council, they listened to an apology sent from Okubara to the assembled crowd that read as follows: "We have just now learned of the incident concerning additional assistance for the post stations. We think your meeting is an appropriate response, and we would like to thank you for your great efforts. During this cold weather, please don't hesitate to let us know whatever it is you need in the way of food or anything else."

The Okubara villagers politely sent the crowd food and hot drinking water, filling everyone with admiration. Two barrels of sake out of the twenty were placed before the alter to the god. The remaining eighteen were sent to Nareuma village which owned the land on which the Onnabake Inari shrine stood. The reason no one among the crowd drank even one drop was because everyone feared the disorder sake brings, and they wanted to refrain from lawless violence.

On the evening of the nineteenth, burning bonfires turned night into day. The noise of tumult—blasts from conch shell trumpets and shouts of war cries—reverberated through heaven and earth loudly enough to crumble mountains. Summoned by the noise, an endless stream of queries poured forth from the villages regarding their own safety. At the meetings that night, the peasants reached a decision.

Between seven and nine o'clock on the morning of the twenty-first, the crowd began its march on Watōji in Kuno village. Everyone in the ranks wore bleached cotton headbands so as not to make the mistake of attacking friends and allies. Each carried bamboo spears, broadaxes, hatchets, saws, fire hooks, or staves. Now blowing conch shell trumpets, now shouting war cries, the multitude advanced forward with such force as to crumble mountains with one hundred thousand thunderbolts. What demon's deeds could have caused this riot, people in nearby villages muttered to each other.

Reports of what was coming threw the people at Watōji's of Kuno into confusion. Just in the length of time it took to slip on a pair of straw sandals, the wheel of fortune turned and wreaked a frightening retribution for his evil deeds.

In the early afternoon of that day, the crowd burst on the scene. Full of vim and vigor, everyone broke into the house all together, each vying to be first. They smashed the doors and paper screens with axes and hatchets; they threw all of the tatami mats outside, where others in the crowd trampled them underfoot and tore them to pieces. Going around to the kitchen, they used their broadaxes to shatter seven large and small pots to smithereens. They wrecked the trunks and chests of drawers with fire hooks and hatchets. They tore up all the clothing. They broke into the storehouses, hauled out the bags of grains and provisions, and threw them all down a well. Two or three unusually strong men threw the bags into the well just as though they were tossing in clods of earth. Truly this did not look like something ordinary men could do. Then some men sawed through the middle of the pillars supporting the house, the store-houses, and sheds. The whole crowd got together and pushed so hard with all its might that the buildings collapsed like a folding stool. Everything was completely smashed up. It really did look like the deeds done by demons. Those who saw this sight must have feared the retribution exacted by fate.

Having smashed things up just as they pleased and slaked their resentment, over six thousand men all raised their voices in volleys of war cries, blew the conch shell trumpets, and returned to the Fox Woman Plain.

Before dawn on the twenty-second, the crowd, blowing conch shell trumpets and shouting war cries, gathered once more to march on Asaya Jizaemon at the Ushiku post station. There the men promptly smashed his tools, shattered the household furnishings, and tore the clothes to smithereens. Next they had intended to break into Jizaemon's branch store across the street from Asaya, but just then its manager, being a quick-witted fellow, set official government lanterns out in front of the store.

Seeing them, one of the commanders in the advance party shouted, "Do not make the mistake of showing contempt for our lord. Our aspirations hold no room for resentment or hatred against strangers. We only hold rancor against Watōji, Gonzaemon, and Jizaemon. Do not make a careless blunder or lift a hand against any-one else." In this way the Asaya branch store was left untouched.

Afterward, the crowd hastened to gather once more at the Fox Woman Plain, where they made plans to advance on Gonzaemon's house in Ami village. Ami lay over fifteen miles by road northwest of the Ushiku post station in the Tsuchiura domain, so first the crowd retired to the Inari shrine, where the men rested for a little while and prepared food and drink. Then early in the afternoon, people evidently gathered once more to push toward Ami. The procession filed forward in two lines. As it had done previously, each unit advanced under its own flag. The thud of serried marching feet throbbed through the neighborhood like the tremors from thunderbolts raising a cloud of dark smoke. Feeling nothing but fear, the people who lined the road ran to hide themselves away.

The crowd arrived at Ami village just as the sun was setting. When Gonzaemon heard what had happened, he realized that there was nothing to be done, so all the members of his household fled.

"Here it is," the attacking forces shouted. They ran riot in a torrent of destruction. Then they went to Gonzaemon's branch store at a place called Akashi. There too they broke in and spent some time smashing things up.

At last they had achieved their aspiration to slake their rage and resentment. Every single one of them clapped his hands in rhythm, raised his voice in war cries, and blew his conch shell trumpet. Then the troops returned to the Fox Woman Plain in ranks as correct as when they had started out. Everyone worshiped the god in heartfelt thanks for having achieved their great wish. Once they had expressed their joy to each other at having satisfied their heart's desire, the six thousand men who had gathered there each returned to his own home.

To suppress the riot for the bakufu, the castellan of Tsuchiura in Hitachi, Lord Tsuchiya Hosaburō, the castellan of Sakura in Shimōsa, Lord Hotta Ōkuradayū, and the Kanto district supervisor Akiwara Yagobei all received orders to dispatch their troops immediately. The lineup was as follows:

Tsuchiya Hosaburō provided thirty cavalry divided into three troops, plus three hundred foot soldiers and various irregulars for a total of five hundred men arrayed in three columns. Flags with his family crest snapped in the breeze. The troops marched off to guard the Ushiku post station with tall paper lanterns, policemen's goads, U-shaped prongs curved like yak horns to pin criminals down by the neck, bows, spears, guns, and cannons all carefully placed in position. Without permitting the slightest disorder in their ranks, these splendid warriors waited in awesome majesty.

Hotta Ōkuradayū provided a total of seven hundred horsemen, foot soldiers, and irregulars. In anticipation of camping in the fields, his troops carried vast quantities of military supplies and food for man and beast. His preparations were so thorough that the people who saw them knit their brows for fear that war would soon break out.

Akiwara Yagobei, Takegaki San'emon, and Okada Seisuke, who were responsible for the Wakashiba post station, set up camp there so they could attend to their duties. On the fourth day of the eleventh month, they and the intendant's staff went to inspect the places where the villagers had gathered on the Fox Woman Plain. In the area around the shrine they found the traces of 150 bonfires. Nevertheless, the three men compassionately realized that if they reported what they had found exactly as it was, the peasants would suffer great hardships. Therefore they reported to the bakufu that they had inspected the plain, but it appeared that the talk of mass meetings was nothing but rumor. The traces of fires found there seemed to be from bonfires set because the weather had been cold. Aside from that, there was absolutely nothing to suggest that anything suspiciously smacking of conspiracy had occurred.

People felt deeply thankful for the officials' benevolent handling of this affair. Had they reported what had really happened—that while the men had been gathered there for two or three days they had cooked their meals over bonfires—the peasants most probably would not have escaped being punished for conspiracy. Their handling of this affair shows that the Kanto district supervisor and the members of the intendant's staff were truly splendid fellows who exercised great compassion, mercy, and love for the people.

But then, at the end of the eleventh month, the following men set out for Tsunouchi Shinden to serve as the official investigators into the villages involved in the recent riot: officials attached to the office of the superintendent of finance, Yoshioka Torajirō and Okumura Kotarō, the tribunal secretary Matsumura Tokusaburō, and his apprentice Yashiro Shinhachirō.

Tsunouchi Shinden was originally part of a village called Tsunouchi which lay at least sixteen or seventeen miles by road northwest of the Ushiku post station. In the neighborhood were many places where the paddies had been ruined by water damage. To help the peasants, a government office for redeveloping the waste fields had been set up at Tsunouchi Shinden, staffed by the Kanto district supervisor Takegaki San'emon who had succored the villagers through his efforts at restoration. After the recent Ushiku post station riot, it was proposed that the participants be summoned to Edo where they could be interrogated one by one, but Takegaki took compassion on the masses for the sufferings they would have experienced, so they were questioned at Tsunouchi Shinden instead.

Every man down to the last tenant farmer from fifty-six villages in the eastern section and fifty villages in the western section was summoned to appear before the officials, who interrogated everybody one by one. As a result, five men were arrested for having led the riot. The others were sent back to their villages. A small hut was erected at Tsunouchi Shinden where the prisoners were held under guard during the investigation. The three hundred men under Tsuchiya Hosaburō hung curtains and decorated them with policemen's goads, U-shaped prongs, bows, arrows, guns, and other military equipment. Tsuchiya himself took rooms at an inn, but during the course of the interrogation he frequently served at the government office where he kept a strict watch.

In the mountains nearby, from ancient times down to the present, strange things have happened.

Finally the five men designated the leaders of the riot, Yūshichi and Kichijūrō from Koike, and Heiemon, Rihachi, and Shōkichi from Katsura, were sent to Edo in litters that looked like bird cages. The government officials all returned to their duties in the capital. At the Edo office, the five men were ordered put in prison, where they remained through the end of that year without anything being done about them. By the spring of 1805, three of the five had died.

According to everyone questioned during the course of the investigation, the first men who petitioned the government had argued that many villages had previously supplied porters and horses to the post stations, but in recent years they had relieved themselves from this duty. Those in the post stations responsible for providing relays of porters and horses had suffered extreme hardships. For this reason, the first petitioners had requested that supplies of men and horses be delivered by the same villages that had done so in the past. Gonzaemon and Asaya Jizaemon of Ami village, who were part of this first group, had not agreed to the plan to increase the number of villages servicing the post stations from the original 50 in the eastern section to 106. That was done by Watōji of Kuno village, who had insisted on presenting a petition that everyone called absolutely outrageous. Nevertheless, the bakufu had no intention of accepting the peasants' appeal, presented by their general representatives, calling for an exemption from post station duty for the 106 villages.

Yūshichi and Kichijūrō of Koike and Heiemon of Katsura died in prison while being interrogated. To pursue the investigation into the leadership displayed by the five men, their village officials and the headmen from the village leagues were summoned to Edo, where they were instructed to have searched the houses belonging to the five men's families. Among the waste paper found in the bedrooms of Heiemon, Kichijūrō, and Yūshichi was a list of names of all the poor peasants from the 106 villages involved in the riot of 1804, a rough draft of the poster that had been plastered on the official sign boards at that time, and the protocols signed by the villages when they met with their neighbors. As a result, the three men were unmistakably declared to have been the leaders. Their families were all forced to apologize for their misdeeds.

No suspicious papers were found at Rihachi's or Shōkichi's. It appeared that they had merely exerted themselves at the forefront of the crowd. Nevertheless, it had been really careless of the headmen for the 106 villages not to have put a stop to things when the riot started. Therefore, at the bakufu tribunal on the thirteenth day of the eighth month of 1805, in the presence of three magistrates, the following announcement was made:

> It was inexcusable for Watōji from Kuno to have insisted on getting additional villages included when he presented his petition, so he is forbidden to come within twenty-five miles of Edo in any direction. His fields and household goods are to be handed down to his wife and children.
>
> Based on precedents showing that the fifty-six villages in the eastern section had provided porters and post horses to the post stations in past years, these villages are ordered to service the Ushiku post station for ten years beginning in the eighth month of 1805.
>
> Asaya Jizaemon should continue to serve as an official freight dispatcher as he has done up to now. Gonzaemon of Ami is free to go about his business.
>
> Were Kichijūrō and Yūshichi of Koike and Heiemon of Katsura still alive, we would order them to be severely punished, but we have decided to show benevolence by

having them disinherited instead. Rihachi and Shōkichi are to be flogged fifty times, then forbidden to approach within twenty-five miles of either Edo or their villages.

For their carelessness in allowing the riot, the headmen of the 106 villages are ordered to pay a fine of two hundred *mon* per one hundred *koku* of village taxable yield to the district supervisor's office.

Everyone who has heard this decree must submit to it respectfully. If anyone disobeys, he will be judged in the wrong. This concludes the statement.

1805, eighth month, thirteenth day

An itinerant ascetic making a tour of the provinces once arrived at the village plain of Nareuma in Hitachi just as day and night, east and west, were becoming indistinguishable. Unable to find any sign of human habitation, and not having any idea of where he should go, he was aimlessly wandering around when in the far distance he caught sight of the light from a cooking fire. Walking in that direction soon brought him near. Looking inside, he saw an old woman cooking food over a fire. He came closer and earnestly begged a place to stay for the night.

"Stay if you can stand such an ugly broken-down hut," she replied. He washed his feet, and she gave him some food.

Once they had finished their dinners, the old woman sat bowed by painful memories. She told him the story of how last year on this same plain, men from the 106 villages nearby had held meetings to foment a conspiracy. They had been punished for this by the authorities. Some men had even died. Not only had the villagers been severely punished, but the expenses connected with the trials had cost them vast sums of gold and silver. It was truly deplorable that the whole thing had come about through the wicked designs of evil people.

Knitting his brows with grief, the ascetic listened to her tale. He decided to write down all that he had heard as a demonstration of his strong sympathy for the peasants.

As the first gray light of dawn spread across the morning sky, the old woman and her hut disappeared. In their place, the shrine precincts became visible. Therefore, this account is entitled, "A Tale of a Dream from the Fox Woman Plain."

The place called Fox Woman Plain was a broad wasteland on the flat soil of Katchi district in the province of Hitachi; it stretched for seven miles in all directions. In its middle stood a shrine to the Great August Deity Inari, the goddess of rice. Seven miles by road distant from this plain to the east lived a peasant in Nemoto village called Chūgorō. This is something that happened years ago in the Tenshō era [1573–91].

Chūgorō had relatives at a shop called Toriya in Tsuchiura. One day he went to Tsuchiura on business. As he was about to go home, having finished his task, he put in his purse three *ryō* that he had received from Toriya to take to Kamaya in Takegasaki. As he was going back across the plain, he saw a fox taking a nap in the shade of a bush by the side of the road. He also saw a hunter getting his gun ready to shoot her. Chūgorō thought how distressing it would be for the fox to lose her life like that, but he had no idea what he should do. He merely coughed to clear his throat as he turned to leave. That startled the fox, who opened her eyes and ran off to where no one could follow her.

The hunter was furious. "Just as I was about to shoot the fox, you made so much noise that she was able to escape," he scolded Chūgorō. "That was a really dirty trick you played. I think maybe I'll kill you instead," he ranted and raved.

Chūgorō stood amazed. "I had no idea that there was anyone here on this road, neither you nor the fox. Since I was just going along minding my own business, there is no way that I could have intended to disturb you. Please forgive me." But no matter how much he apologized, the other refused to listen.

"You must be carrying some money for your travel expenses. Pull it out and use it to pay for your crime," the hunter said in irritation.

Chūgorō had no choice but to apologize sincerely and hand over the three *ryō* that he was supposed to take Kamaya in Takegasaki from Toriya in Tsuchiura. At last he managed to escape and start back to his own home. He worried about what he was going to do the whole way.

When he got back home, he told his wife everything that had happened to him. At first she was delighted that he had returned safely. Nevertheless, since the unhappy couple already lived a miserable existence, they were at a loss as to how they were going to repay the three *ryō*. They were forced to sell their clothing and everything else in order to procure the entire amount and send it to Kamaya in Takegasaki.

Thereafter the couple suffered even greater misfortunes in trying to survive from day to day. The wife was already afflicted with heart disease, and all of her troubles simply made it worse. At last she pitifully passed away. Chūgorō was left all alone to make his sorrowful way in the floating world.

One day Chūgorō went to Tsuchiura on business. On his way home, a woman of over thirty appeared before him. She approached and fell on her knees.

"May I know where you're going? There is something that I must ask you, and I need to tell you what it is."

"I am nothing but a miserably lonely man," Chūgorō replied.

"Precisely because you're alone, I feel that I can trust you. I beg of you please to make me your wife."

"Here I am, a man with only meager clothing and food. There's no way that I could make you my wife. That's simply the way things are so please don't even think about it."

"I have spoken thus because although I'm a mere woman, I know I can relieve your pains and afflictions," she said in all sincerity.

"If what you've said is true, you may come along if you like for I have indeed been lonely."

With this, the woman's mind was set at ease. The two returned to Chūgorō's house together.

After that the couple passed the days and nights in harmony. With the passage of the years, the woman gave birth to one daughter and two sons. The eldest child they called O-Tsuru, the next Kamejirō, and the youngest Takematsu. Of these three, Kamejirō was sent to work for the peasant Kakuzaemon in Kuriyama. After the third child, Takematsu, grew up, he lived on Sanjō Street in Kyoto, where he had his own son. When this son grew up, he called himself Kuribayashi Jirō Yoshinaga and joined the followers of Okami Jifudayū. In later years he became known as the great general Shimōsa no kami Yoshinaga. A son-in-law was adopted for their daughter O-Tsuru. All four, the parents and the young couple, succeeded in working so diligently that they lacked for nothing in their daily life. Chūgorō's previous hardships had become a tale of the distant past.

Chūgorō planted his paddies in rice. After his crop had been transplanted and allowed to grow throughout the summer, the plants excelled all others in their beauty and quality. Nevertheless, even by the middle of autumn the rice had not yet come into ear, and the green stalks bent over halfway to the ground.

That year government officials in charge of assessing the land tax came to inspect the crops. Taking pity on Chūgorō, they agreed that the best thing to do would be to exempt him from paying any land tax at all on his rice crop. The village officials reported that the entire family had really exerted themselves in working as hard as they could at farming, so the officials felt special compassion for them and gave them rice seed and food supplies.

Then, about the beginning of the tenth month, color appeared in the rows of rice. When the ears were cut, threshed, and hulled, the grains were far superior to those of normal years, and the harvest turned out to be much bigger than in ordinary times. Being an honest and upright man, Chūgorō reported what had happened to the village headman.

"When we inspected the hulled rice that we harvested this year, we discovered that we had collected much more than we do in ordinary years, so please allow us to pay taxes on it," he told the headman.

"My, my, you certainly are an honest fellow. Anyone else who managed to bring in a large harvest would have faked ignorance. We must inform the government office of what you've done," the village officials replied.

When the time came to submit the land tax for that year, the headman reported what Chūgorō had told him. The government officials were deeply impressed. They decided that Chūgorō must have been able to acquire such a large harvest because the gods and Buddhas had responded favorably to his honesty. Nevertheless, they would have to issue him new instructions because the government had already exempted him from paying any land tax. The headman was ordered to go home at once and come back again bringing Chūgorō with him. He hurried home and returned to the government office with Chūgorō. The officials then made the following announcement: "It has reached our ears that you have really been extremely diligent in your efforts at farming, you are exceptionally honest, and you follow the path of righteousness. For that reason we are giving you an award of two pieces of silver."

The headman and Chūgorō thanked the officials and returned to their own homes. News of what had happened spread like the wind through the neighborhood to delight everyone who heard it. Stories about the award and especially about the rice grains that matured in the stalk became the talk of Chūgorō's and other villages. Thereafter at the time of the festival for bountiful harvests offered to the god of the wind, people in all the villages prayed that the ears of rice would ripen in the stalk so as not to be subject to damage from water or drought and bountiful harvests would be theirs forever.

Chūgorō's wife continued to toil as faithfully as she could, never doing anything contrary to her husband's wishes. One day she was especially busy putting everything in order. She swept and cleaned their rooms using her tail as a broom. Just then some neighborhood children caught sight of her.

"Hey, lady, you've got a tail growing from your butt," they shouted in surprise.

Because they had seen her, the poor woman had to suffer the pain of parting from her husband. She could not even say good-bye to the children with whom she had lived for so many years. Feeling as though her heart would burst, she desperately wanted to write a line to her husband before anyone else caught sight of her. And thus she left behind the following poems written on a sheet of paper:

> I have repaid my obligation to you with eight years of faithful service that passed like a dream.

> In the course of time, I gave birth to three children.
> On the verge of parting, my heart yearns to stay.

> *[In Chinese]*

> If you love me,
> Come search for me at the sound of the evening bell
> On the Fox Woman Plain.

> *[In Japanese]*

The followers of Lord Oda Ujiharu, a descendant of Minamoto no Yoshiie, built forty-eight fortifications in the eastern provinces. One of them, the lord of Tsuchiura, Shinoda Izumi no kami, had lived in the famous castle called Kamei, but he lost it to the lord of

Fujisawa, Lord Suga Yazaemonjō Masamitsu. Lord Masamitsu was slain by Hōjō Ujinao. For many generations, the rulers at Tsuchiura have been the descendants of a retainer of Takeda Shingen. The present lord is Tsuchiya Hosaburō.

The lord of Sakura in Shimōsa was Hotta Kaga no kami, who was transferred there from Matsumoto in Shinano. He erected a new temple at which to pray for peace in the realm. It remains down to the present. There is a popular song sung while hulling wheat about the building of that temple:

"Who built the new temple at Sakura where the sun does not shine on the fields?

"Lord Kaga's hills were seven with seven bends.

"The eightfold cherry blossoms at the Sakura castle fell, becoming as dust in the yard."

His legitimate son Kōzuke no kami was bewitched by some sort of demon. During his reign, the headman of Kōzu village, Sōgorō, was punished for having made a direct appeal. Many years after that, the lord became Hotta Ōkuradayū, who reigns at present.

In Katchi district, Hitachi, there were thirteen villages in the domain of Ōkubo Aki no kami. Peasants from three of them, Kami Ōtsuka, Usukura, and Shimo Itabashi, joined the league of villages active in the recent riot. About that time a government office had been built at Shimo Itabashi, with officials placed there to oversee the domain. When they heard news of the riot, they reported what had happened to their lord's mansion in Edo, and the lord himself gave orders to dispatch troops immediately. A total of two hundred men, cavalry and foot soldiers, divided into two divisions, set out before dawn on the twentieth day of the tenth month of 1804 and arrived at Itabashi by late afternoon the same day. Notwithstanding that no orders had been issued by the bakufu, these men were dispatched to quell disorder in the domain and nearby areas. Everyone, even the commoners, talked about what a splendid idea it was, just what one would expect from Aki no kami.

One day Ōkubo Aki no kami's ancestor, Gorōzaemon, was out fishing at a pond in the mountains when his pet dog started to bother him. With one stroke of his sword, he chopped off the dog's head.

Instantly it flew up into a pine tree, where it attacked a huge serpent that had been hiding there. Gorōzaemon promptly killed the serpent. Then he realized that his dog had acted just like a real retainer. Thereafter all members of the Ōkubo family put the character for dog on their crests as a mark of good fortune. Several generations had passed before the Ōkubo Aki no kami known today.

The Ushiku post station was the site for the government headquarters of Lord Yamaguchi Suō no kami, so it was guarded very carefully. Troops were dispatched to the post station and to the domain boundaries where they staunchly defended their territory.

Ponder this well when you read this story. When a person comes to lose his life, he should die like Ōkubo Gorōzaemon's dog described above. Heiemon, Kichijūrō, and Yūshichi simply got lots of people in an uproar; they did not even manage to get an exemption from the regular number of porters and horses assigned to post station service, and they did more harm than good for the multitudes in the villages. For this reason, they were far inferior to Ōkubo Gorōzaemon's dog and the fox who transformed herself into a woman. This shows that if you save other people out of benevolence, even if you die, you will be praised. You should never act in such a way as to make yourself inferior to mere animals. Ponder this carefully.

1863/11/22   *Copied by Sekiguchi Tosuke*
                                      Owned by Jinbei of Hitachi province,
                                      Katchi district, Shimo Ōtsu village

A Tale Told in a Dream of a Eulogy to Filial Piety

THIS EULOGY TO FILIAL PIETY takes as its context the 1866 riot in the Tsuyama domain of western Japan. It is the story of what happens to a peasant family when its head is imprisoned for having led an uprising, but centered throughout the narrative are his two daughters, whose devotion to their parents exemplifies virtue. As women of Japan they did not participate in the riot itself; their knowledge of what happened comes to them through dreams. Like "A Tale of a Dream from the Fox Woman Plain," the text derives its ability to recapitulate events from an unverifiable source.

One of many peasant uprisings that erupted during the last years of Tokugawa rule, the 1866 Tsuyama riot forced the ruling authorities to reverse policies disliked by the peasants and indirectly helped bring to power an anti-bakufu faction within the domain, less than two years before the collapse of the entire Tokugawa system. Its significance was not lost on its contemporaries; a number of men wrote and copied accounts that tried to explain how such an event could have occurred. According to Nagamitsu Norikazu, who unearthed vast collections of documents that tell of social protest in what is now Okayama prefecture, the most complete records sympathetic to the peasants are "An Account of the Disturbance That Led to Political Reform," written by Kobayashi Sōsuke, a samurai doctor; "The Story of the Beggars' Riot in Mimasaka," written by a member of the Maebara family of deputy district headmen; and "A Eulogy to Filial Piety," whose author probably knew about the "Political Reform" text but whose own achieves a completely different emphasis.[1]

"The Story of the Beggars' Riot" begins with a survey of key national events, beginning in 1853, when the American commodore

Matthew C. Perry arrived in Japan. In 1860, the bakufu strongman Ii Naosuke was assassinated. In 1863, the shōgun made a formal visit to Kyoto, and peasants and samurai revolted at Gōjō and Ikuno. Fires and rebellions broke out in succeeding years. In 1866, the shōgun sent an expeditionary force to crush Chōshū. Thus the author astutely located the peasant uprising in his own domain against the background of political turmoil all over Japan. This grasp of national politics is completely lacking in "A Eulogy to Filial Piety," perhaps because women could not be expected to have knowledge of the wide world outside, even in a dream.

"A Eulogy to Filial Piety" also restricts its explanation of the causes for the uprising to a bare minimum. Only once does it hint that the peasants were dissatisfied with the way their taxes were measured. Instead it points to crop failures caused by natural disasters. Other texts with their wider masculine vision emphasize the domanial reforms introduced in 1861 and 1863, which increased the amount of rice peasants had to include in each bale and required strict inspections to insure that only the highest-quality rice ended up in government storehouses. "If the peasants brought in ten bales of rice, three of the bales were returned, four or five had to be done over, and only two or three would be accepted without question."[2] Village headmen petitioned repeatedly for leniency, but burdened with the extraordinary expenses incurred by sending an army to assist the bakufu in subduing Chōshū, the domanial authorities denied their requests.

The account given in "A Eulogy to Filial Piety" radically reduces the scale of the uprising. It fails to mention that the girls' father, Naokichi, incited unrest by writing a circular to send through the villages, but instead portrays him as a self-made hero who, after peace has been restored, resolves to take the peasants' crimes on himself for the sake of the community. It barely alludes to the scenes of destruction that fill other histories depicting the peasants' march on Tsuyama. The attack on the castle town itself is abbreviated, nor is there any mention that the urban poor joined the peasants. All records agree that the crowds manage to scatter the warriors guarding the barrier on the city outskirts, but when they try to cross the bridge leading to the castle itself, they are defeated with firearms. Only in "A Eulogy to Filial Piety" does the lord himself placate the crowd with gifts of grain. In the other accounts, the peasants at first refuse to be put off with offers of food and promises to consider their demands at a later date. Instead they revile as rascals and wretches the officials who humbly call them honorable peasants. Forced to retreat from the castle when four of their number are shot, bands of poor peasants then roam through town and countryside, smashing up houses, looting, and fighting the soldiers sent against them. For almost two months sporadic riots continue to trouble the domain until a combination of armed troops and donations of food finally pacifies the peasants.[3] These peripheral events are recorded in "A Eulogy to Filial Piety" only as lawlessness and violence, a horrifying way to oppose the lord.

Like other accounts of peasant uprisings, "A Eulogy to Filial Piety" presents an ambiguous perspective on peasant action. Driven by necessity, the peasants protest under only the most extreme duress. By discriminating between good and evil in responding politely to offers of food and to their lord, they demonstrate that they are virtuous. The text omits scenes of destruction and the peasants' attack near the castle to deny the soldiers' justification for firing on the crowd, an act seen as traitorous to the lord and one that harms the peasants, the "treasures of the country." On the other hand, peasants who refuse to be put off with promises of relief are castigated as guilty of the horrible crimes for which Naokichi will have to pay. In extreme circumstances, protest may be justified, but violence is always abhorred.

Like "One Thousand Spears at Kitsunezuka," "A Eulogy to Filial Piety" exposes the conflict between community and family interests. The former offers a meditation on the corrupting power of money; the latter gives a critical perspective on the relations between the family and the youth association. In the traditional village, the youth association was responsible for maintaining community conformity. It regulated festivals, and, in some regions at least, it controlled the sexual activities of the village women. Especially notorious was the practice of "night visits" *(yobai)*, when men would sneak into the bedrooms of unmarried women, and married women whose husbands were absent. This practice was condoned as long all the parties involved were of approximately equal status, but it was resisted when parents decided that the imperative of family continuity required them to choose their children's marriage partners from families whose property matched their own. The tension between the youth association/community and the family cropped up repeatedly in the narrative until Naokichi's daughters were safely settled.

"A Eulogy to Filial Piety" utilizes few of the devices so often appropriated by histories of peasant uprisings to represent crowd action. The stereotypical battle scenes that lend drama and excitment to "A Record of How the Four Orders of People in Mimasaka Ran Riot" and "The Story of the Beggars' Riot in Mimasaka" are completely missing. Exaggerations appear only in language denoting totality, for example, the announcement that everyone in the domain gathered in a long shed to await the officials' verdict. Even Naokichi's decision to sacrifice himself as Sakura Sōgorō had done is mentioned only briefly. This does not mean, however, that "A Eulogy to Filial Piety" lacks its own intertextual context.

Buddhist practices permeate this text. The death of Naokichi is described in terms that emphasize the evanescence of existence. Important too are the memorial services held for him after death. Buddhist imagery can be seen in the repeated references to the three treasures, which usually refer to the Buddha, the sutras, and the priests. In this text they represent what was most important to the peasants. *Wasan,* translated in the title as "eulogy," is a Buddhist term for hymns of praise sung to extol the deeds of the Buddhas and high priests. Like hymns, poetry, recitative and dramatic literature, the "Eulogy" is written in a 7/5 syllabic meter difficult to replicate, at least by this translator, in English. This meter can be seen as one more reflection of the belief in the magical power of ordered words.[4] Here the solemn format is ironically appropriated to praise a peasant girl.

The text also engages in a dialogue with the worldview often closely associated with nativism. To call the peasants the treasures of the country was a favorite phrase of those who valorized agricultural work as the source of wealth.[5] The ambiguous portrayal of Naokichi's foibles presents a more rounded personality than the usual stereotypical descriptions of peasant martyrs. He dies, but by ending with a wedding and a promise that the family will continue, the story affirms life. Depicted in detail is the idyllic existence of the retired peasant, taking his ease, pipe in hand, with his family at his beck and call. The contrast between the dignity of the peasants' labors and the filth in which they are performed highlights a concern for the fabric of everyday life. Even the peasants' most private parts are exposed. A homonym for the son's name, Bōji, using the same first character as the name, means "sexual intercourse." And given the name's proximity in the text to a reference to Bōji's penis, it appears that the author may have been making a small joke, perhaps also alluding to the nighttime proclivities of the youth association so feared by the girls' mother. In this text what was previously taken as a matter of course, the separation of the heroic from practical and everyday life, disappears.[6]

This story is not about the politics of peasant rebellion nor yet Buddhist priests; it is about women and filial piety. Stories about filial piety abound in the Chinese and Japanese literary canon. In the temple schools or *terakoya* that spread across Japan in the early nineteenth century, a favorite text for children was the Chinese "Classic of Filial Piety," often supplemented with exemplary tales of filial behavior. To these were joined stories about people who in Japan had demonstrated extraordinary devotion to their parents. In 1843 a village headman living near Edo published his own precepts for children under the title "A Miscellany of Filial Piety" *(Kōkō mezashigusa).*[7] "Tales of Filial Children in Higo" on the island of Kyushu told how the peasant daughter Sata worked in the family fields and cut mountain grasses and reeds, which she sold in the market to buy clothing, candy, and sake for her invalid, ill-tempered father and blind mother. Reports of her filial conduct reached the ears of the Hosokawa domanial officials, who in 1743 granted her a stipend. Similar tales were collected in books like "Tales of Filial Piety from Geibi" and "Biographies of Filial Children and Good People in Chikuzen."[8] These collections included more stories of samurai than peasants and more stories of men than women.

Lords and commoners were involved in a complicity to guide women in the path of righteousness by invoking examples of virtuous wives, mothers, and daughters. In Obama on the Japan Sea coast of western Japan, a young nursemaid named Tsuna defended her master's son from a rabid dog, but at the cost of being bitten herself. She died in agony. In 1769, the Sakai domain lord honored her by erecting a gravestone in her memory. Textbooks such as "A Mirror for Virtuous Women" *(Teijo no kagami)* told of women who refused to marry a second time, even after divorce, behavior more befitting a samurai woman than a peasant. Mothers were encouraged to act like the peasant Kohei's second wife, who treated her stepson as her own. In her last testament as she lay dying of measles, she said, "I regret only that I was unable to raise the child until he was at least ten."⁹ Textbooks for women were published in ever increasing quantity and variety in the early nineteenth century, but the message was generally the same: a virtuous woman is one who self-effacingly devotes herself to the interests of men.

"A Eulogy to Filial Piety" demonstrated the devotion of daughters to their parents in ways both ordinary and extraordinary. It was expected that the daughters would try to ease their mother's burdens. More virtuous still was their attention to their father, reprobate though he was. Both sisters were humble and self-deprecating, womanly qualities valued in this society. In the interests of maintaining the family, Kuma accepted without question her arranged marriage to her stepbrother. In these instances, the daughters passively conformed to what was expected of them; they appeared not as individuals but as a stereotype, without a story. Claiming that they were conforming to the dictates of filial piety, however, empowered them to act. By taking action for themselves, they stepped out of the usual confines for women. It was by professing devotion to her father, for example, that Shima could refuse to have sex with men.

Tokugawa-period texts provided women with few opportunities to act. In the histories of peasant uprisings, even peasant men had to go to extraordinary lengths to justify protest, to designate themselves as actors in a system that reserved to only a few samurai bureaucrats the right to act politically. China and India knew of women warriors. Rani Lakshmibai of Jhansi, for example, led her troops into battle against the British in the Great Rebellion of 1857–58,¹⁰ but there were no comparable heroines in the Japanese tradition. In tales of filial piety, however, a few peasant women were depicted in guises that allowed them to give up their normative passivity for the public arena.

"A Eulogy to Filial Piety" participated in an ongoing dialogue about women who acted out of devotion to their fathers. The most famous rendition of such devotion was performed on an Edo Kabuki stage in 1780 as "A Tale of the White Stones Used in Great Battles on a Go Board" *(Go taiheiki shiraishi banashi).* Discussed by the urban intellectuals of the time and published in twenty-six versions between 1766 and 1867, the story appeared from Aomori to Okinawa in folk songs, festival dances, and local plays. Briefly, it told of two sisters who avenged their father's death at the hands of a warrior. In urban versions, the elder sister had been sold into prostitution long before her father's murder. By the time her rustic sister found her, she had become an elegant, high-ranking courtesan. In contrast, rural versions emphasized the meetings between the peasants and the samurai: first when the father vainly performed elaborate apologies for having tossed muddy weeds up on a path where the samurai was walking, and second when the two daughters, having become skilled swordfighters, killed their hated enemy. How did they learn the secret techniques that gave them victory? Why from Yui Shōsetsu (1605–51), an underground hero, who led the last revolt against the Tokugawa shōguns.[11]

The story of the two daughters' revenge is the sole text centered on peasant women that achieved nationwide distribution during the Tokugawa period. Like "A Eulogy to Filial Piety," it transformed dutiful women into the context of heroes. Nevertheless, this dialogue on filial piety contains an implicit contradiction. Under ordinary circumstances, children showed their devotion to their parents by producing progeny to replicate the family. Given the widespread acceptance of adoption in Japan, families without sons could carry on the family line by marrying their daughter to a man who would succeed her father. Naokichi, for example, had married into Chiyo's family as her second husband. To dedicate oneself to revenge or, as Shima did, to resolve to substitute oneself for a beloved parent did not advance the family's long-range interests.[12] In "A Eulogy to Filial Piety," the contradiction is resolved by allowing one daughter to become a nun, thus consecrating herself to her father's memory, while the other daughter marries her stepbrother to perpetuate the family.

"A Eulogy to Filial Piety" is crosscut with conflicting representations of women. Shima undermines the limitations placed on women in her society by making up her mind on her own; her determination to sacrifice herself is not forced on her. The head of the household is not an exemplar of virtue; that role is reserved for his daughters. Appropriate male and female behavior is also called into question when Shima offers to give up her status as a woman to substitute for her father in prison.[13] Under Tokugawa law, the punishments for men and women were carefully differentiated, so much so that when it was found necessary to execute a woman, she was given a man's name. In such cases, the category "woman" was as much a function of social structure as of biology. The message of the text seemingly reinforces the status quo by focusing on family continuity, but it is subverted from within when it centers women as the subjects of action that transgresses gender roles.

One hundred and forty years separate "A Record of How the Four Orders of People in Mimasaka Ran Riot" from "A Eulogy to Filial Piety," and many changes had taken place in the Tsuyama region during that time. Herbert Bix argues that the 1727 uprising was futile and doomed to failure because the state was still unified and able to impose its will on the peasants. The 1866 incident included the same targets as before—taxes and the intermediaries in its collection—but it involved townspeople as well as peasants in a successful struggle against a weak and divided state. Within the countryside, the growth of rural commerce had produced internal class antagonisms between landlords and moneylenders on the one hand and day laborers and tenant farmers on the other, people whom Bix, following the lead of Sasaki Junnosuke, calls the semiproletariat. The significance of the 1866 uprising lies in the entry of this new class onto the stage of history.[14]

Bix makes a careful analysis of the socioeconomic changes that had disrupted the region, but his categories of analysis lead him to distort the changes in local leadership. Like Heiroku, the other leader of this uprising mentioned in "A Eulogy to Filial Piety," Naokichi was a landholding peasant worth over ten *koku*, hardly a member of the semiproletariat. (Heiroku had fields valued at over twelve *koku*.) Bix tries to explain away this anomoly by claiming that Naokichi's large family of eight made his actual existential situation precarious.[15] From the peasants' point of view, however, Naokichi was in an enviable situation with three grown children to provide a source of labor. The other members of the family were probably live-in servants, another indication of prosperity. His relative wealth is further documented by Shima's decision to become a nun, an option requiring family support unavailable to the poor. Whatever reasons incited Naokichi to lead the uprising, his own poverty was not one of them.

Bix contrasts the 1727 and 1866 riots on the level of event, but it is also possible to compare them at the level of text. "A Record of How the Four Orders of People in Mimasaka Ran Riot" defines the deeds of the crowd and its leaders in terms of classical norms of action. Men act as autonomous individuals to perform their destiny. Filial piety is defined in terms of honor. It means respect for the aged, not family continuity. In the balance between family and community interests, the weight falls decisively on the side of the community. "A Eulogy to Filial Piety" is different. From the opening platitute to the concluding wedding ceremony, it valorizes the family. In contrast to the "beggars" or poor peasants for whom the family could only be preserved within the context of the community, the family depicted here relies less on cooperative endeavors than its own resources. Like "A Thousand Spears at Kitsunezuka," this text exposes the conflict between public duty and family responsibility. In so doing, it allows a glimpse at the changes in the values of at least one part of the peasantry—not those on the verge of becoming the proletariat, but the landholders and landlords who remained the dominant force in the countryside throughout the nineteenth century.

A Tale Told in a Dream of a Eulogy to Filial Piety

As a rule, when people act righteously by believing in the gods and Buddhas, respecting their superiors, taking pity on their inferiors, obeying the laws of the state, revering their ancestors, and exerting themselves to show filial piety toward their mothers and fathers, when brothers, sisters, parents, wives, children, and all other household members live in harmony with each other, guarding against extravagance in their everyday life, abhoring making a brilliant show, conducting their business with frugality in all things, and working diligently, then shall they become wealthy and prosper, their descendants will experience eternal good fortune, and the family will continue to greet the New Year forever.

Here was a family that worked in the mountains, where their daughters were raised drinking the clear flowing waters of the Kamo River. Everyone praised their skill with plows and hoes, yes, even sickles and hatchets. Out of filial piety for their mother, every morning and every night they drew water from the well, dexterously swinging the long pole with its rock at one end that balanced the bucket. Whenever they were not otherwise engaged, they set a waterwheel to work grinding wheat and rice. They looked after their mother, likewise their brother.

Once while they were talking together about one thing or another, they said to each other: "All of us who were born into peasant families are splattered with loathsome and disgusting mud. We think of nothing but our strenuous and difficult labors. In the brief respite we gain from farmwork in spring or winter, we spin hemp night after night. We patch each other's clothes. We carefully attend to our needlework, and the members of each household have lived in harmony. But now has come a year of unparalleled disaster. Everywhere everyone is experiencing exceptional crop failures. We have almost no way of paying our taxes."

Then the stepdaughter O-Kuma related the story of a dream she had had, a dream which showed the deepest depths of her step-father Naokichi's heart so that once the members of her family knew what had transpired, they would also know what had been his heartfelt ambition:

"Our father is a man who always helped the weak by over-powering the strong. At the time of the riot, we clung to his sleeves, begging him in tears to stay. He must have some reason for what he did. Perhaps a dream can truly let us know what happened to him.

"Under ordinary circumstances, I would know nothing about what happened. It appears that all the people in the villages have prepared flaming torches to carry in their hands. They steel their resolve, encouraging each other to make it to the pass at Arasaka, each and every one of them. When the time is right, a multitude of people rise up carrying their pine torches to light the night. The sounds of temple bells and war cries swell in a sudden clamor.

"The crowd of people go through Yukishige, Naoi, Momo-momo, and Konakahara. They do not quite vent all their resentment by smashing up Masuya, so by and by they treat the fabled Kakuya in the same way. Then they divide their forces to the east and west along the flowing river. Their shouts make it sound like a tidal wave is coming.

"Some people go through the Ochiai barrier at Ayabe and fill the beach at Tako. Once they withdraw from there, they divide their forces in two, then appear at Nomura. There they have two deputy district headmen guide them in their push forward to the highway between Inaba, Tsuyama, and Bizen.

"The district headman of Oshiire village, Mr. Nemoto, makes all the preparations he can. He tries to restrain the crowd with drawn sword, but he falls at once. It is only to be expected that his gate and walls, houses and storehouses are smashed up. This really is the sort of thing that happens only in a dream.

"Everyone realizes that to hold council here would be pointless, so they hurry off in the direction of Kawabe, a fortified post station east of the castle town of Tsuyama. There the Doi family mansion extends for a block on all four sides. Smack in the middle of the gateway the crowd finds big shallow-bottomed tubs lined up and heaped with all sorts of rough grains. There is a pile of rice looking just like Mt. Fuji, the greatest mountain in the world. As soon as they catch sight of this treasure, the people in the crowd snatch it up with ladles and hands. Many people are thus saved. Happily no damage is done, showing that even men of the soil understand the difference between good and evil. No one brandishes even one staff.

"Thereafter the crowd splits up, going to the east, west, north, and south. At the same time, government officials salute their leaders and set out from the castle town in the direction the crowd is headed. According to what I am told in my dream, their forces number about ten thousand cavalry.

"Suddenly, at the Gyokurin barrier blocking the eastern entrance to Tsuyama, war cries shake heaven and earth. The crowd forces open the barrier before anyone realizes what is going on. More than enough guards are on duty there, but they cannot withstand their opponents. The melee scatters them in all directions. They vanish in a flash.

"Inside the barrier the crowd rushes through Matsubara and Nakanomachi where many townspeople live and pushes forward in the direction of the main bridge to the accompaniment of loud applause. The lord's commander prepares to defend the barrier at the main guardhouse in front of the castle with rows of cannon and guns at the ready. The peasants all align the points of their bamboo spears. The top of the bridge looks like a field covered with plumes of horsetail grass. Here is a sight unheard of even in ancient times. The peasants suddenly raise their voices in war cries which rend heaven and earth with their dreadful noise.

"The lord of the castle himself appears before them: 'I will listen to all the complaints that all the peasants make together, and I will announce my response later on.' Since he shows that he understands their problems, the peasants too say, 'All right, we will withdraw.'

"The wind and waves of disorder are quieted. Then misfortune overtakes the ruler and the commoners alike. The soldiers put the fuses to their guns. They destroy the treasures of the country who

work the lord's fields. While the people are still wondering whether
that thunderbolt was intentional, the soldiers count those who have
fallen. A total of eleven villagers are hit: four die immediately, two
are severely wounded, and another five suffer slight wounds. Then,
'Wait a minute, wait a minute,' a voice calls.

"Lord Furuichi Ukon and Lord Ōshima Heizō appear before the
crowd. There at the bridge they calm the peasants down. Both sides
are talked into lowering their arms. Out of gratitude for the nobles'
kind words, all the peasants accompany them when they take the
road to Tomikawara. On the wide banks of the river plain, officials
from town who serve the government feed rice gruel to the peasants. As night turns to dawn, the peasants receive 13,500 bales of
grain sealed with the lord's black stamp as a temporary food allot-
ment. They are informed that the response to their petition will be
announced at a later date."

[Here ends the story of the riot related by Kuma. The scene
shifts to Naokichi's house, where his wife O-Chiyo remains with his
children.]

The time was early in the twelfth lunar month. O-Chiyo, a
mother, spent a long night in bed holding her children. Her
daughters O-Kuma and O-Shima both fell asleep, but she worried
sorely about her short-tempered husband. Whenever she started to
drowse off, she would fret about her daughters. Finally she fell
asleep tormented by fear of what the neighborhood youth association would do if it knew that she alone was in charge of the house
during her husband's absence.

Soon it was dawn. The elder brother Bōji got up. Grabbing his
penis in his hand, he opened the door. Next O-Shima arose and lit
the cooking fire. While she was preparing breakfast, the rest of the
household awakened. O-Kuma told them the entire story, related
above, that had appeared to her in a lengthy dream. The whole
household was discussing it when the vanguard of a troop of beggars came through the village on their way back home.[16]

"Is that so, is that so," they exclaimed upon hearing O-Kuma's
story. How strange, how very strange it was to have had such an
accurate dream. Gossiping about what had happened. they trooped
back home one after the other.

According to one report, the appeal made en masse directly to
the authorities, which spread to the east, west, north, and south,
enticed more and more people to get involved, and they committed

acts of lawlessness and violence. This is the most horrifying way to oppose the lord. Many people died, making the beggars' crimes even more atrocious.

The girls' father, Naokichi, enumerated these crimes for himself, going from house to house and examining each person. It gradually became apparent that the beggars' frightful crimes concerned the laws governing the measures used to pay taxes to the lord.

"I have made up my mind that I alone will take responsibility for having presented the petition and for being the instigator of the uprising," he announced. "I do this for the sake of all people everywhere and also for the sake of our lord."

He was at least fifty-five years old when he made up his mind to set off in the direction of the government office. Accompanied by one other man from the community association, he waited for the day when he would be imprisoned.

At that time he possessed a number of things he would never use again. He also had two poems:

Children, take good care of your parents.
Parents, love your children and your grandchildren.
You must never part from one another.

Although we have not scattered one from another,
The mountain cherry blossoms are
Simply caught by whichever wind that blows.

Naokichi wrote these poems to send back home. The person whom he asked to take them told the family everything that had happened. Their grief was indescribable. Finally his daughter O-Shima stood up in tears.

"How selfish can he be? His sole ambition was to become the savior, all by himself, of the people of the soil who inhabit this 110,000 *koku* domain. Had he any human feeling at all, he would have told my mother, my sister, and myself a little bit of what was going on. Then we grumbling women would have prattled on about whatever came into our heads like we're doing right this minute. Had he deigned to listen to us, you would not now see us weep these bitter tears."

Ever since the beginning of autumn, O-Shima had been muttering nonsense.

205

"From the time of his youth, our father disobeyed the roadside prohibition-edict boards by indulging in his secret fondness for gambling. Even after he became the head of the household, he still indulged in wine, food, and sex, bustling about doing whatever he pleased regardless of the consequences. Once he reached the age of fifty, he who had once been our guardian resolved to retire. He had our elder brother Bōji take over the household's affairs. Then he had the bedding taken completely out of an interior room in the house to make a place for himself where he could sit and smoke.

"When we his daughters were able to take time away from our work, we sat to his left and right, attending to his needs and making sure that we served him his tea. Whenever he lacked for anything, he would clap his hands, relying on us to come see what was needed. Had we argued with him to stop him from going out and amusing himself, that would have been unfilial. Out of deference for the blessings we have received from you, father, we ask your forgiveness." This shows just how his daughter felt when she expressed her apologies.

Finally the last day of the year arrived. Everyone in the province was allowed to return to his own home. Even the officials who had been dispatched to the countryside were allowed to withdraw because it appeared that order had been restored.

The old year was rung out; the first day of the new year of 1867 arrived auspiciously. In all the villages of the countryside, morning celebrations welcomed a propitious spring. Each household also performed its own first rites of the year. For the seasonal greetings made early in the New Year, people went back and forth, paying visits to one another all over the country. They gathered in groups large enough to rival Mt. Fuji, the greatest mountain in the world. Their chatter pounded as continually as the waves at Tago Inlet in Suruga.[17] Conditions livened up; everyone enjoyed the excitement. In the newly found peace and tranquility, the events of the preceding year were quickly forgotten.

The members of the neighborhood youth association came to perform the greetings of the season at the gate to the Naokichi house. Family members responded with their own greetings. They brought out the three treasures of a farmer—the sake cups, the sake bottles, and side dishes—and opened the sliding paper doors. Ashamed to let others catch sight of their anxieties, they held back their tears while with proud faces they performed the salutations prescribed by Buddhist law. Once they had bid the association farewell, they reentered the house.

The family lived in constant anxiety over what would become of their father. Then in the fourth month of 1867, a notice arrived from the village headman's office stating: "Everyone in the villages, the headmen, group leaders, and ordinary peasants, are all required to appear at the Tsuyama government office."

Assuming that everyone had been pardoned, they all went there joyfully. Everyone asked what was going on, but no one had any idea, and so the entire population of the domain simply waited in a long shed.

Soon the criminals were all summoned into the officials' presence. Those who had committed lesser crimes were pardoned; those with more serious offenses were imprisoned for life. Out of the lord's great love for his people, the children and relatives of the latter were told: "Take your farewells for you will never again see each other in this life." Everyone felt grateful for his compassion.

Weeping beside the road, the two daughters heard their father say: "Daughters, take care of my grandchildren." These were his final words of parting. They saw him off, they saw him off as far as prison, bound as he was in a rope three inches thick for having committed a crime.

Then the two daughters turned and went back to their own home, where they knelt before their mother: "The summons today concerned our father, who has been imprisoned forever for the crime of having been the instigator of the appeal made en masse directly to the authorities. We have taken our final parting from him. Out of the lord's compassionate mercy, we were allowed to exchange words of farewell there before the prison. Now we have returned home in tears."

When they had thus reported to their mother what had happened, her face showed that she was truly the wife of her husband. "We must maintain the family," was all she said as she tried to soothe her children.

Her daughter O-Shima made up her mind what she was going to do, tightened her obi, and made a pilgrimage to the shrine. In the audience room for the god,[18] she knelt down.

"I have a petition to make, O god of our family. Please grant my prayer concerning my father, who has been imprisoned forever for the crime of having made an appeal en masse directly to the authorities. In return, even if I find a man to love, I will keep him company without doing anything that pollutes my body or corrupts my prayers. I will give up tobacco, and I will not drink sake. These three things will I abstain from to show my sincerity in making this plea. I earnestly entreat you, Ò goddess of mercy, to grant that he return to our village."

Night after night at dusk she made her pilgrimage. The house where she lived became a house of widows. She put on a chastity belt. In the innermost recesses of her heart, she set up a prohibition saying, "Men forbidden," but none of this showed in her face. For many long months and days, members of the neighborhood youth association tried to get her to open up by sticking their hands in her robe, but she sent them home with red faces.

Her friends jested: "Isn't it ridiculous, yes really ridiculous that our lady O-Shima has put on a chastity belt in the bloom of her youth." Nevertheless, O-Shima continued to live as though she had not heard their idle gossip. Then one night she too had the dream related in this story.

One day the family was gathered together discussing how Heiroku from Komi in Ōba had been the instigator in the west for the appeal made en masse directly to the authorities. Since he had committed the same crime as Naokichi, he too was bound and put in prison.

Then someone said: "Our father was the instigator of the riot in the east, and Heiroku was the instigator of the riot in the west. Rumor has it that he is young, but still he showed great ingenuity. How strange it is that a rumor and the story told in a dream should match so well."

After thinking for awhile, the daughter O-Shima spoke: "He may have been resourceful as the leader of the riot, but he also is a source of strength for our father who has no one to rely on while he is in prison. They live together in harmony." There is good reason why in her heart she had secretly joined her hands together in making her pitch. Gradually she pulled herself together.

"Our dear father is fifty-six years old, he had already retired, and he is no longer responsible for looking after the family. Heiroku is but thirty-eight in the prime of his manhood. Indeed, he is constantly tormented by thoughts of what he should be doing for his parents, wife, and children to maintain his house. Surely all of you have considered this in the innermost recesses of your thoughts."

Straightening herself up, she continued through her tears: "I beg of you please to forgive me for having said nothing about my secret visits to the prison." How pitifully did she apologize.

According to another account, the daughter O-Shima gradually pulled herself together. "Everyone, I beg of you please to listen carefully to what I have to say. It is to be expected that both of them are being patient because I sent word to them in prison that, ashamed though I am of this impure woman's body, I have nevertheless dared to remonstrate with the gods and Buddhas in offering up a fervent prayer. Sooner or later they will be released as a sign my prayers have been heard."

Gradually 1867 drew to a close, and without much happening, the year ended. For the celebrations on the first day of the new year 1868, people followed the customs of Yamato, the land of Japan, with plants symbolizing gold and silver, good fortune and long life. Flowers blossomed everywhere in the tranquility of spring.

"No one in this world knows what I feel in my heart." While O-Shima was repeating this to herself, the winds of rumor brought her the news that her father had fallen ill in prison. She whose heart was deeply imbued with filial piety thought up a plan. Then, with her whole being firmly resolved on a course of action, she knelt before her mother.

"Mother, you have discerned with the wisdom of your years that I need to talk to you. Until now I had hesitated to make an appeal which might harm you for that would be to show a lack of filial piety, but I must do something. I beg of you to let me appeal for an exemption to the order that we never communicate with my father again in this life. If you will be pleased to grant my request, I plan to petition the government office to take away my status as a woman and substitute me for the life imprisonment to which they have subjected my father who has no one else to rely on. This is what I have made up my mind to do. I beg of you, please let me do it."

Hearing these words, the elder sister said: "Younger sister, you were raised as the natural child of both our mother and father. I more than you have an obligation to our honored father. My duty to repay this obligation is very important to me, and I ask you, my sister O-Shima, to do your work here at home looking after our mother who has no one else to rely on." Thus O-Kuma demonstrated the strength of her resolve.

These were two remarkable women. The younger sister spoke:

Chapter Five

"Elder sister, are you not one of our parents' children? For you as the eldest to leave the other children behind and not do everything you can to help our mother would mean that what you think of as filial piety would become unfilial. Please don't do it, O elder sister."

While they were arguing back and forth, their elder brother Bōji came in. "This is not a task for little girls. I am the one who will make the appeal."

The three of them were still disputing who would make the appeal when the head of the main house and headman of the village, a man of strong will, appeared and said, "The three of you should not be arguing like this. I have already decided on what we should do. Accompanied by the elder brother Bōji and the younger sister Shima, I will make an appeal to ask that the authorities decide whether they would prefer that the boy or the girl substitute for the father. After that, we shall see. The two of you should go make your preparations." With these parting remarks, the headman returned to his own home.

O-Shima immediately put on her outfit. Underneath she wore pristine white underwear of the type worn by people who depart this world for the next. Next to her skin she placed a dagger. For her outer garment she wore something to dazzle the eye. Her elder brother dressed himself in the same way before they went together to the headman's house.

For his clothing that day the headman wore a long, full, dark brown coat embroidered with his family crest. Indeed, accompanied by this pair he hardly looked like a headman at all, right down to the swords that he carried at his waist. O-Shima's girlish heart beat fast as they crossed the Arasaka Pass, hurrying along the road to reach the government office even sooner than they had anticipated.

Having come on a matter of considerable urgency, the two children threw themselves on their knees in the wide garden before the entry way inside the government compound. The headman placed his hands together and spoke:

"The matter on which I have come to entreat the honorable officials concerns the illness of Naokichi, who was ordered into life imprisonment for the crime of having been the instigator of the beggars' riot. We have received word that his condition has gradually become very grave indeed. Having found it impossible to ignore the principle of filial piety, his son Bōji and his younger daughter Shima would like to be substituted for their father. They implore you to allow them to be put in prison.

"I must humbly report that they were unacquainted with the regulations of this government office," he continued. "In my own poor house I tried to explain how things are, but they refused to listen to me at all. They merely insisted that they felt compelled to nurse their father even if only for a single day. In all deference I entreat you to be understanding concerning what I have just said."

"We will have to ask for instructions. Wait here a moment." With these orders, the officials shut them up in the long shed.

After they had waited for awhile, they were summoned into the presence of higher officials. The elder brother Bōji was ordered placed in prison, and the daughter Shima was made to go back to the inn where government supplicants stayed. Indeed O-Shima's determination to be filial, which had driven her to make the appeal, caused a change in governmental regulations rarely seen even in ancient times. For someone condemned to life imprisonment to be released is unheard of, but it happened here.

"Tomorrow our father will return home." All the villagers bought refreshments and waited to receive him. His relatives and people from the entire community association went out to greet him. Everyone on the road made merry. Because Naokichi was sick, however, he returned home riding in a palanquin.

Because he was so sick, his family massaged him on all sides. They even called a doctor to take care of him. Nothing was neglected in the efforts made to nurse him, but he was enticed away by the inescapable evanescent wind. After seven days of nursing, the fifty-seven years of his life disappeared like the dew in a single morning.

Through the guidance of the chief priest at Shinfuku-ji, the parish temple for his village, he was given the posthumous name of Riyū Shōdō Shinshi [the gentleman who believes in the correct way for the separation from grief].[19] The cremation and burial were carried out with all due ceremony. His daughter O-Shima resolved to become a nun so that she could perform Buddhist memorial services to bring him instant enlightenment and a place in Nirvana. For all future generations, she left this "Tale Told in a Dream of a Eulogy to Filial Piety."

A Later Report

Once the cremation and burial had been completed with all due ceremony, the members of the household and the relatives all collapsed where they were without thinking about what had happened or what the future would bring. Only the head of the main house and headman of the village thought about what should be done to secure the family succession. He opened the sliding paper doors to bring some light into the house, roused everyone, and had them clean the living room until everything was neat and tidy. In the meantime he established himself in the back room, where he had the maid O-Nami bring him some tea. He took it from her hand, and while he was drinking it, he even went so far as to light up his pipe. The smell of tobacco burning in his pipe tasted good even to the god of longevity. While he was puffing away, he received visits from each member of the household.

"It may sound like I'm just rambling on, but please calm yourselves and listen to what I have to say. Previously we received a poem from Naokichi while he was in Tsuyama that went like this:

Parents take good care of your children,
Children love your parents; parents love your grandchildren
And never part from each other.[20]

"This is what he wrote. Now Bōji feels a keen sense of duty toward his stepmother. The daughter O-Kuma feels the same way toward both her parents and also feels strongly obligated to her stepfather. Nevertheless, this brother and sister are no more related by blood than are strangers. Furthermore, it seems to me that your father himself has told his children to get married. For that reason, to read the last line of the poem as 'And never part from each other' implies without saying so that it is a phrase privately requesting someone to perform the role of go-between for the marriage. Based on this interpretation, I as your guardian will act as the go-between. If that is not what it means, please tell me now if any member of the household or any one of the relatives objects to what I have said."

Not one person among all the members of the household and all the relatives made any objection at all. They merely said, "It's all right with us," and the discussion ended.

"We should not do anything during this period of mourning," the headman continued. "When it comes time for the ceremonies to

212

be performed for the wedding rites, then I will serve as the go-between." That being all for the present, everyone returned to their own homes.

Slowly, slowly, the days and nights passed. In the middle of the fourth month, an urgent message arrived at the headman's office from the lord of the domain. When it was opened and read, it was found to say: "The brother and sister involved in this incident must come to the government office accompanied by everyone from their community association."

Everyone immediately made their preparations and set out. At the government office they were met by an agent, who took everyone involved together with the community association into the courtroom.

"It has reached our ears that you, brother and sister, have shown great filial piety toward your parents. Our lord has made up his mind to give you a monetary reward. For all ages this is a rare event. Now get out of here."

In accordance with the lord's orders, they received a reward. Then they returned to their own home accompanied by the headman. Together with the brother and sister, he promptly informed the members of the household of what had happened. Everyone was delighted. They talked for a long time, alternating tears and laughter.

While they were still carrying on, the headman bustled about acting as the go-between by getting rice cakes pounded and so forth. He had the bath heated, the family took baths, and they prepared a fine repast. In the meantime, the day quickly turned to night, so the headman returned to his own home.

The next day was the day for the Buddhist memorial service held on the forty-ninth day after death. The brother and sister combined the monetary rewards they had received from the lord to buy a mortuary tablet. For the memorial services held on the one hundredth day after death to be performed with all due ceremony, they welcomed the priest from their temple and summoned the headman, their relatives, the members of their community association, and their neighbors.

"We ask you please to perform the memorial service," they said, setting the mortuary tablet that they had purchased in front of the chief priest.

"Until today we have had to use a temporary mortuary tablet

made of unfinished wood because things happened so quickly, but now I would like to explain how we got the mortuary tablet we have placed before you," O-Shima said. "It came to our lord's attention that we had been deeply filial to our parents. Out of the reward he gave us, we have purchased this tablet. Would it not stand to reason that every day we should first worship our lord and then worship our father? But maybe this is just something that only a foolish and complaining woman would say."

After she had made her statement, the priest merely replied, "I see, I see."

Since none of the other people had anything else to say, the priest took up the mortuary tablet, copied on it Naokichi's posthumous Buddhist name, and then set it back down in front of the statue of the Buddha. After he had finished reciting the sutras for enshrining a newly made mortuary tablet, everyone went together to make a pilgrimage to the grave. The chief priest returned to his temple immediately thereafter. Everyone else went back home too.

A little later the head of the main family who was also the village headman appeared. He plopped down and summoned to him everyone who had been involved in the incident.

"The period of mourning has been completed with all due ceremony, and the Buddhist memorial services have been performed for the one hundredth day anniversary of the death. Since these have all been taken care of, we should now break our fast. Let's have some refreshments brought in for this auspicious occasion. Not to change the subject, but there is something else I want to talk to you about. Look everybody, how would it be if we had those marriage rites performed that we've agreed on?"

The entire group and all the members of the household cheered, "Yes, then we'll have a successor."

"Now that my mind has been set at rest, make preparations for the ceremony."

As soon as he had said that, people passed out the three treasures of a farmer—the sake cups, the sake bottles, and the side dishes—and even some chopsticks. Nothing was lacking. For her part, the mother O-Chiyo placed the three treasures of a farmer right in front of the go-between.

"Our headman, we're relying on you," she said and went right back into the kitchen.

At the signal made with all good grace by the headman, the peasants' marriage ceremony got well underway, like the turning of a stone mortar to grind grain. Then the headman called out: "Bōji, come here. O-Kuma, come here." The members of the household all lined up together. The couple passed the cups of sake back and forth. People toasted them with sake, wishing them one thousand years of happiness. Joyful voices rose everywhere. O-Kuma performed the tea ceremony. This auspicious marriage ceremony came to an end, with voices singing the Noh song Takasago.[21]

Through the steadfast efforts of the headman, a successor was found who would continue the house for one hundred thousand years, and guardians remained who would look after it forever.

Unworthy though I am, I have repolished this old mirror.
I look to see if it reflects my heart.

Author

Copied by Yūraku.

Rereading Peasant Histories of Peasant Uprisings

T O BEGIN WITH THE STORY OF Sakura Sōgorō who died in the mid-seventeenth century and to end with an account of the 1866 beggars' riot in Tsuyama is to impose a false chronology on the texts for this history of peasant uprisings. For the modern reader, the events represented here are linked in a temporal sequence unknown and unknowable through written narrative to the Japanese peasants directly involved in them. From a strictly textual point of view, the 1726 uprising described in "A Record of How the Four Orders of People in Mimasaka Ran Riot," ought to come first; last should come "A Thousand Spears at Kitsunezuka," about the 1764 post station riot; the Sōgorō story should fall somewhere between. To select and arrange these histories according to the order of the events they narrate or even to analyze them according to the sequence of textual production is thus an artifact of our present-day understanding.

These histories of peasant uprisings were written to recall something not present—disruptions of the social order already receding into memory. For local historians desirous of discovering an oppositional consciousness to ruling authorities that precedes the modern period, it is sufficient that these histories exist. For the most part the analysis of their content has focused on "peeling away the fictive elements" to get at the "real facts"[1] in order to show that the struggle for the sake of the community has a noble pedigree. The immediacy of this political purpose is largely lost on a foreign audience. While respecting the tradition of resistance to authority constructed by Japanese scholars, I have sought the significance of these texts at a different level. I wish to interpret them in ways meaningful to people like myself, yet retain a consciousness of the demonstrable difference between early modern Japan and today.

It is important to remain conscious of difference while reading these histories of peasant uprisings. Like all narrative discourse, they possess the same temporal structure as the historical events they represent. People everywhere seem to feel a need to give meaningful shape to the raw material of experience beyond its character as mere sequence. On the constant flux of existence they impose a beginning, a middle, and an end. They exclude some events, for example, the specific details of how the poor organize protest, and overemphasize others, perhaps exaggerating the autonomy of the leaders, binding together disparate elements, and bringing order to disorder through description in such a way as to moralize these events or make them exemplary. The construction of narrative is indeed "a universal cultural activity."[2] For that reason, we seemingly have less trouble understanding a text that presents a history of a peasant uprising than understanding a haiku or the principles of Zen Buddhism. It is not hard to uncover the moral to these histories, for rather than appeal to a notion of objectivity in crafting their narratives, the authors in rural Japan believed in making their aims explicit, unsympathetic though they may be to modern readers seeking evidence of revolutionary destructiveness.

Histories of peasant uprisings are plain tales. They derive their force from repetitions of images and language and other mnemonic devices, not from the skillful display of wit. They rely on the terms of everyday life, especially those found in religion and administration. They develop not richly imaginative phrases but summon those hackneyed through overuse. These modes of description are as important as the objects described. They indicate that what the audience found important was not originality but a series of familiar subtexts. At the same time, it is clear that the form determined the content. Out of the flux of existence that encompassed events of protest, writing histories imposed a notion of sequenciality. The act of writing forced the writers to select what they would discuss according to the dictates of logic and causality. Writing itself made sense out of protest.

Writing narratives is both the most logical and the most satisfying way to represent past events, but its meaning is not self-evident. Narrative is "especially well suited to the production of notions of continuity, wholeness, closure . . . that every 'civilized' society wishes to see itself as incarnating, against the chaos of a merely 'natural' way of life."[3] On another level, narrative is necessary because it transforms crude existence into art, art not merely as entertainment but as a "symbolic gateway" to the world of deities and spirits, making them tangible and visible. This is especially true of what Plutschow calls ritual literature, often written anonymously, which suggests that it originated not so much with the individual, creative artist, but with a group.[4] Histories of social disorder emerged from an exchange among different strata within the peasantry. Although the people who wrote them came from the landholding if not the landlord sector, and their accounts tell about obedience to the moral code of filial piety that exemplifies what they saw as the ordering principle of society, voices that think otherwise can never be completely erased from the text. These histories are fraught with discontinuities, gaps, and lacunae where traces of what has been excluded can be sought. These exclusions also mean that total intelligibility is an illusion, and that no set of texts, including the one constructed here, reveals its world completely. The analysis must give due weight to the authorial voice that constructed them; at the same time, however, to show the different messages that the texts emit and to decode them using non-narrative means, the analysis must encompass what has been left out.

Peasant Heroes

It is well to remember, as Palmer has said, that in precapitalist societies, "class is less of a presence, socially and economically, and more of a metaphor encompassing a range of tensions, antagonisms, and conflicts," and so it is with the texts presented here.[5] Taking over war tales for the purpose of talking about peasant uprisings transforms the nature of the tales. Like other categories of literature, the genre is fluid; what is meant in the context of medieval warrior society changes radically in peasant society. Stephen Greenblatt has pointed out that the boundaries of literature are "contested, endlessly renegotiated, and permeable."[6] These contestations and negotiations are all social insofar as they involve the efforts of subordinate as well as dominant classes. To contextualize his argument in the specific case of Tokugawa Japan, I argue that histories such as "A Record of How the Four Orders of People in Mimasaka Ran Riot" and "A Thousand Spears at Kitsunezuka" draw on the heroic epics of an earlier time, but in so doing, they reconstitute and challenge the social status of the hero.

Histories of peasant uprisings with unpeasantlike, conventional heroes tend to come earlier rather than later in the Tokugawa period. "A Record of How the Four Orders of People in Mimasaka Ran Riot" can be read as an example of the transition between the men with aristocratic pretensions that fill the medieval war tales and the full-blown peasant hero. Tokuemon is neither a warrior nor a peasant, but a man whose identity confuses the boundaries between both. In later tales, this obfuscation becomes less necessary. Most men who lead peasant uprisings make no bones about their peasant identities. What they do instead is claim a noble lineage, like Sōgorō, whose ancestor was Taira no Masakado, a hero in eastern Japan who tried to overthrow the emperor in 940. The men whom the author of "A Thousand Spears at Kitsunezuka" depicts as opposing the conspiracy of freight transporters have longstanding connections with the shōgun. The hero of "The Record of the Watanabe Doheiji Riot," written about an attack on sake brewers in 1787, alleges descent from a follower of Hōjō Ujimasa (1538–90), a general defeated in the strife-torn sixteenth century. By the end of the Tokugawa period, however, the social status of the heroes apparently begins to devolve still further. On the Kabuki stage in urban areas, bandits and gangsters become the protagonists of choice; in the countryside, Naokichi of Tsuyama, a wastrel, a drunkard, and a womanizer, becomes the worthy recipient of his daughters' devotion.[7]

In reconstituting the status of the hero, the histories of peasant uprisings fundamentally alter the heroic genre of the war tales. Greenblatt's article on murdering peasants shows how peasant rebellion, in this case the German Peasants' War of 1524, was represented by members of the class who suppressed it.[8] Paradoxical meanings underlay their representations, however, because for the nobility to remain noble and retain a sense of honor, it had to have a noble foe which the peasants definitely were not. The perspective found in these Japanese histories of peasant uprisings is different. Here the peasants are as often the subject as the object of the murdering, a reversal that calls into question the whole notion of honor. For Sakura Sōgorō, who had to watch his children die before his very eyes, honor did not acrue to the officials who ordered his death. It did not abide with him either, for those called the "honorable peasants" *(onbyakushō)* achieved their status through paying taxes, not resisting authority.[9] When honor no longer acrues to heroes, the meaning of each term becomes problematical. The headman Hyōnai was superior to the warriors, but the author of "A Thousand Spears at Kitsunezuka" hardly saw him as someone to be emulated.

One meaning of the stories about heroes lies in the extreme penalties they suffered in punishment. Greenblatt has suggested that at particular historical moments, the ruling elite conjures images of repression so harsh that they can double as images of protest.[10] Commoners in Japan performed this trick for themselves. According to "A Record of How the Four Orders of People in Mimasaka Ran Riot," the authorities dragged their prisoners out to be executed without acceding to any of the peasants' demands. In return, Tokuemon cursed his tormenters, expressing his unrepentant hatred of the system by slandering its officials. Later texts saw peasants appropriate images of repression for their own purposes. Without denying the harshness of the penalty, they juxtaposed it to its reward—the abatement of heavy taxes. In "A Tale in a Dream of a Eulogy to Filial Piety," written as the Tokugawa regime collapsed, repression and protest were ironically resolved in representations of conciliation between the peasants and their rulers.

A close reading of these texts suggests that heroes meant different things to different strata of the peasantry. Let us leave aside Tokuemon, a transitional figure whose character owes much to the circumstances of his creation. The male leaders who dominate the other narratives appear at different moments in the story, assume their role more or less willingly, and speak to different assumptions regarding the importance of social activism. In "A Tale of a Dream from the Fox Woman Plain," the rioters and their communities are seemingly united in a harmonious resolve to eschew unnecessary violence, and the deeds done by the leaders almost completely disappear. In chapters 3 and 5, Hyōnai and Naokichi appear almost as an afterthought, their presence made necessary by the authors' unspoken supposition that ordinary peasants were incapable of organizing themselves. As Yokoyama has pointed out, assimilating the deeds of the peasant masses to one man can indeed make protest less meaningful.[11] Nevertheless, a distinction can be drawn between Hyōnai and Sōgorō. Both were village headmen, but Sōgorō was much more a man of the people. Hyōnai spoke to the aspirations of the rural elite; Sōgorō reminded everyone of the nobility of sacrifice for the community.

The Social Dimension of Meaning

In analyzing peasant histories of peasant uprisings, the ultimate goal is to understand what people thought—their assumptions and values, their definition of the central issues of family, sexual activity, alliance formation and its obverse, the fear of strangers—and how these changed over time. These texts articulate the perceptions of different groups: first the group telling the stories, the sources only vaguely identified in the text; next and foremost, the group writing or copying them; and finally the audience that reads or hears them. As David Warren Sabean has said, "What is common in community is not shared values or common understanding so much as the fact that members of a community are engaged in the same argument, . . . the same discourse, in which alternative strategies, misunderstandings, conflicting goals, and values are threshed out."[12] The presence of these diverse groups means that embedded in the texts are subordinated voices and plural views of the past that further complicate their social function.

Before taking on the subordinated voices within the texts, let us define the dominant voice, its concerns, and its values. It is masculine and self-important; like all peasants in this society, it fears dearth and hates greed. It is obsessed with survival, but it ties survival to making and keeping money and to a commitment to the continuity of the family. The local notables who speak with this voice find themselves trapped in an ambiguous position between their overwhelming importance to rural society and their political powerlessness vis-à-vis the policymakers and samurai administrators. In their writings, this ambiguity appears in an always uncomfortable tension between dominance over local society and submission to the ruling authorities. At the same time, however, the men who see themselves as the natural leaders of rural society share many of its emotions.

The histories of peasant uprisings expose the enmities, jealousies, and conflicts of interest that run through peasant society. Even if from the same economic class, strangers are feared. Instead of joining in the attack, the poor rally to the aid of local leaders who both protect and exploit them. The wealthy do not hesitate to betray each other. In "A Thousand Spears at Kitsunezuka," Gonzaemon, one of the men accused of conspiring to increase the number of villages supplying porters, treacherously informs the authorities that Sanzaemon from Mihonoya has given aid and assistance to the rioters. As in Germany, where "solidarity with one's fellows extends only so far as it is a question of excluding the outsider," in Japan, villages on the plain might see their neighbors in the mountains as enemies. In both countries "a practical plan of action based on a perception of a link between events in the everyday life of the village and more inclusive political and social structures remains elusive."[13]

Based on the knowledge that came in the form of generally received notions, rumors, reports, and opinions which then had to be processed, the fluctuating and ambiguous emotional boundaries to Japanese peasant communities shifted with the influx of information. For this reason, alliances might stretch a surprising distance and encompass thousands of peasants, or they might end abruptly where the uprising outran the manifestos and reports that justified its actions. These boundaries sometimes but not always excluded priests and even the gods themselves. Priests were welcomed and respected for their piety and erudition, but they were denounced for their avarice. They might be viewed as ambivalent, perhaps even amoral, beings whose help was always arbitrary. The gods were likewise. In "A Thousand Spears at Kitsunezuka," it was a god who identified evildoers, but he also encouraged the peasants to perform acts of destruction later severely criticized. The guidance he gave the rioters became a curse upon their arrest.

European folktales taught peasants that the world is harsh, dangerous, arbitrary, and amoral. It is folly to expect anything more than cruelty from a cruel social order. Calamities are inscrutable and inexorable. No one can be certain that virtue will be rewarded.[14] Instead of positing some higher meaning to existence, folktales simply demonstrate that life is nasty, brutish, and short. This attitude is seldom exposed in histories of peasant uprisings, not because the poor would have rejected it but because the men who wrote these histories had the wherewithal to take a more benign view of the world. They depicted brutality, but they undercut it with representations of people who acted according to the moral code of benevolence and filial piety. Unlike the audience for folktales, the group concerned with writing these histories aspired, perhaps, to standards of behavior that mitigated when they did not entirely alleviate the worst conflicts between human beings.

The producers of these histories abhorred the very deeds they uneasily centered in their narratives: violence, the destruction of property, and the taking of life. Unlike the war tales, histories of peasant uprisings seldom describe heroic deaths in battle. Even in "A Record of How the Four Orders of People in Mimasaka Ran Riot," the clash of swords ends ignominiously in the capture of the uprising leaders. The only people who die are the unnamed masses. Enthusiastic descriptions of violence often mark oral narratives, but in "A Tale of a Dream from the Fox Woman Plain," scenes of destruction are abbreviated almost to the point of disappearing from the text.

There is, nevertheless, an undercurrent of recognition that violence is sometimes necessary, a recognition which gives rise to conflicting impulses toward speech and reticence. We know from other documents generated by peasant uprisings that they tended to become more violent over time, especially after 1750. Japanese historians have pointed to a breakdown in communal bonds; the poor, no longer trusting in the rich and aware that their misery had a human agency, attacked their neighbors accused of having wronged them. In these histories, however, we see two contradictory attitutes: one that abhorred violence, held most probably by those most likely to be its targets, and another that celebrated its cleansing properties. In "A Thousand Spears at Kitsunezuka," the legitimacy of violence was recognized even as it was condemned. The local historian Sasaki Kyōichi reported he heard stories of the Nanbu Sanhei uprising of 1853 from his grandmother, but when he asked people in his community about the incident, they said, "Our ancestors did a bad thing a long time ago, and we don't talk about it."[15] Perhaps because she was marginalized by society, a woman could speak more freely than the men constituted at its center. Perhaps too, men not directly involved in the events or families so poor that they had no property to protect would have found it easier to speak what was otherwise left unspoken.

Family and Community

The plurality of voices within the peasantry also gave different weights to the family and community. Robert Muchembled has demonstrated that in some parts of France before 1750, the family was void of emotional and affective content: "It was merely a shield against pressing dangers, kinship was more important than conjugal relations, and what was essential in social life took place outside the conjugal nucleus."[16] A similar conception of the family may have been prevalent among the poor peasants in Japan, who supported community organizations including the village youth group, but it gradually died out in those families that produced histories of peasant uprisings. In "A Record of How the Four Orders of People in Mimasaka Ran Riot," family honor was implicated in Higuchi Jirō's dilemma. Whether he obeyed his mother and continued to fight or disobeyed her to follow the dictates of filial piety, his primary concern was his reputation. Sakura Sōgorō was famous for sacrificing his family for his community, but the sacrifice was so clearly fraught with conflicting impulses toward family preservation versus the communal good that it justified his revenge against his lord. The later texts emphasize the preservation of the family as the most important concern a peasant can have. Less important are notions of family honor, and left unspoken is the conflict with poor peasants who could survive with or without their families only if they were protected by a common access to collective resources.

The conflict between family preservation and community requirements generates a tension that pervades the later texts, but they are reticent on the constituents of family formation. Rather than being structured externally through community sanctions or through the restrictive custom of arranged marriages, these families are formed internally along the nexus of parent and child, man and woman. Conjugal affection left implied in the story of Sakura Sōgorō is incorporated into the realm of human feelings in both "A Thousand Spears at Kitsunezuka" and "A Tale of a Dream from the Fox Woman Plain." Filial piety is emphasized in chapters 2, 3, and 5. In these texts, it valorizes a structure of relations in which, with few exceptions, both men and women appear in pairs of sexual opposites.[17]

This is an overly determined heterosexual and family-oriented world.[18] As such it stands in stark contrast to samurai traditions and practices and to the themes of illicit love developed in urban literature. In the *Taiheiki* from the fourteenth century, the dictates of filial piety and family honor concern men first and foremost. Sons fight to avenge their fathers; their mothers play a distinctly secondary role. Ruth Benedict pointed out that "homosexual indulgences are part of traditional 'human feelings.' In Old Japan these were the sanctioned pleasures of men of high status such as the samurai and the priests . . . it falls among those 'human feelings' about which moralistic attitudes are inappropriate."[19] When he was not describing the temptations of the pleasure quarters, the great novelist Ihara Saikaku (1642–93) wrote about the love of samurai men for boys, including one book translated as *The Great Mirror of Male Love*, but for a peasant to have appeared in his stories was so incongruous as to be inconceivable. A recent translator of Saikaku argues for "the cultural assumption that romantic love was to be found not in the institution of marriage but in the realm of prostitution," an assumption belied in "A Thousand Spears at Kitsunezuka" and one that exposes the gulf between urban and rural tastes.[20] Wealthy peasants occasionally took concubines, and peasants of every rank committed adultery, but these pursuits found no place in the histories of peasant uprisings. Nor were peasants incapable of same-sex bonding, otherwise the uprising composed entirely of males would have been impossible. In general, sacrifice for the other meant sacrifice for the community as a whole, not a retainer's sacrifice for the ruler or a friend's for a friend (both male-male). The community was privileged as the justification for protest, but what is valued in histories of peasant uprisings is the family in which women as well as men play a part.

An important undercurrent in these histories of peasant uprisings is a narration of both the social relationships between the sexes and the roles of women in this society. In what is almost a universal constant, "the dominant images of femininity are male fantasies" in which women "conform to the patriarchal standards imposed on them."[21] Thus women appear in their role of nurturing mother, and they are implicated in filial piety when they voice masculine concerns in urging their sons to fight for the family honor. Yet it is clear that women are not portrayed with "the same sympathy, variety, and depth as men," a lack which marginalizes them in these histories and exposes the invisible sexual politics of this literature. In the Western enduring myths of power, males are honorable, brave, and cunning, and we have seen many examples of these characteristics; women are beautiful, submissive, and treacherous.[22] Japanese peasants were suspicious of beauty; even the fox wife was described as a mature rather than an attractive woman. Neither in these histories nor in any of the others I have read, with the exception of "A Tea Canister in the Rain," does a woman appear as a villain. What gives these depictions of women interest is not a focus on the social relationships conducive to protest, but the concern for conjugal relations. In shifting their emphasis to examine the content of family life, the histories create a gap between topic and subject that allows a different voice to appear.

Allowing women to speak about love and to express sexual desire could easily be interpreted as making use of a stereotype to displace emotions felt by, but suppressed in, men.[23] Nevertheless, women had a significant role to play in maintaining the dyads constituting male-female relations. Unstated in "A Tale Told in a Dream of a Eulogy to Filial Piety" is the assumption that without the wife Chiyo to stay home and guard the house and without Kuma's agreement to marry her stepbrother, the family would have become extinct. "A Record of How the Four Orders of People in Mimasaka Ran Riot" implies that it was the widow who sought out Tokuemon's grandfather and enticed him to spend time with her. Her poem and those written by the fox wife expressed the emotional content of their relationships. By including these and other passionate statements such as that spoken by Hyōnai's wife, the histories refuse the opportunity to "institute themselves as fictive totalities, as organized, coherent, homogeneous, logical systems" that establish closure by excluding women.[24]

The differences in the ways women are depicted in these texts suggest changes in how male-female relationships were represented between the seventeenth and the nineteenth centuries and among different segments of the rural population. The wanton and aggressive widow in "A Record of How the Four Orders of People in Mimasaka Ran Riot" constituted a fitting introduction to a hero who himself belonged to neither the ruling class nor the peasantry. Women found in the later texts were different; although they seldom received the dignity of a name, they were embedded in the family relations that defined their role in society. Yet here too contradictory impulses were at work. I have already argued that the creators of Hyōnai were among the most erudite and elite of the peasant population. Hyōnai's wife as well had the luxury to consider only her own feelings. In contrast, all the other women were mothers. The portraits of Sōgorō's and Naokichi's wives and the fox wife ironically imply the world of the hardworking peasant woman, who nurtures her children and helps her husband.

Insofar as these texts figure the social relationships between the sexes, they emphasize courtship, marriage, and parenthood.[25] If they are in some sense normative and describe social life as it ought to be lived rather than imitating actual experience, then within them lies a paradox. "A Tale Told in a Dream of a Eulogy to Filial Piety" ascribes impossible virtues to two filial daughters, confining them in a narrow and remarkably circumscribing realm of behavior, but possession of these virtues also provides the daughters with the justification to take action. In chapters 2 and 4, love allows women to break the boundaries of social conventions, to pursue the men they want, and to give voice to private human emotions. In this world, and it must be confined to the dominant group of local intellectuals and wealthy landholding peasants, conjugal togetherness has apparently come to be valued for itself.

Emmanuel LeRoy Ladurie has pointed out that male writers see only half of the world; they ignore women's concerns and problems. Some aspects of women's experiences are reconstituted and absorbed, but most are disqualified from the constructed field of public relevance.[26] In histories of peasant uprisings as well, men dominate the production of meaning, but women nonetheless are not reduced to complete silence. "A Tale Told in a Dream of a Eulogy to Filial Piety" encompasses a theme that goes against the grain of the main argument. Almost as an aside, as a point not to be taken seriously, this text makes problematic the relationship between unmarried daughters and the village youth group to raise the issue of a woman's control of her own body. Despite a stratified society in which authority is everywhere invested in men, Shima asserts her intention to restrict the access to her person. In so doing, she exposes private values and questions of power over women that implicate the ultimately political nature of these texts.

Insofar as they depict one view of society to the exclusion of others and reinforce one set of values and attitudes rather than another, these texts make political statements, though the clearest statements concern the immediate arena of peasant society and not the wider world. The argument could also be made that they transcend everyday life in their concern with the universal human values of honor and self-sacrifice, as long as those values are understood to have a distinctly Japanese cultural context and to be biased in the direction of masculine interests. In addition, the contrast between what scholars today think actually happened, the objective reality of peasant protest, and the subjective reality of peasant revolt inscribed in these texts could be analyzed to show how these histories gave sense and meaning to the world as tools in the formation of a revolutionary socialist consciousness. By examining what they call into question, however, I read in them an expression of the issues inscribed in village discourse that signals the need for social reform.[27]

Let us recall a curious section in "The Sakura Sōgorō Story" where peasants crucify a domanial official. This episode can be read on several levels. It provides a parallel to the violence done to Sōgorō at the end of the story. It perhaps represents the peasants' deep-seated longing for revenge for the real and imagined injuries suffered at the hands of their betters. Killing officials was a common peasant fantasy. It appears in other histories of peasant uprisings and also in the stories of the two sisters from Adachi who avenged their father's murder. Like the legends of the mountain where the aged are abandoned (Obasuteyama), it demonstrates the power of the imagination to transform the fear of dearth and feelings of resentment into tales of horror. On another level this episode allows a glimpse of the nineteenth-century social reality in which insolence to officials had become an ongoing problem for the ruling class. By bringing the official down to the level of the populace, it demonstrates that the samurai were not a separate order of beings but men who bled and died just like their social inferiors.

Cautiously and with a good deal of subterfuge, these texts question the relationship between peasants and officials. One message they emit is the desire to resolve doubts regarding the ability of rulers to rule. Neither "A Record of How the Four Orders of People in Mimasaka Ran Riot" nor "A Thousand Spears at Kitsunezuka" ends with the restoration of benevolent government and the re-creation of the category of honorable peasant. Officials are castigated for being greedy and inept. Yet for all the criticism of domanial and bakufu policies and officials, the will to knowledge that informs these texts is curiously silent concerning its own aims. Only a statement such as the assertion that the headman Hyōnai was superior to the warriors suggests that the goal was to center peasant leaders in a state that allowed them the autonomy to run their family enterprises and their villages according to the principles, in Western terms, of enlightened self-interest.

The silence at the center of these texts is political. Unlike the dominant literary discourse of the time which insisted on the absolute separation of literature, politics, and ideology, histories of peasant uprisings invoked matters of state in ways that Saikaku's *Five Women Who Loved Love* do not. Nevertheless, metaphors of natural disasters deny autonomous action and politicality to the peasants; individual officials may be criticized, but issues of system are never raised. Shaped by both dominant and oppositional ideological strategies which they variously affirm and contest, these texts partially expose the power cloaked by the authority of Tokugawa rule, but they conceal the place of peasants in making changes.

The discourse enscribed in the nineteenth-century texts also leaves unspoken the place of the peasant leaders in their communities. If the men who led peasant uprisings, themselves traditionally village headmen, were not to be emulated, what then was the village official to do? On what basis was he to command the allegiance of the peasants who praised Sōgorō because he was willing to sacrifice his interests for theirs? Yet insofar as this discourse was the site of contestations, providing the terms for peasants to talk and disagree with each other, it also limited what could be said about the issue that concerned them the most—the struggle for survival within the village itself, which could only be expressed in the kind of language that cloaked competition in the guise of harmony. The stakes in constituting a narrative discourse were indeed high; involved was nothing less than control over the definition of not just extraordinary events but daily life itself.

Histories of peasant uprisings continue to be written in modern Japan, but they differ radically from the texts translated here. Those composed by contemporary scholars emphasize the structural forces at work, the class contradictions and antagonisms, the impersonal trends and processes that inhibited the peasants' ability to make lasting changes. Those written for a popular audience usually center peasant martyrs, giving a face to the men involved even in large-scale protests, describing them in greater and more personal detail, and permitting them self-awareness. Descriptions of nature fill many pages. The plots are fitted with a climax, the participants engage in heated dialogues, and the passionate avowels of love spoken by women are constrained within the confines of family duty when they are not completely absent. Missing from these texts is a sense of the complex interaction between this world and the next. Most dismiss as superstition the power of angry spirits or treat it as a psychological problem.[28] The texts are important for what they say about how people today recall their past to address concerns in the present, but both in form and content they represent a different reality from their textual ancestors.

Neither a strictly Marxist reading which decries the lack of a class consciousness nor a solely feminist reading which denies them a concern with gender issues can do justice to these texts. Nevertheless, both are valuable for sensitizing the reader to the presence of male power and class power. Using these tools and others fashioned through my encounters with critical theory, historiography, and Japanese history, I have crafted ways of reading these texts. I invite my readers to try their own.

Notes

Introduction

1. Herbert Bix gives the number three thousand for all incidents excluding legal appeals, but he omits the village disturbances which totaled almost twenty-five hundred between 1700 and 1870. See *Peasant Protest in Japan, 1590–1884* (New Haven: Yale University Press, 1986), xxi; and Anne Walthall, *Social Protest and Popular Culture in Eighteenth-Century Japan* (Tucson: University of Arizona Press, 1986), 96. For a graphic representation of where the most significant uprisings of the Tokugawa period took place, see the maps in Aoki Michio, Irumada Nobuo, Kurokawa Naonori, Satō Kazuhiko, Satō Shigerō, Fukaya Katsumi, Minegishi Sumio, and Yamada Tadao, eds., *Kōza ikki*, vol. 2: *Ikki no rekishi* (Tokyo: Tokyo Daigaku Shuppan Kai, 1981), 385–87.

2. James Clifford, *The Predicament of Culture: Twentieth-Century Ethnography, Literature, and Art* (Cambridge: Harvard University Press, 1988), esp. 46, 51, 53.

3. Bryan D. Palmer, *Descent into Discourse: The Reification of Language and the Writing of Social History* (Philadelphia: Temple University Press, 1990), 40, 188.

4. Aron Gurevich, *Medieval Popular Culture: Problems of Belief and Perception*, trans. Janos M. Bok and Paul A. Hollingsworth (New York: Cambridge University Press, 1988), 2–3.

5. Fukaya Katsumi has defined the four central criteria of the status system: (1) It relied on an inherited social division of labor based on the concept of service *(yaku)* to the state; (2) it established vertical relationships within each status as well as between statuses, relationships marked by the opposing attitudes of respect and scorn; (3) it was used in an effort to perfect a thoroughgoing control over the personality of the ruled; (4) it provided the ruling class with an extra-economic means of coercion. "Kinsei-shi kenkyū to mibun," *Rekishi hyōron*, no. 369 (January 1981): 50.

6. James W. White, "State Growth and Popular Protest in Tokugawa Japan," *Journal of Japanese Studies* 14.1 (Winter 1988): 1–25.

7. The lunar cycle is useful for agriculture because it helps peasants ascertain when to plant their fields, but it does not quite fit the passage of time marked by the sun. Every few years an extra month would have to be inserted, called an intercalary month. I have used the Japanese numbering system for the months, but the reader should be aware that the first month marked the beginning of spring. Era names have also been retained, but their inclusive dates have been incorporated in the text for the benefit of readers for whom Tenshō may not conjure the period of time between 1573 and 1592.

8. This kind of personification is a common occurrence in early modern societies. Robert Darnton has pointed out that in prerevolutionary France, people outside the court saw politics as a kind of nonparticipant sport involving villains and heroes but no issues: "Politics was living folklore." *The Literary Underground of the Old Regime* (Cambridge: Harvard University Press, 1982), 203–4.

9. Hilton L. Root, *Peasants and King in Burgundy: Agrarian Foundations of French Absolutism* (Berkeley: University of California Press, 1987), 176.

10. Thomas C. Smith, *The Agrarian Origins of Modern Japan* (Stanford: Stanford University Press, 1959), 172.

11. David Warren Sabean, *Power in the Blood: Popular Culture and Village Discourse in Early Modern Germany* (New York: Cambridge University Press, 1984), 18.

12. Bix points out that in Tsuyama on the eve of the 1726 uprising, tribute rates had risen to almost 70 percent of the harvest. *Peasant Protest in Japan*, 13.

13. Susan B. Hanley and Kozo Yamamura, *Economic and Demographic Change in Preindustrial Japan, 1600–1868* (Princeton: Princeton University Press, 1977), 342.

14. Philip C. Brown, "The Mismeasure of Land: Land Surveying in the Tokugawa Period," *Monumenta Nipponica* 42.2 (Summer 1987): 115–55.

15. William W. Kelly, *Deference and Defiance in Nineteenth-Century Japan* (Princeton: Princeton University Press, 1985), 42–43.

16. Sabean, *Power in the Blood*, 5.

17. Root, *Peasants and King in Burgundy*, 10. In Japan, participation in village assemblies was limited to the *honbyakushō*, making it even more likely that the spokesmen for the community represented the interests of the landholders.

18. Watanabe Takashi's analysis of one rich peasant family shows that they owned a city block in Edo between 1795 and 1819 on which they built

twenty rental units. "Kinsei no Edo to Kantō nōson," *Ronshū kinsei*, no. 9 (December 1984): 1–23.

19. Thomas C. Smith, *Native Sources of Japanese Industrialization, 1750–1920* (Berkeley: University of California Press, 1988), 15–49.

20. Root, *Peasants and King in Burgundy*, 10.

21. In a long and intriguing text on the social and economic problems suffered in Higo around 1800, the anticlericalism of the rich peasants is quite evident. They even mocked the gods, to the horror of the poor. Heinrich Martin Reinfried, the translator, assumes that the text was written by an official whose low rank blurred the distinction between peasant and samurai. *The Tale of Nisuke: Peasant and Authorities in Higo around 1800* (Wiesbaden: Otto Harrassowitz, 1978), 315, 329.

22. Katsumata Shizuo, *Ikki* (Tokyo: Iwanami Shoten, 1982), 22–23. Gatherings at shrines could also be interpreted as an attempt "to represent not in texts or institutions but rather in a dramatic gesture" the replacement of political by religious authority. Other "motives" behind the act would include a search for a large area capable of holding a crowd and the need for a central and a well-known location. As J. Victor Koschmann has pointed out, however, "political, economic, and social considerations do not affect symbolic meaning." "Action as Text: Ideology in the Tengu Insurrection," in Tetsuo Najita and J. Victor Koschmann, eds., *Conflict in Modern Japanese History: The Neglected Tradition* (Princeton: Princeton University Press, 1982), 99.

23. Aron Gurevich has pointed out that this was true for medieval Europe as well, where traditional magic and Christianity blended together in syncretic practice. *Medieval Popular Culture*, 91, 220. For a history of how Buddhism was assimilated to Shintō see H. E. Plutschow, *Chaos and Cosmos: Ritual in Early and Medieval Japanese Literature* (Leiden: E. J. Brill, 1990), 148–51.

24. Robert Muchembled opposed this worldview to Christian Manichaeism, a notion inconceivable to Japanese of whatever status. *Popular Culture and Elite Culture in France, 1400–1750*, trans. Lydia Cochrane (Baton Rouge: Louisiana University Press, 1985), 222.

25. This characterization of religious consciousness was formulated by Shibata Minoru in 1964 and quoted in Miyata Noboru, *Ikigami shinkō: Hito o kami ni matsuru shūzoku* (Tokyo: Hanawa Shobō, 1970), 113.

26. Miyata Noboru, *Kinsei no hayarigami* (Tokyo: Hyōronsha, 1975), 140.

27. H. D. Harootunian, *Things Seen and Unseen: Discourse and Ideology in Tokugawa Nativism* (Chicago: University of Chicago Press, 1988), 49–50.

28. Peter Nosco, *Nativism and Nostalgia in Eighteenth-Century Japan* (Cambridge: Harvard University Press, 1990), xi, 8–9.

29. H. D. Harootunian, pers. comm.

30. Suzuki Bokushi, *Snow Country Tales: Life in the Other Japan*, trans Jeffrey Hunter with Rose Lesser (Tokyo: John Weatherhill, 1986), xxxvii.

31. Bix, *Peasant Protest in Japan*, 77.

32. Herman Ooms, *Tokugawa Ideology: Early Constructs, 1570–1680* (Princeton: Princeton University Press, 1985), 107.

33. The author of "Mikawa monogatari," Ōkubo Hikozaemon, became a popular figure in historical narratives which used accounts of his life to criticize the bakufu. One text based on his history, "The Ōkubo Stirrup from Musashi" *(Ōkubo Musashi abumi*—the Musashi stirrup was famous nationwide, and this title implies that Ōkubo was likewise), contains some elements also found in texts for the "Mankoku Riot" of 1711 and the story of Sakura Sōgorō and places Hikozaemon at the Shimabara Christian rebellion of 1637. Tamura Eitarō, *Jitsuroku shōsetsu-kō* (Tokyo: Yūzankaku, 1960), 171–80.

34. Some of the difficulties with Andō Shōeki's thought are explained by Bitō Masahide in his introduction to Shōeki's work in Ienaga Saburō, Shimizu Shigeru, Ōkubo Tadashi, Odaka Toshirō, Ishihama Juntarō, and Bitō Masahide, eds., *Nihon koten bungaku taikei*, vol. 97: *Kinsei shisōka bunshū* (Tokyo: Iwanami Shoten, 1966), 569–85.

35. Robert Darnton has pointed out that in the age of absolutism in France, those responsible for gathering information on the activities of others knew that simply to know is power. *The Great Cat Massacre and Other Episodes in French Cultural History* (New York: Basic Books, 1984), 159. After the 1918 rice riots in Japan, the Home Ministry tried to ban any news whatsoever from being printed about the disturbances. Arthur Young, "The Rice Riots of 1918," in Jon Livingston, Joe Moore, and Felicia Oldfather, eds., *Imperial Japan: 1800–1945* (New York: Pantheon, 1973), 324.

36. Yamazumi Masami and Nakae Kazue, *Kosodate no sho* (Tokyo: Heibonsha, 1976), 2: 204–18.

37. Ooms, *Tokugawa Ideology*, 295–96.

38. One collection of farmhouse documents located in Aoki village in the mountains of Nagano prefecture includes an account, copied in 1854, of the 1637 Shimabara Christian rebellion. In his survey of the theatrical representations of the Yoshitsune story, Gunji Masakatsu pointed out that in northern Japan, itinerant players always had to include a bit on Yoshitsune, otherwise the audience would be dissatisfied. "Budai no Yoshitsune," *Taiyō*, no. 111 (September 1972): 76. Yoshitsune, Masashige, and Amakusa Shirō are three of the heroes described by Ivan Morris in *Nobility of Failure: Tragic Heroes in the History of Japan* (New York: Holt, Rinehart, and Winston, 1975).

39. Fukaya Katsumi, "Rekishi no naka no Amakusa/Shimabara no ran", *Kumamoto shigaku*, no. 66–67 (1990): 8. Fukaya points out that to call this event the Shimabara rebellion acquieses in the perspective of the ruling class, whereas Amakusa signifies the islands where the peasants lived. Typical titles of the seventeenth-century texts were "Shimabara gun monogatari" and "Amakusa gassen-ki."

40. Suzuki Bokushi, *Akiyama kikō, yonabegusa*, ed. Miya Eiji (Tokyo: Heibonsha, 1971), 199.

41. Max Lüthi, *The European Folktale: Form and Nature*, trans. John D. Niles (Bloomington: Indiana University Press, 1982), introduction and chap. 1.

42. Not all stories about warriors were war tales. The *Azuma kagami*, translatable as "Mirror of the Eastern Provinces," the title of a history of the Kamakura bakufu written at the end of the thirteenth century, was written in an undramatic, unlyrical Chinese style, making it unsuitable for ritual purposes; thus it does not fit within the category of placatory tale or *gunki monogatari*. Plutschow, *Chaos and Cosmos*, 222, 226–27.

43. Carlo Ginzburg, *The Cheese and the Worms: The Cosmos of a Sixteenth-Century Miller*, trans. John Tedeschi and Anne Tedeschi (New York: Penguin Books, 1982), xii.

44. Margaret Spufford, *Small Books and Pleasant Histories: Popular Fiction and Its Readership in Seventeenth-Century England* (Athens: University of Georgia Press, 1981), 144–45. Drawing on the insights of Robert Redfield, Peter Burke emphasized the two-way traffic between the great and the little tradition throughout Europe. *Popular Culture in Early Modern Europe* (New York: Harper and Row, 1978), 24, 26, 59–60. In the nineteenth century, sympathetic observers of the French countryside wrote at least two "historical fictions" about social protest. Eugen Weber, *Peasants into Frenchmen: The Modernization of Rural France, 1870–1919* (Stanford: Stanford University Press, 1976), 242.

45. Richard H. Okada, "Translation and Difference: A Review Article," *Journal of Asian Studies* 47.1 (February 1988): 29.

46. Earl Miner, "On Distinctions, Functions, and Hard Words to Translate," *Monumenta Nipponica* 36.1 (Spring 1981): 91. For a description of the historical tales and their place in Japanese literature, see Edward Putzar, *Japanese Literature: A Historical Outline*, adapted and translated from *Nihon bungaku*, ed. Hisamatsu Sen'ichi (Tucson: University of Arizona Press, 1973), 60–113.

47. Plutschow, *Chaos and Cosmos*, 226.

48. Darnton applies this insight to folktales, but it can obviously encompass other genres as well. *Great Cat Massacre*, 15.

49. Akiko Hirota, "Ex-Emperor Go-Toba: A Study in Personality, Politics, and Poetry," Ph.D. diss., University of California, Los Angeles, 1989.

50. Frederic Jameson, *The Political Unconscious: Narrative as a Socially Symbolic Act* (Ithaca, N.Y.: Cornell University Press, 1981), 86, 89.

51. Donald Keene, trans., *Chūshingura: The Treasury of Loyal Retainers* (New York: Columbia University Press, 1971).

52. Nagamitsu Norikazu, ed., *Bizen Bitchū Mimasaka hyakushō ikki shiryō* (Tokyo: Kokusho Kankōkai, 1978), 4: 1218—19.

53. Aoki Michio, "Kinsei minshū no seikatsu to teikō," in Aoki Michio, Irumada Nobuo, Kurokawa Naonori, Satō Kazuhiko, Satō Shigerō, Fukaya Katsumi, Minegishi Sumio, and Yamada Tadao, eds., *Kōza ikki,* vol 4: *Seikatsu, bunka, shisō* (Tokyo: Tokyo Daigaku Shuppan Kai, 1981), 168.

54. One of the most interesting collections of stories about the leaders of peasant uprisings can be found in Komuro Shinsuke's *Tōyō minken hyakkaden,* reissued with an introduction by Hayashi Motoi (Tokyo: Iwanami Shoten, 1957). Ono Takeo includes portions of significant texts in *Hyakushō ikki sōdan,* vols. 1 and 2 (Tokyo: Tōkō shoin, 1927), but he altered them all. In 1930, Tamura Eitarō published *Nihon nōmin ikki roku* (Tokyo: Nanban Shobō), which also includes edited texts.

55. The clearest account of the 1866 uprising is by Patricia Sippel, "Popular Protest in Early Modern Japan: The Bushū Outburst," *Harvard Journal of Asiatic Studies* 37.2 (December 1977): 273—322.

56. Natalie Zemon Davis, *Fiction in the Archives: Pardon Tales and Their Tellers in Sixteenth-Century France* (Stanford: Stanford University Press, 1987), esp. 18, 141.

57. Shōji Kichinosuke, Hayashi Motoi, and Yasumaru Yoshio, eds., *Nihon shisō taikei,* vol. 58: *Minshū undō no shisō* (Tokyo: Iwanami Shoten, 1970), 170—84. Documents generated in the course of this riot include another history entitled *Hoei azuma kagami.* Hoei ikki kenkyūkai, ed., *Mito han Hoei ikki shiryōshū* (Tokyo: Hoei Ikki Kenkyūkai, 1988), 48—58.

58. Aoki Kōji, Mori Kahei, and Harada Tomohiko, eds., *Nihon shomin seikatsu shiryō shūsei,* vol. 6: *Ikki* (Tokyo: San'ichi Shobō, 1968), 96. Tottori was ruled by a tozama daimyō. Edward Shorter's study of the *veille* in France indicates that the "old tales" told when farm families gathered to talk at night did not include an oral history of collective exploits. "The Veille and the Great Transformation," in Jacques Beauroy, ed., *Popular Culture in France from the Old Regime to the Twentieth Century* (Saratoga, Calif.: Anma Libri, 1977), 135. The evidence presented here suggests that occasionally things were different in Japan.

59. The text of this document is in Aoki, *Nihon shomin seikatsu shiryō shūsei,* 6: 423—46. See also the collective biography of men who partici-

pated in or were connected with uprisings, written by Fukaya Katsumi, *Hachiemon, Heisuke, Hansuke* (Tokyo: Asahi Shinbunsha, 1978).

60. Nagamitsu, *Bizen Bitchū Mimasaka hyakushō ikki shiryō*, 2: 659–60. For a slightly different assessment of authorship see also Aoki, *Nihon shomin seikatsu shiryō shūsei*, 6: 657–58.

61. This text was never published in any official local histories because town officials feared that the animosity shown toward the Uesugi, the domain lords, might cause Uesugi descendants still living in the region to take revenge on them. Shingyū Takemi, *Tangan shinhitsuroku* (Tokyo: Shingyū Takemi, 1977).

62. His "Prison Memorandums and Letters" *(Gokuchūki)* have been analyzed by Herbert Bix, "Leader of Peasant Rebellion: Miura Meisuke," in Murakami Hyoe and Thomas J. Harper, eds., *Great Historical Figures of Japan* (Tokyo: Japan Culture Institute, 1978), 243–60. This text and another prison diary, one by Kanno Hachirō, can be found in Shōji, *Nihon shisō taikei*, 58: 15–86, 88–168. See also the biography by Fukaya Katsumi, *Nanbu hyakushō Meisuke no shōgai* (Tokyo: Asahi Shinbunsha, 1983). The other two documents written by uprising leaders are mentioned by Yasumaru Yoshio in "Chihō to bungakuteki hōga," in *Iwanami kōza bungaku* (Tokyo: Iwanami Shoten, 1976), 6: 331.

63. Janet Batsleer, Tony Davies, Rebecca O'Rourke, and Chris Weedon, eds., *Rewriting English: Cultural Politics of Gender and Class* (New York: Methuen, 1985), 81.

64. Judith N. Rabinovitch, trans., *Shōmonki* (Tokyo: Monumenta Nipponica, 1986), 43.

65. In his detailed study of what commoners read, Nagatomo Chiyoji reports that the war tale most frequently cited in their poetry was the *Taiheiki.* "Edo jidai shomin no dokusho," *Bungaku* 45.9 (September 1977): 101. Like other imperial loyalists of the eighteenth and nineteenth centuries, Takayama Hikokurō (1747–93) was addicted to the *Taiheiki* and carried it with him on his travels to northern Japan. Andō Hideo, *Kansei sankinin den* (Tokyo: Yamato Shobō, 1976), 78–79, 84–85. Many different texts on military strategy and even agronomy were titled *Taiheiki.* Wakabayashi Tatsusaburō, "Kinsei no nōseiron to *Taiheiki no hiden,*" *Nihon rekishi,* no. 227 (April 1967): 85–86. The history of Yui Shōsetsu was called *Keian taiheiki* (Keian era: 1648–51). Tamura, *Jitsuroku shōsetsu-kō,* 30. See also Helen Craig McCullough, trans., *Taiheiki: A Chronicle of Medieval Japan* (New York: Columbia University Press, 1959), xvii–xviii.

66. Bix, *Peasant Protest in Japan,* 115.

67. J. Rahder, "Record of the Kurume Uprising" *Acta Orientalia* 14 (1937): 83, 105.

68. As late as 1910 the foot soldier *(ashigaru)* Itō Kiyoshi wrote an account of the 1853 Nanbu uprising to fulfill a promise he had made to Miura Meisuke's sister. Kanda Kensaku, Takeda Isao, and Hayasaka Motoi, "Nanbu giminden ni kansuru ichikōsatsu," *Hirosaki daigaku nōgakubu gakujutsu hōkoku,* no. 47 (June 1987): 42–90.

69. Yokoyama Toshio, *Ueda han nōmin sōdōshi,* rev. ed. (Nagano-ken, Ueda-shi: Heirindō Shoten, 1981), 269–300. Herbert Bix has translated a different though still samurai, version of this incident, "An Account of the Peasant Uprising in Ueda Fief" *(Ueda sōdō jikki)* in the same volume, 214–38.

70. Michael Bommes and Patrick Wright, "Charms of Residence: The Public and the Past," in Richard Johnson, Gregor McLennan, Bill Schwarz, and David Sutton, eds., *Making Histories: Studies in History Writing and Politics* (Minneapolis: University of Minnesota Press, 1982), 258.

71. J. Victor Koschmann has pointed out that in the Mito branch of Tokugawa ideology, "the 'ignorant' [common] people' *(gumin)* were expected merely to respond loyally and submissively, not to act." "Action as Text," 89. In the *Taiheiki,* the occasional mention of peasants shows them as passive objects of warrior action. McCullough, *Taiheiki,* xx.

72. Aoki Kōji, *Nihon shomin seikatsu shiryō shūsei,* 6: 487.

73. Ibid., 6: 33–34.

74. Itō Tadashi and Kishino Toshihiko, "Mikawa-kuni Kamo-gun hyakushō ikki kikigaki," *Rekishi hyōron,* no. 389 (September 1982): 66–68. See also Kishino Toshihiko, "Tenpō-ki bunjin no shisōteki sekai—Watanabe Masaka to 'Kamo no Sawadachi' no saikentō," *Rekishi hyōron,* no. 375 (July 1981): 75–80.

75. Officials in late fifteenth-century Spain hoped to suppress vernacular tongues by imposing an official grammarian's language that would help consolidate the royal authority. Ivan Illich, *Shadow Work* (Boston: Marion Boyars, 1981), 33–56.

76. Quoted in Fukaya Katsumi, "Tokugawa Peasants and the Three Rs," *Japan Interpreter* 13.1 (Summer 1980): 127. Peasants were helped along by a variety of "how to" books. The libraries of farm families in Aoki village, Nagano prefecture, contain models for the documents written formally to the authorities *(hyakushō ōrai)* and models for business letters *(shōbai ōrai).* I thank Saitō Jun for taking me to this village.

77. Aoki Michio, *Taikei Nihon no rekishi,* vol. 11: *Kindai no yokō* (Tokyo: Shogakkan, 1989), 9. Kimura Motoi's surveys of farmhouse libraries points to a dramatic increase in the number of documents stored there beginning in the early nineteenth century. The same was true for the openings of village schools called *terakoya. Mura no kataru Nihon no rekishi* (Tokyo: Soshiete Kabushiki Kaisha, 1983), 164–66.

78. Herman Ooms, *Charismatic Bureaucrat: A Political Biography of Matsudaira Sadanobu, 1758–1829* (Chicago: University of Chicago Press, 1975), 87. The impact of their return on rural areas is attested to by Hayashiya Tatsusaburō, "Shomin seikatsu to geinō," in *Iwanami kōza Nihon rekishi,* vol. 12: *Kinsei* 4 (Tokyo: Iwanami Shoten, 1976), 207–8.

79. Fukaya, "Tokugawa Peasants and the Three Rs," 128.

80. Yokoyama, *Ueda han nōmin sōdōshi,* 302–17.

81. Yasumaru, "Chihō to bungakuteki hōga," 323–40.

82. For a recent assessment of Baba Bunkō's place in the history of Japanese political satire, see Yamada Tadao, "Seiji to minshū bunka," *Rekishi hyōron,* no. 465 (January 1989): 26–29.

83. Sugiura Minpei, *Ishin zen'ya no bungaku* (Tokyo: Iwanami Shoten, 1977), 1–22.

84. Yokoyama Toshio, *Hyakushō ikki to gimin denshō* (Tokyo: Kyōikusha, 1977), 201.

85. Yokoyama Toshio, *Gimin denshō no kenkyū* (Tokyo: San'ichi Shobō, 1985), 343–66.

86. Stephen Vlastos, *Peasant Protests and Uprisings in Tokugawa Japan* (Berkeley: University of California Press, 1986), 70, 163. The slogan first appeared in 1796 when three men martyred after an uprising in the Tsu domain were worshiped as *yonaoshi daimyōjin.* Itō Tadao, "Hyakushō ikki to minshū jiji," in Rekishigaku kenkyūkai, ed., *Kōza Nihon rekishi* (Tokyo: Tokyo Daigaku Shuppan Kai, 1985), 6: 105.

87. Bix, *Peasant Protest in Japan,* 77.

88. Ibid., 33, 49, 98.

89. Ibid., 36, 98, 100, 115, 175.

90. Walthall, *Social Protest and Popular Culture,* 173–204.

91. Anne Walthall, "Narratives of Peasant Uprisings in Japan," *Journal of Asian Studies* 42.3 (May 1983): 571–87.

92. Sabean, *Power in the Blood,* 3.

93. Roland Barthes pointed out that "to give the text an author is to impose a limit on the text, to furnish it with a final signified." *Image, Music, Text,* trans. Stephen Heath (London: Fontana, 1977), 147.

94. Mark Morris, "Desire and the Prince: New Work on *Genji Monogatari:* A Review Article," *Journal of Asian Studies* 49.2 (May 1990): 298.

95. For the issues surrounding the task of the translator, see Susan Bassnett-McGuire, *Translation Studies* (New York: Methuen, 1980), esp. 13–36 and 100–104.

96. Walter J. Ong, *Orality and Literacy: The Technologizing of the Word* (New York: Methuen, 1982), 148.

One / The Sakura Sōgorō Story

1. David E. Apter and Nagayo Sawa, *Against the State: Politics and Social Protest in Japan* (Cambridge: Harvard University Press, 1984), 37.

2. Conversation, in Utsunomiya, July 9, 1983.

3. Irokawa Daikichi, *The Culture of Meiji Japan*, trans. Marius B. Jansen (Princeton: Princeton University Press, 1985), 254.

4. Shibata Hajime, "Nōmin ishiki to nōson bunka no dentō," in Chihōshi kenkyūkyōgikai, ed., *Chihō bunka no dentō to sōzō* (Tokyo: Yūzankaku, 1976), 1887.

5. Aoki Kōji, *Nihon shomin seikatsu shiryō shūsei*, 6: 17–18, 30. Memorial services were performed for the three headmen in 1717, 1743, 1810, and 1860.

6. See Anne Walthall, "Japanese Gimin: Peasant Martyrs in Popular Memory," *American Historical Review* 91.5 (December 1986): 1085; Shibata, "Nōmin ishiki," 187; Chadani Jūroku, "Nanbu Sanhei ikki to minshū bunka," *Rekishi chiri kyōiku*, no. 296 (October 1979): 17; Hosaka Satoru, "Kakuchi no Sōgo jinja," *Rekishi Hyōron*, no. 441 (January 1987): 151. Yasumaru mentions that Sōgorō became the protective deity for the 1859 riot in the Minamiyama district in the Ina Valley, in "Chihō to bungakuteki hōga," 336.

7. Suzuki Tōzō and Koike Shōtarō, eds., *Kinsei shomin seikatsu shiryō: Fujiokaya nikki* (Tokyo: San'ichi Shobō, 1988), 4: 434–39. Twice Yūzō refers to Sōgorō as a *gimin* or righteous man, the first time this phrase is known to have been applied to a peasant martyr.

8. The other is *Go taiheiki shiraishi banashi*. It is discussed in chapter 5. Samuel L. Leiter, *Kabuki Encyclopedia* (Westport, Conn: Greenwood Press, 1979), 321; Earle Ernst, *The Kabuki Theatre* (Oxford: Oxford University Press, 1956; Honolulu: University of Hawaii Press, 1974), 210. A detailed history of theatrical productions is found in Ōzumi Masao, Saigō Nobutsuna, Sakashita Keihachi, Hattori Sachio, Hirosue Tamotsu, and Yamamoto Kichisayū, eds., *Nihon kakū denshō jinmei jiten* (Tokyo: Heibonsha, 1986), 232–33. My thanks to Henry D. Smith II for bringing this book to my attention.

9. Ivan Morris tells the story of Amakusa Shirō, leader of the Christian rebellion in 1637, whose family background was probably that of a low-ranking warrior. *Nobility of Failure*, 143–79. See Bix, "Miura Meisuke," 243–60. A much older book, by Edward S. Stephenson and W. Asano, *Famous People of Japan* (Yokohama: Kelly and Walsh, 1911), a series of one-page sketches, includes Sōgorō on page 133.

10. A. B. Mitford, *Tales of Old Japan* (Rutland, Vt.: Charles E. Tuttle Co., 1966), 161–91. Michiko Y. Aoki and Margaret B. Dardess, eds., *As the Japa-*

nese See It (Honolulu: University of Hawaii Press, 1981), 275–82. A book about Sōgorō that includes many of the elements incorporated into his story in the modern period is by Viscount Tadasu Hayashi, *For His People: Being the True Story of Sōgorō's Sacrifice Entitled in the Original Japanese Version "The Cherry Blossoms of a Spring Moon"* (New York: Harper and Brothers, 1903). Another account in English, well worth reading, comes from a lecture given by K. Ando to the Japan Society of London on February 9, 1910. "Sakura Sōgorō, Martyr," *Transactions and Proceedings of the Japan Society* 9 (1909–10): 72–95. Shorter versions have appeared in biographical dictionaries.

11. Barbara Ruch, "Kakuichi's Complaint: Homer and the Heike Hazards," *Japan Interpreter* 11.2 (Autumn 1976): 229.

12. I got this translation from Hirota, "Ex-Emperor Go-Toba." She points out that *kotodama* integrates "words and things, art and life" (299). Plutschow discusses *kotodama* in *Chaos and Cosmos*, 11, 75, 82, 91. For examples of word magic in medieval Europe see Gurevich, *Medieval Popular Culture*, 189, 212. Ong has pointed that "oral people commonly, and probably universally, consider words to have great power and magical potency." *Orality and Literacy*, 32.

13. Yamaguchi Masao argues that the most ancient local histories in Japan, the *Fudoki* (713, 925 A.D.) explain place-names in terms of the destruction wrought by morally ambivalent or "rough" gods. Their deeds can be seen as analogous to the angry spirit of Sōgorō. *Bunka to ryōgisei* (Tokyo: Iwanami Shoten, 1975), 7.

14. Yamaguchi Masao, "Kingship, Theatricality, and Marginal Reality in Japan," *ASA Essays in Social Anthropology* (Philadelphia: ISHI, 1977), 157.

15. Shimada Komao, *Nōshi no kokoro* (Tokyo: Shindaiya Sangyō Kabushiki Kaisha, 1977), 1.

16. Barbara Ruch, "Medieval Jongleurs and the Making of a National Literature," in John W. Hall and Toyoda Takeshi, eds., *Japan in the Muromachi Age* (Berkeley: University of California Press, 1977), 305–6.

17. Rabinovitch, *Shōmonki*. Plutschow points out that the Buddhist priest who wrote this tale blamed Masakado's rebellion and death on his wicked deeds in his previous life, an interpretation growing out of the Buddhist theory of karma. *Chaos and Cosmos*, 227.

18. Ono Masaji, *Jizō-dō tsuya monogatari* (Chiba-ken, Ryūsan-shi: Ron Shobō, 1978), 12–13.

19. Stephen Addiss, ed. *Japanese Ghosts and Demons: Art of the Supernatural* (New York: George Braziller, 1985), 53.

20. Quoted in Plutschow, *Chaos and Cosmos*, 205. See 203–16 for an extended discussion of what he calls "evil" spirits.

21. According to the Fujiokaya diary, the Hotta erected two shrines to

Sōgorō, one in the domain and one in the garden attached to their Edo mansion in Asakusa. *Fujiokaya nikki*, 4: 435.

22. Margaret H. Childs, "Martyrs, Serpents, and Nuns: Jealous Women in Japanese Literature," lecture presented to the Rocky Mountain/Southwest Japan Seminar, April 9, 1988, Lawrence, Kansas. The prototypical example of the belief in angry spirits *(goryō shinkō)* is the cult to Sugawara Michizane (845–903 C.E.), said to have brought destruction to his enemies after his death in exile. Ichiro Hori, *Folk Religion in Japan* (Chicago: University of Chicago Press, 1968), 115; Plutschow, *Chaos and Cosmos*, 210–11. Similar beliefs could be found in early modern Germany, where villagers well knew that enmity, envy, and hate could lead to magical attack. Sabean, *Power in the Blood*, 54.

23. I know of two triptyches, one at the Tsubouchi Memorial Theatre Museum at Waseda University and the other at the Spencer Museum of Art. Addiss, *Japanese Ghosts and Demons*, 70–71.

24. *Fujiokaya nikki*, 437; Plutschow, *Chaos and Cosmos*, 10, 72, 251, 254.

25. Tsutsumi Kunihiko, "Weird Tales from Tokugawa Times: Connections with Buddhist Fable," *Undercurrent: The Japan Scene, Past and Present*, no. 1 (March 1983): 37. Thomas Blenman Hare has some provocative statements on the different Buddhist attitudes toward language in "Reading Writing and Cooking: Kūkai's Interpretive Strategies" *Journal of Asian Studies* 49.2 (May 1990): 253, 254.

26. In Kanto villages, this sutra was read once a year to expel evil spirits. For this purpose, it had to be read as loudly as possible. Yamaguchi, *Bunka to ryōgisei*, 69–70.

27. Normal Field, *The Splendor of Longing in "The Tale of Genji"* (Princeton: Princeton University Press, 1987), 54.

28. Susan Matisoff, *The Legend of Semimaru: Blind Musician of Japan* (New York: Columbia University Press, 1978), 116.

29. Walthall, "Japanese Gimin," 1084. See the representation of this episode in Henry D. Smith II, *Kiyochika: Artist of Meiji Japan* (Santa Barbara, Calif.: Santa Barbara Museum of Art, 1988), 66.

30. Ruch, "Medieval Jongleurs," 286–87, 301, 305. Alfred B. Lord, famous for his study of oral epics, pointed out that in Europe, stories came into being to serve not art but religion. *The Singer of Tales* (Cambridge: Harvard University Press, 1960), 220. Plutschow argues that stories could not serve religion unless they were artful because art transforms chaos into order. *Chaos and Cosmos*, x, 35, and *passim*.

31. Clarke Garrett, "Spirit Possession, Oral Tradition, and the Camisard Revolt," in Marc Bertrand, ed., *Popular Tradition and Learned Culture in France* (Saratoga, Calif.: Anma Libri, 1985), 53.

32. Matisoff, *Legend of Semimaru*, 34, 114—16.

33. In the course of transmission, various elements were added to these stories to bring them up to date. Some included an official position established in the early nineteenth century or the name of a samurai prominent in the 1750s. Conversation with Hayashi Motoi, July 15, 1979.

34. Kenneth Dean Butler, "The Textual Evolution of the Heike Monogatari," *Harvard Journal of Asiatic Studies* 26 (1966): 5—51.

35. Ono, *Jizō-dō tsuya monogatari*, 11. Takeo Hagihara based his translation for Aoki and Dardess, *As the Japanese See It* on this text, but he excerpted only part of it, drastically truncating the narrative, misreading the character of Hotta Masanobu, and omitting the entire second half.

36. Lord, *Singer of Tales*, 100.

37. Helen Craig McCullough has noted that a distinguishing feature of the Heike narrative is the use of action-stopping devices to emphasize noteworthy situations, events, and people. *The Tale of the Heike* (Stanford: Stanford University Press, 1988), 466. Another reason for such seeming digressions is to relax the tension. Erich Auerbach, *Mimesis: The Representation of Reality in Western Literature* (Princeton: Princeton University Press, 1953), 4.

38. According to Conrad Totman, Masanobu's brother took over the family line in 1667, and he was assigned to the Annaka domain. *Politics in the Tokugawa Bakufu* (Cambridge: Harvard University Press, 1967), 158.

39. The peasants knew that if they left the public road for their lord's private quarters without a promise of safe passage, they might be arrested and tortured without anything being done about their petition.

40. A famous temple in Edo, more formally known as Sensō-ji, built to worship Kannon, the Buddhist goddess of mercy.

41. During the Edo period, the heads of executed criminals were usually exposed to the public by hanging them on the gateways to prisons.

42. Kan'ei-ji is a temple on a hill in Ueno called Tōeizan, a large temple complex that protected the capital from evil spirits coming from the unlucky northeast direction. It was built in 1625 by the shōgun Iemitsu as a branch temple of Nikkō where Ieyasu was enshrined.

43. Kumigashira were in charge of the five-family groups, the bottom cell of village organization, and were responsible for seeing that all the people in their group behaved themselves and were aware of government regulations.

44. Doi Toshikatsu (1573—1644) became lord of Sakura in 1610 and left there in 1633.

45. Matsudaira Yasunobu succeeded his father as lord of Sakura in 1638.

46. This is a fictitious name; there was no Araki Shima no kami according to the list prepared of family geneologies in the 1790s.

47. Danzaemon was the leader of the *eta* or outcasts, the people responsible for performing executions, among other loathsome tasks.

48. The Pure Land is the paradise promised by the Amida Bodhisattva to all true believers.

49. Dewa is a province in northern Japan. The lord of this domain in 1649 was Sakai Tadatsune, for whom it was created in 1647, but he was never called Iwami no kami.

50. This paraphrases a quotation from *Hagakure,* a manual of conduct for the warrior class.

51. This is also a fictitious name; there is no Doi with the title of shōshō listed in the family geneologies of the 1790s.

Two / How the People in Mimasaka Ran Riot

1. This translation is based on "Mikoku shimin ranbōki," ed. Nagamitsu Norikazu, in Shōji, *Nihon shisō taikei,* 58: 186–206. The same text with the same editor is in *Bizen Bitchū Mimasaka hyakushō ikki shiryō,* 2: 121–38. For a recent summation of this event that emphasizes what the peasants gained from their uprising, see Takeuchi Makoto, *Nihon no rekishi,* vol. 10: *Edo to Osaka* (Tokyo: Shogakkan, 1989), 156–58.

2. Nagamitsu, *Bizen, Bitchū, Mimasaka hyakushō ikki shiryō,* 1: 58; Hayashi Motoi, "Preface," in Sanchū ikki gimin kenshōkai, ed., *Mimasaka-kuni sanchū ikki shiryō* (Okayama: Yūhara-chō Kyōiku linkai, 1957), iii.

3. Bix, *Peasant Protest in Japan,* 32. James McMullen has argued that Bix's title for this text, "An Account of the People's Revolt in the Province of Mimasaka," gives it "a proletarian nuance dubiously present in the original." Review of *Peasant Protest in Japan,* by Bix, *English Historical Review* 103.408 (July 1988): 687.

4. Plutschow emphasizes that what he calls ritual literature, that read aloud at specified times during the year, includes both *The Tale of Genji* read at the "Little New Year" and *The Tales of the Heike. Chaos and Cosmos,* 5, 13.

5. Nagamitsu Norikazu, "Kaisetsu," in Shōji, *Nihon shisō taikei,* 58: 471. According to Tamura Eitarō, warriors left masterless after the battle of Sekigahara in 1601 made telling the *Taiheiki* their profession. *Jitsuroku shōsetsu-kō,* 9. Wakabayashi Tatsusaburō has pointed out that research on the *Taiheiki* flourished in the Tokugawa period. Agricultural reforms made in the Kaga domain were modeled on "Secret Teachings of the *Taiheiki,*" a text probably written in the early 1600s and widely known among village

officials by the end of the century. "Kinsei no nōseiron to *Taiheiki* no hiden," 85–86.

6. Saiki Kazuma, Okayama Taiji, and Sagara Tōru, eds., *Nihon shisō taikei*, vol. 26: *Mikawa monogatari, hagakure* (Tokyo: Iwanami Shoten, 1974), 14, 581. *The Tale of the Soga Brothers* has been translated by Thomas J. Cogan (Tokyo: Tokyo University Press, 1987).

7. Herman Ooms has pointed out that *Mikawa monogatari* was written as a private document and never meant to be circulated. It was never printed during the Tokugawa period because it spoke too directly to Ieyasu's military power in his conquest of Japan. *Tokugawa Ideology,* 107.

8. Butler, "Textual Evolution of the Heike Monogatari," 10–11. My colleague in Chinese literature, Stephen Durrant, informs me that a concern with chronology goes back at least to the Chinese historian Sima Qian (145?–90? B.C.E.), who paid much more attention to dates than his Western analogue Herodotus.

9. Field, *Splendor of Longing,* 128–29. Poems written by commoners show that by the eighteenth century, books and the tedium of the rainy season went together. Nagatomo, "Edo jidai shomin no dokusho," 105.

10. Ong, *Orality and Literacy,* 133.

11. Yamaguchi discusses this role of the outsider in *Bunka to ryōgisei,* 120.

12. Bix, *Peasant Protest in Japan,* 3–30.

13. Other domains notable for leaving samurai in the countryside were Satsuma and Tosa, both far from Edo, and Mito, just a few days north of the capital. See Marius B. Jansen, "Tosa in the Seventeenth Century: The Establishment of Yamauchi Rule," in John W. Hall and Marius B. Jansen, eds., *Studies in the Institutional History of Early Modern Japan* (Princeton: Princeton University Press, 1968), 115–30; and J. Victor Koschmann, *The Mito Ideology: Discourse, Reform, and Insurrection in Late Tokugawa Japan, 1790–1864* (Berkeley: University of California Press, 1987), 132.

14. Burke, *Popular Culture in Early Modern Europe,* 174.

15. Feminists have been more sensitive to the complexity of human relations than have many Marxists. For this perspective on peasant consciousness, which would sound quite familiar to a practitioner of Confucianism, I reformulated a statement found in Judith Newton and Nancy Hoffman, "Preface," *Feminist Studies* 14.1 (Spring 1988): 9.

16. Roland Barthes, "The Reality Effect," in Tzvetan Todorov, ed., *French Literary Theory Today: A Reader* (New York: Cambridge University Press, 1982), 11–17.

17. Catherine Belsey, *Critical Practice* (New York: Methuen, 1980), 144.

18. Bix, *Peasant Protest in Japan,* 33–50.

19. Ibid., 50.

20. Ibid., 43; Ooms, *Tokugawa Ideology,* 65, 76.

21. Hatake Kichū, *Sanchū ikki to kubinashi jizō* (Tsuyama-shi: Kubinashi Jizō Hōzonkai, 1981), 42.

22. In peasant petitions, *jihi,* the Buddhist word for benevolence, was the term of choice, not *jinsei,* with its Confucian overtones favored by modern historians. According to Ooms, even in high bakufu circles, Confucian terminology took a long time to replace this Buddhist term. *Tokugawa Ideology,* 67–68.

23. Ibid., 44.

24. In the Japanese text, his name is given as Ama no Shirō or Amano Tokisada. *Ama* is the Japanese pronunciation for the Chinese character *ten* or "heaven," dissociated from any specific geographical locality, but to maintain continuity and because "Amakusa" is the more commonly known name for this man, I have retained it in this translation. Claiming descent from heroes was not uncommon. Ooms reminds us that Oda Nobunaga (1534–82), the first of the great unifiers in the sixteenth century, changed his name to Heike. Ibid., 34.

25. Emiko Ohnuki-Tierney has analyzed the complex meanings of the proverb given here, *"tōrō ga ono, enkō ga tsuki,"* as follows: Both animals are ridiculous in striving for the impossible, therefore one must not try to achieve beyond one's means lest misfortune strike. At a more abstract level, the monkey's reaching for the moon can be interpreted as striving to reach a transcendental self. Regardless of the possibility for success, what is significant is the effort. *The Monkey as Mirror: Symbolic Transformations in Japanese History and Ritual* (Princeton: Princeton University Press, 1987), 62, 151, 240.

26. Higuchi Jirō Kanemitsu was one of the heroes in *The Tale of the Heike.* McCullough trans., 15.

27. Tokisada is a name by which Amakusa Shirō was known. Taifu is derived from an ancient title and position, the assistant to the bureau chief. Here these titles suggest that the masterless warrior was descended from the great leader of the Christian rebellion in 1637, who is himself said to have been descended from the ancient court aristocracy.

28. A scholar of physiognomy in China during the Three Dynasties period (1818–722 B.C.E.).

29. A swordsmith from Mino who lived in the early sixteenth century.

30. The chief actors in a succession dispute in the Matsudaira family of Echigo between 1679 and 1681 that led the bakufu to confiscate their domain.

31. To make it easier for the domain to ship tax rice, local merchants

would exchange certificates to be redeemed at a later date for the rice, but if the domain got a new ruler, the old certificates would become worthless, and the peasants assumed that the merchants would keep the rice.

32. One domanial reform was to refuse the peasants permission to plant wheat until all taxes had been paid. Stories about the riot exaggerated the peasants' hardships by claiming that they were not allowed to plant wheat at all. Taniguchi Sumio, ed., *Okayama ken no rekishi* (Tokyo: Yamakawa Shuppansha, 1970), 121.

33. Two famous military strategists from the Spring and Autumn period of Chinese history (722—481 B.C.E.)

34. This strategy for use in mountainous areas is taken from the *Lu T'ao*, a Chinese text. The troops are divided into small units and allowed to operate at will.

35. According to official records, Sōemon was arrested simply because he was Tokuemon's brother. Nagamitsu, *Bizen Bitchū Mimasaka hyakushō ikki shiryō*, 1: 208.

36. "Nonhuman," *nibinin*, is a Buddhist expression found in *The Tale of the Heike*.

37. Ōmori Hikoshichi was one of Ashikaga Takauji's generals. He appears in the *Taiheiki* as the man who forced Kusunoki Masashige to commit suicide.

Three / A Thousand Spears at Kitsunezuka

1. Shimazaki Tōson, *Before the Dawn*, trans. William E. Naff (Honolulu: University of Hawaii Press, 1987). Among the many modern accounts of peasant uprisings that privilege the history of the people over the national history is an account of this riot written by a local schoolteacher in 1973. Kitazawa Fumitake, *Meiwa no dai ikki* (Tokyo: Hata no Shobō, 1973).

2. Constantine N. Vaporis, "Post Station and Assisting Villages: Corvée Labor and Peasant Contention," *Monumenta Nipponica* 41.4 (Winter 1986): 401—10. See also Walthall, *Social Protest and Popular Culture*, 67—68.

3. Vaporis ignores the plans to have these outlying villages take over transportation assistance on a regular basis. Instead he points to the burden the peasants assumed they would incur when the shōgun traveled to Nikkō in 1765 to commemorate the 150th anniversary of Ieyasu's death. "Post Station and Assisting Villages," 411. Other sources argue that there was probably no connection between the procession to Nikkō and the riot. See Shishi hensanka, *Higashi Matsuyama-shi no rekishi* (Higashi Matsuyama-shi, 1985), 245. See also Bix, *Peasant Protest in Japan*, 140—41, and Takeuchi, *Nihon no rekishi*, 10: 162—63.

4. Kujirai Chisato, "Ikki denshō to minshū ishiki no tenkai: Nakasendō Meiwa tenma sōdō o taizō ni shite," *Rekishi,* no. 55 (1980): 59, 68–69. For an analysis of what Kidayū intended to do with this memorial service, see also Walthall, "Japanese Gimin," 1085.

5. This text can be found in Shōji, *Nihon shisō taikei,* 58: 208–35. See the explanation of the text on 473–76. Other texts pertaining to this riot are in Aoki Kōji, *Nihon shomin seikatsu shiryō shūsei,* 6: 199–252.

6. Carmen Blacker, *The Catalpa Bow: A Study of Shamanistic Practices in Japan* (London: George Allen and Unwin, 1975), 51, 56–57, 60–61, 66. Even today some Japanese believe that their richer neighbors keep foxes to help them make money. See Bradley K. Martin, "In Japan, Being Foxy Isn't the Same as It Is in America," *Wall Street Journal,* May 10, 1984, 1. Eugen Weber has pointed out that in rural France before the twentieth century, "so rare was the incidence of wealth that when a villager managed to grow rich, his success was likely to be attributed to trafficking with the devil or to criminal activity." *Peasants into Frenchmen,* 13.

7. Miyata Noboru has pointed out that Daikoku was originally the kitchen god, but in the mid-eighteenth century, he was transformed into a *marebito,* a traveler who brings good fortune from outside. Spread by priests from Izumo, the Daikoku cult was practiced more by individuals and their families than by communities as a whole. *Kinsei no hayarigami,* 111–12.

8. *Higashi Matsuyama-shi no rekishi,* 244.

9. Fukaya Katsumi, *Zōho kaiteiban: Hyakushō ikki no rekishiteki kōzō* (Tokyo: Azekura Shobō, 1986), 138–45.

10. Katsumata, *Ikki,* 104–5, 129, 134.

11. Gurevich, *Medieval Popular Culture,* 11.

12. Bix, *Peasant Protest in Japan,* 141–42.

13. *Higashi Matsuyama-shi no rekishi,* 247–56.

14. Kujirai, "Ikki denshō to minshū ishiki no tenkai," 67.

15. Harootunian, *Things Seen and Unseen,* 240, 256–7, 298, 312.

16. Ivan Morris, *Nobility of Failure,* 67–105.

17. Donald Keene, trans., *Essays in Idleness: The Tsurezuregusa of Kenkō* (New York: Columbia University Press, 1967).

18. Burton Watson, trans., *Chuang-tze: Basic Writings* (New York: Columbia University Press, 1964).

19. David Pollack, review of *Ikkyū and the Crazy Cloud Anthology,* by Sonja Arntzen, *Journal of Asian Studies* 47.2 (May 1988): 369–70.

20. Paul K. T. Sih has pointed out that "The Classic of Filial Piety" has a relatively easy style and a vocabulary of less than four hundred different characters. "No other work contains such an important selection of charac-

ters within such a simple grammatical context." "Introduction," in Mary Lelia Makra, trans., *The Hsiao Ching* (New York: St. John's University Press, 1961), xi.

21. In neither "A Record of How the Four Orders of People in Mimasaka Ran Riot," nor in this history does the conclusion point to a restoration of benevolent government. Instead the focus remains on the peasant martyrs.

22. Harootunian, *Things Seen and Unseen*, 248–51.

23. Ibid., 306–7. For his perspective on the issue of nativists and wealth, see especially 216, 227, 229.

24. Ibid., 247, 248.

25. In Japanese, the words in parentheses are puns on the preceding phrases.

26. This is a quotation from the *I ching*, the Book of Changes, an ancient Chinese classic written before 200 B.C.E. and still used today for divination.

27. Both of these passages are slightly garbled. The first begins, "Following the laws (way) of nature," the second ends with "widows and widowers" in place of "the masses." For the Chinese text and a slightly different translation, see Makra, *Hsiao Ching*, 12–13 and 16–17.

28. Those who know the story of the Kannon statue enshrined at Sensō-ji in Asakusa will recognize its parallels to the following story.

29. Kimura Yumiko, *Ibaraki-ken no hyakushō ikki to gimin densō* (Ibaraki-ken, Tsuchiura-shi: Chikuba Shorin, 1985), 1: 76–77.

Four / A Tale of a Dream from the Fox Woman Plain

1. Ueda Toshio, *Ibaraki hyakushō ikki* (Tokyo: Fūtōsha, 1974), 81–82.

2. Plutschow, *Chaos and Cosmos*, 228.

3. Suzuki Hisashi, *Kōyaku jōku kantan yume monogatari* (Ibaraki-ken, Tsuchiura-shi: Chikuba Shorin, 1979), 84. Portions of some of these texts have been reproduced in Ami-chō hensan iinkai, *Ami chōshi hensan shiryōshū* (Tsuchiura-shi: Ami-chō Hensan Iinkai, 1978), vol. 1. Official records of the riot but no narratives can be found in Aoki Kōji, ed., *Hennen hyakushō ikki shiryō shūsei* (Tokyo: San'ichi Shobō, 1981), 8: 148–76. Suzuki Hisashi has also mimeographed his own handmade versions of the texts in two volumes, "Ushiku sōdō onnabake nikki" and "Onnabake hara yume monogatari." I am grateful to Suzuki Hisashi for sending me copies of these texts.

4. Ueda, *Ibaraki hyakushō ikki*, 118.

5. Katsu Kokichi, *Musui's Story: The Autobiography of a Tokugawa Samurai*, trans. Teruko Craig (Tucson: University of Arizona Press, 1988), xix.

6. For this argument I have taken out of context some remarks made about ethnography by James Clifford in "Introduction: Partial Truths," in *Writing Culture: The Poetics and Politics of Ethnography* (Berkeley: University of California Press, 1986), 4, 15.

7. This was a knotty problem for many Japanese thinkers. According to Herman Ooms, scholars like Arai Hakuseki and Ogyū Sorai accepted the *I ching*'s concept of change but insisted that man is still the author of his history. "Hakuseki's Reading of History," *Monumenta Nipponica* 39.3 (Autumn 1984): 148.

8. Stephen Durrant has informed me that this was the practice followed by Sima Qin, and it even appears in such erotic classics as *Rou butuan* (The prayer mat of flesh).

9. Suzuki Hisashi, *Koyaku jōku kantan yume monogatari*, 89.

10. See Walthall, "Japanese Gimin," 1090–91.

11. Komuro, *Tōyō minken hyakkaden*, 317–54, esp. 342.

12. Other histories of peasant uprisings also raise this issue. See, for example, the prologues to "Uchū no kanzu" about a conflict between townspeople and the magistrate of Fushimi in 1785 and "Abenodōjimon" about the 1786 uprising in Fukuyama. Aoki Kōji, *Nihon shomin seikatsu shiryō shūsei*, 6: 273, 343. I discussed these prologues in Walthall, *Social Protest and Popular Culture*, 174–75. Even a leader of the famous Ōhara riot in Hida in the late eighteenth century took this approach, calling his recollections of the riot simply "A Tale of a Dream." Watanabe Masayasu, ed., *Zoku Hida sōsho*, vol. 1: *Yume monogatari* (Gifu-ken, Takayama-shi: Hida Chūō Insatsu Kabushiki Kaisha, 1974).

13. Jan Vansina has pointed out that etiological myths for particular features of the landscape also constitute an important part of European folklore. *Oral Tradition*, trans. H. M. Wright (London: Routledge and Kegan Paul, 1965), 158.

14. Fanny Hagin Mayer, *Ancient Tales in Modern Japan* (Bloomington: Indiana University Press, 1984), 31–32; idem, ed., *The Yanagita Kunio Guide to the Japanese Folk Tale* (Bloomington: Indiana University Press, 1986), 31–32; Richard M. Dorson, *Folk Legends of Japan* (Rutland, Vt.: Charles E. Tuttle Co., 1962), 132–33; Joanne P. Algarin, *Japanese Folk Literature* (New York: R. R. Bowker, 1982), 79, 167.

15. His story and a discussion of the texts are given in Kaneko Bin, *Kitsune kara umareta otoko* (Ibaraki-ken, Tsuchiura-shi: Chikuba Shobō, 1978).

16. For this distinction between folktale and legend, I relied on Lüthi, *European Folktale*, vii, x, xi, 6, 11–12, 16–17, 21, 32, 37, 55–56.

17. Suzuki Hisashi, *Koyaku jōku kantan yume monogatari*, 70.

18. Dorson, *Folk Legends of Japan*, 166–67.

19. Harootunian, *Things Seen and Unseen*, 38.

20. Suzuki Bokushi, *Snow Country Tales*.

Five / A Tale Told in a Dream of a Eulogy to Filial Piety

1. Documents pertaining to this incident have been collected in Nagamitsu Norikazu, ed., *Bizen Bitchū Mimasaka hyakushō ikki shiryō* (Tokyo: Kokusho Kankōkai, 1978), 3: 759–1042. The text translated here, "Kōkō wasan yume monogatari," is on 801–7. It was probably written soon after the event, perhaps in the early 1870s. Two copies of the manuscript have been found, one in Yukishige village, home of Naokichi and his family, and the other in what is now a suburb of Tsuyama city. Some of the same texts, though not "A Eulogy to Filial Piety," can also be found in Aoki Kōji, ed., *Nihon shomin seikatsu shiryō shūsei*, vol. 13: *Sōjō* (Tokyo: San'ichi Shobō, 1970), 293–377.

2. Nagamitsu, *Bizen Bitchū Mimasaka hyakushō ikki shiryō*, 3: 811.

3. A detailed account of the riot that relies on "An Account of the Disturbance That Led to Political Reform" and "The Story of the Beggars' Riot" can be found in Bix, *Peasant Protest in Japan*, 175–82.

4. Plutschow, *Chaos and Cosmos*, 10.

5. See, for example, the nativist and rich peasant Miyauchi Yoshinaga's comparison of the peasants versus everyone else, in Harootunian, *Things Seen and Unseen*, 251.

6. Analyzing the French heroic epic, Erich Auerbach pointed out that it succeeds in representing only a narrow portion of objective life. *Mimesis*, 121. This narrowness of representation was also characteristic of *The Tale of the Heike* and other war tales, and indeed most histories of peasant uprisings. "A Eulogy to Filial Piety" thus puts not only new actors but a different slice of reality into words.

7. Yokohama kaikō shiryōkan, *Nanushi nikki ga kataru bakumatsu* (Yokohama: Yokohama Kaikō Shiryōkan Fukyū Kyōkai, 1986), 47.

8. Nishioka Toranosuke, *Nihon josei shikō* (Tokyo: Shinhyōronsha, 1956), 225–28.

9. Ibid., 229.

10. Joyce Lebra-Chapman, *The Rani of Jhansi: A Study in Female Heroism in India* (Honolulu: University of Hawaii Press, 1986).

11. Of the 104 cases of revenge officially recorded for the Tokugawa period, only 2 involved peasants against samurai: the two daughters from Adachi and a male peasant adopted into a warrior household. A detailed study of the Adachi story and its diffusion through the great and little tradi-

tions can be found in Chadani Jūroku, "'Ōshū shiraishi banashi' no seiritsu to tenkai," *Minzoku geijutsu kenkyūjo kiyō*, no. 2 (1975): 112–41.

12. The text insists that Naokichi was freed because his children's willingness to take his place had moved the hearts of the officials, but a different reading can also be placed on his release. In other incidents, when a prisoner was known to be dying, he would be released to spare the officials the trouble of having to deal with his body. Local historians say that all the leaders of the 1866 uprising were freed under a general amnesty granted by the Meiji emperor in 1868. Kamo kyōdo-shi kenkyūkai, *Gimin monogatari: Mimasaka kaisei ikki* (Okayama-ken, Kamo-chō: Mimasaka Kaisei Ikki Gimin Kenshōkai, 1956), 12.

13. According to Alfred B. Lord, in the European tradition and the Greek myths, it was the son who helped free his father by allowing himself to become hostage in the father's place. *Singer of Tales*, 161.

14. Bix, *Peasant Protest in Japan*, 189–92.

15. Ibid., 177–78.

16. The word in the text is *hinin*, an outcast or beggar, but in this riot the peasants used it, perhaps ironically, to refer to themselves.

17. A poetic figure of speech. See for example a poem by Fujiwara no Okikaye written c. 910, in Arthur Waley, *Japanese Poetry: The "Uta"* (London: Lund Humphries, 1965), 72. Note too the geographical affinity of Mt. Fuji and Tago, both places far from Tsuyama. A poem in the *Man'yōshū* (ninth century) by Yamabe no Akahito states: "Coming out from Tago's nestled cove, I gaze; white, pure white the snow has fallen on Fuji's lofty peak." *The Thousand Leaves*, trans. Ian Hideo Levy (Princeton: Princeton University Press, 1981), 78.

18. The word here, *on-kōzen (o-hiromae)*, is one typically used by adherents of Konkō-kyō.

19. Shinshi (gentlemen believer) is a posthumous name awarded to commoners of exceptional merit and high social position. For it to be given to an uprising leader was proof of the respect the villagers had for him, but it is highly unlikely the authorities would have approved.

20. The word order and words given here differ slightly from the ones in the poem given above. Either the transcriber did not bother to check back or the difference in emphasis is intentional.

21. The song of Takasago taken from the Noh drama by Zeami accompanies an auspicious dance often performed at celebrations.

Six / Rereading Peasant Histories of Peasant Uprisings

1. In *Fiction in the Archives,* Natalie Zemon Davis defines this as what has been the task of "we scientific historians," 3.

2. Victor Turner has called narrative "the supreme instrument for binding the 'values' and goals which motivate human conduct into a situational structure of meaning . . . a universal cultural activity." "Social Dramas and Stories about Them," *Critical Inquiry* 7 (Autumn 1980): 167. The following discussion is drawn from my reading of Hayden White, *The Content of the Form: Narrative Discourse and Historical Representation* (Baltimore: Johns Hopkins University Press, 1987), x, 1–25, 86–87, 169–75, 208–13, and *passim.*

3. White, *Content of the Form,* 87. Gail Greene and Coppélia Kahn have pointed out that the concept of neither nature nor culture is a "given." Their meanings vary depending on time and place, class and gender, a variability of which White seems unaware. "Feminist Scholarship and the Social Construction of Women," in Gail Greene and Coppélia Kahn, eds., *Making a Difference: Feminist Literary Criticism* (New York: Methuen, 1985), 10.

4. Plutschow, *Chaos and Cosmos,* 34–35.

5. Palmer, *Descent into Discourse,* 139.

6. Stephen Greenblatt, "Introduction," in Stephen Greenblatt, ed., *Representing the English Renaissance* (Berkeley: University of California Press, 1988), vii. I am grateful to Barry L. Weller for directing me to Greenblatt's ideas on representation.

7. Putzar has pointed out that the major novelist of the early nineteenth century, Takizawa Bakin (1767–1848), introduced a new hero, the ruffian. *Japanese Literature,* 158.

8. Stephen Greenblatt, "Murdering Peasants: Status, Genre, and the Representation of Rebellion," *Representations,* no. 1 (February 1983): 1–29; reprinted in idem, *Representing the English Renaissance,* 1–29.

9. Fukaya Katsumi was the first historian to emphasize the importance of the concept *onbyakushō,* in "Hyakushō ikki no shisō," *Shisō,* no. 584 (February 1973): 206–14. A reprint with the title "Hyakushō ikki no ishiki kōzō" is in his collected essays, *Hyakushō ikki no rekishiteki kōzō* (Tokyo: Azekura Shobō, 1986), 63–97. American historians who have drawn on his language for his interpretation of peasant consciousness include myself, *Social Protest and Popular Culture,* 55–57, and Irwin Scheiner, "Benevolent Lords and Honorable Peasants: Rebellion and Peasant Consciousness in Tokugawa Japan," in Tetsuo Najita and Irwin Scheiner, eds., *Japanese Thought in the Tokugawa Period, 1600–1868: Methods and Metaphors* (Chicago: University of Chicago Press, 1978), 45–47.

10. Greenblatt, "Murdering Peasants," 11.

11. Yokoyama, *Hyakushō ikki to gimin denshō*, 201.

12. Sabean, *Power in the Blood*, 29.

13. Ibid., 143.

14. Darnton, *Great Cat Massacre*, 38, 53–54.

15. Sasaki Kyōichi, "Nanbu Sanhei hyakushō ikki no minken denshō," *Minzoku geijustu kenkyūjo kiyō*, no. 2 (1975): 39.

16. Muchembled, *Popular Culture and Elite Culture in France*, 35–38.

17. In Western thought, the patriarchal value system is structured in terms of binary oppositions—activity/passivity, sun/moon—in which the feminine side is always seen as the negative, powerless instance. Toril Moi, *Sexual/Textual Politics: Feminist Literary Theory* (New York: Methuen, 1985), 104. In Japanese thought, however, each includes elements of the other. Drawing on Lao-tzu, Suzuki Bokushi wrote, "All things bear the yin and embrace the yang. This is the principle of harmony. By this principle, a wife who does not contain within her yin self a bit of the yang is not in accord with heaven." *Snow Country Tales*, 50.

18. I derived this notion from reading Louis Adrian Montrose, "Shaping Fantasies: Figurations of Gender and Power in Elizabethan Culture," in Greenblatt, *Representing the English Renaissance*, esp. 32–36.

19. Ruth Benedict, *The Chrysanthum and the Sword* (New York: Houghton Mifflin, 1946), 187–88.

20. Ihara Saikaku, *The Great Mirror of Male Love*, trans. Paul Gordon Schalow (Stanford: Stanford University Press, 1990), 1. An earlier translation of this book is *Comrade Loves of the Samurai*, trans. E. Powys Mathers (Rutland, Vt.: Charles E. Tuttle Co., 1972).

21. Moi, *Sexual/Textual Politics*, 57.

22. Batsleer et al., *Rewriting English*, 120, 79. Adrienne Munich has emphasized the importance of reading texts, even those written by men, for their female themes as well as for their male themes to explain, among other things, the "invisible" sexual politics of literature. "Notorious Signs, Feminist Criticism, and Literary Tradition," in Greene and Kahn, eds., *Making a Difference*, 251.

23. The great nativist Motoori Norinaga (1730–1801) emphasized "the sensation and emotionalism of immediate, fleeting, 'feminine' experience such as kindness, affection, tenderness, and love. Despite recent opinion associating these values with women, he writes, such expressive emotionality belonged to the original spirit of all." Harootunian, *Things Seen and Unseen*, 95.

24. Leslie Wahl Rabine, "A Feminist Politics of Non-Identity," *Feminist Studies* 14.1 (Spring 1988): 13.

25. I derived the interpretation in this paragraph and the one that fol-

lows from Emmanuel LeRoy Ladurie, *Love, Death and Money in the Pays d'Oc,* trans. Alan Sheridan (New York: George Braziller, 1982), 66, 145; Montrose, "Shaping Fantasies," 32; Moi, *Sexual/Textual Politics,* 27; and Herbert Gans, *Popular Culture and High Culture: An Analysis and Evaluation of Taste* (New York: Basic Books, 1974).

26. Bommes and Wright, "Charms of Residence," 261.

27. My understanding of these three perspectives is derived from Batsleer et al., *Rewriting English,* 66.

28. An account of Sakura Sōgorō written in 1903 by Viscount Hayashi Tadasu attributed the death of Lord Hotta's consort and his own madness to hallucinations, depression, and remorse. Viscount Hayashi Tadasu, *For His People,* 210–21.

Index

"Account of the Disturbance That Led to Political Reform," 193
"Account of the Peasant Uprising in Ueda Fief (Ueda sōdō jikki)," 240n.69
Agronomy textbooks, 16
Amakusa Shirō, 17, 79, 82, 85, 87, 91, 242n.9, 248n.27
Amakusa Tokisada, 81, 91, 92, 94, 97, 98, 101–3, 105–7, 248n.24; capture of, 108–9; death of, 117; praise for, 110
Amida Bodhisattva, 11, 41
Andō Shōeki, 16
Angry spirits (onryō), 13, 16, 39–42, 169, 173, 243n.13; in modern Japan, 231; in "Record of How the Four Orders of People in Mimasaka Ran Riot," 82, 85, 110, 117–18; Sakura Sōgorō as, 47, 67–69; in the Sakura Sōgorō story, 40–41; as Sugawara Michizane, 244n.22
Anticlericalism, 11, 223, 235n.21; in "Record of How the Four Orders of People in Mimasaka Ran Riot," 116; in Sōgorō story, 43, 46, 65; in "Thousand Spears at Kitsunezuka," 127, 131, 155
Aoki Koji, 36
Aoki Michio, 21
As the Japanese See It, 38
Azuma kagami, 237n.42

Baba Bunkō, 29
Bakufu, 5

Barthes, Roland, 83
Before the Dawn, 120
Beggars, 4, 204
Benedict, Ruth, 226
Benkei, 127, 156
"Biographies of Filial Children and Good People of Chikuzen," 197
Bix, Herbert, 15, 24, 30–31, 200, 233n.1; on peasant consciousness, 81; and "Record of How the Four Orders of People in Mimasaka Ran Riot," 83; on taxes, 8
Blood festival (chimatsuri), 85, 105
Bōji (brother), 197, 204, 210, 212, 215
Bonten (god of purification), 125
"Book of Changes" (I ching), 171, 177, 251n.26, 252n.7
Brown, Philip, 8
Buddhism, 11–13; in "Record of How the Four Orders of People in Mimasaka Ran Riot," 78, 84–85, 102, 115, 117; in Sōgorō story, 63–64, 67, 68–69; in "Tale Told in a Dream of a Eulogy to Filial Piety," 196, 201, 207, 211, 213–14; in "Thousand Spears at Kitsunezuka," 153
Buddhist priests, 11
Burgundy, 6, 8, 10, 13
Burke, Peter, 81

Catharsis of pity, 19
Censorship, 16, 85

"Child from Abeno's Questions, The" *(Abenodō jimon)*, 24
Children, 64–65
Chinese classics, 77, 125, 127, 128, 153, 171, 197
Chinese military strategy, 87, 88, 101, 106
Chiyo (mother), 204, 214, 227
Chōja, 122
Chuang-tze, 127, 131
Chūgorō (husband of fox wife), 175, 176, 187–90
"Clamor of Ducks" *(Kamo no sawadachi)*, 20, 22, 26, 30
"Classic of Filial Piety," 27, 127–28, 153, 197, 250n.20
Clifford, James, 2
Commercial agriculture, 9–10
Commercial economy, 120, 121, 167, 200
Community versus family, 31, 126, 195, 201, 225–29
Confraternities *(kō)*, 13–14
Confucianism, 84
Conjugal relations, 126, 163, 225, 227, 228
Consort of Hotta Kōzuke no suke, 67–69
Corvée, 8, 119, 121
Country samurai *(gōshi)*, 4, 7, 80–81, 93, 103, 105, 106–7, 112
Creation deities, 163
Crucifixions, 63–67, 117

Dai-gongen, 12
"Daily Record of the Riot over Ten Thousand Koku" *(Mankoku sōdō nichiroku)*, 36
Daimyō, 4, 120
Danzaemon, 246n.47
Daughters, 64, 198, 201, 206, 228
Davis, Natalie Zemon, 21
Decapitation Falls, 143

Demons, 180, 181
Deputy district headmen *(chūjōya)*, 7, 90, 93, 94, 193, 202
Desire *(yoku)*, 84. *See also* Greed
District headmen, 94, 95, 202
Dog, 76, 84, 191–92, 197
Dreams: in histories of peasant uprisings, 252n.12; in "Tale of a Dream from the Fox Woman Plain," 173–74, 186; in "Tale Told in a Dream of a Eulogy to Filial Piety," 193, 202, 204, 208

Edo city magistrates, 164
Elders *(toshiyori)*, 7
Era names, 234n.7
Essays in Idleness, 127, 130
Evanescence of life, 13, 67, 196, 211
Executioner, 64, 66
Executions, 85, 105, 111, 114–15, 166. *See also* Crucifixions

Family versus community, 31, 126, 195, 201, 225–29
Festivals, 11–13, 190, 195
Filial piety, 84, 125, 197–99, 200–201, 219; in "Record of How the Four Orders of People in Mimasaka Ran Riot," 113, 115, 225; in *Taiheiki*, 226; in "Tale Told in a Dream of a Eulogy to Filial Piety," 201, 206, 209, 210, 211, 213; in "Thousand Spears at Kitsunezuka," 160–62
Five Women Who Loved Love, 230
Folk arts *(mingei)*, 27
Folklore, 2, 31, 122, 175, 252n.13; women in, 40
Folktales, 3, 18, 23, 171, 173–75; European, 223

*For His People: Being the True Story
    of Sōgorō's Sacrifice,* 243n.10
Fox wife, 171, 174, 188–90, 192,
    227
Fox Woman Plain, 174, 176, 178,
    181, 182, 183, 187
Foxes, 14, 122, 174, 187, 250n.6
France, 225
Freight dispatchers *(toiya),* 170,
    185
Fuchiwatari Shukei, 46, 48, 50, 70
Fujiokaya Yūzō, 37
Fukaya Katsumi, 27, 123, 233n.5,
    255n.9

Garrett, Clarke, 43
General *(taishō),* 12, 102. *See also*
    People's commander
German Peasants' War, 220
Germany, 7, 8, 223, 244n.22
Gimin, 242n.7
God of wealth (Daikoku), 129,
    130, 131, 132, 133, 250n.7
Goddess of Mercy (Kannon), 153–
    54, 245n.40
Great August Deity *(dai-myōjin),*
    12; Inari, 187; Kōriyama, 153;
    Sōgorō as, 36, 37, 46, 47, 74,
    75
Great Mirror of Male Love, 226
Greed, 80, 84, 93; in "Tale of a
    Dream from the Fox Woman
    Plain," 178; in "Thousand
    Spears at Kitsunezuka," 122,
    129–31, 133, 147
Greenblatt, Stephen, 219, 220–21
Group leaders *(kumigashira),* 7,
    245n.43
Gurevich, Aron, 124

Hagakure, 46, 246n.50
Harootunian, H. D., 14, 126, 128

Hatamoto (shogunal bannerman),
    176
Hayashi Hachiemon, 22
Hayashi Motoi, 25
Hayashi Tadasu, 243n.10
Higashiyama Sakura Sōshi, 40
Higuchi (Ya)jirō, 84, 86, 97, 98,
    104, 112–13, 117, 225
Hirota, Akiko, 19
Historical tales *(rekishi mono-
    gatari),* 19
Histories of peasant uprisings:
    arrests in, 61, 100–102, 107–
    9, 112–14, 150, 160, 163, 184;
    authorship of, 23–28, 29, 31,
    32, 78, 171, 219; battles in, 3,
    22, 31, 82, 107–9, 139, 143,
    152, 156, 224; chronology in,
    217, 247n.8; and conflict
    within the village, 6; context,
    14–17; contradictions in, 125,
    199, 227–28; criteria for
    selection, 20–23; dreams in,
    202, 204, 208, 252n.12; genre,
    17–20; historiography, 28–33;
    military strategy in, 80, 82, 86,
    101, 104–6; in modern Japan,
    230–31; names in, 82, 86, 91–
    92, 96–97, 111–12, 113–15,
    123, 133, 149; as narrative, 2,
    28, 218–19; numbers in, 140,
    150, 157, 196, 204; poems in,
    87, 88, 131, 146, 147, 150,
    157, 159, 190, 205, 207, 212,
    215; politics in, 229–30;
    prologues to, 31, 47, 86; songs
    in, 191; strangers in, 222–23;
    translations of, 33–34, 83;
    variant versions of, 124, 141,
    151, 169, 171, 173, 193;
    women in, 226–28
Hoei azuma kagami, 238n.57
Hoei taiheiki, 22

Hōjō Ujimasa, 220
Homosexuality, 226
Honorable peasants *(onbyakushō)*, 221, 229, 255n.9
Hosaka Satoru, 44
Hoshi Ukichi, 22
Hotta Chikuzen no kami, 74
Hotta Kaga no kami Masamori, 44–45, 47, 191
Hotta Kōzuke no suke Masanobu, 35, 44, 47, 191; madness of, 68–72; as senior councillor, 47–48; verdict on Sōgorō, 60–61
House elders *(karō)*, 5; in Sakura Sōgorō story, 48, 50, 60–61, 62, 70
Hyōnai (in "Thousand Spears at Kitsunezuka"), 124, 140–42, 145; arrest of, 162–63; confession of, 165; as peasant martyr, 121, 125, 221; vis-a-vis warriors, 151, 221

Ichikawa Kodanji, 41
Ihara Saikaku, 226, 230
Ikki, 79, 123, 165, 172
Ikkyū (priest), 127, 131
Ina Hanzaemon, 6, 141, 144, 145, 151, 164
Inari, 14, 174, 176, 178, 181, 187
Inns for daimyō, 133–34, 143–44, 145
Inspectors *(metsuke)*, 5
Intercalary month, 234n.7
Intertextuality, 19–20, 26, 36, 45–46, 78–79, 126–28, 170, 196–97
Itakura Shigemasa, 127, 149
Itinerant priest, 78, 173, 186

Jien, 40
Jinbei (ferryman), 37, 42

Jiyū shinbun (Liberal Newspaper), 172
Jizō, 14, 39

K'ung Ming military arts, 87
Kabuki, 37, 41, 126, 220
Kami (Shintō deities), 12, 125, 145, 163, 190, 219, 223. *See also* God of wealth, Inari
Kan'ei-ji, 245n.42
Kanto district supervisor (Kantō *gundai bugyō)*, 183
Kantō *gundai*, 5, 6
Karasumaru Mitsuhiro, 17
Karma, 13, 41–42, 84, 85, 181
Kelly, William, 8, 30
Kiso Yoshinaka, 143
Kobayashi Sōsuke, 193
Kojima Shikibu, 50, 60–61, 62, 73
Koku, 8
Komuro Shinsuke, 172, 238n.54
Korean delegation, 121, 123, 134, 138, 140
Koschmann, J. Victor, 235n.22
Kotodama, 39, 196, 243n.12
Kubo Chikahira, 89–90, 94–95, 101, 110
Kuma (daughter), 204, 209, 212, 214–15, 227
Kumasaka Chōhan, 127
Kuribayashi Yoshinaga, 174–75, 176, 188
Kusunoki Masashige, 17, 82, 102, 249n.37

Landholding peasants *(honbyakushō)*, 6, 9, 44, 201, 219, 234n.17
Landlords, 9–10, 201, 219
League headmen *(ōjōya)*, 7
Legends, 1, 174–75
LeRoy Ladurie, Emmanuel, 228
Literacy, 3, 26–28, 171, 240n.76

Loans to the government
(goyōkin), 8, 138
Lord, Alfred B., 44
Lu T'an, 249n.34

Magistrate in charge of roads, 134,
135, 150, 164, 165
Maki Tokuemon, 79, 91
Maki Tōsuke, 86, 104, 105
Mankoku riot, 236n.33
Marriage ceremony, 214–15
Martial arts, 152, 156
Masterless warriors (rōnin), 4, 26,
78, 79–81, 246n.5
Matisoff, Susan, 42
Medieval Europe, 3, 39, 235n.23,
243n.12
Meiji Restoration, 120, 254n.12
Memorial monument (kuyō-hi),
169
"Mikawa monogatari," 15–16,
78, 247n.7
"Military Chronicle of a Quarrel"
(Deiri gunhōki), 28
Minamoto no Yoshitsune, 16, 127,
143, 236n.38
Minamoto Tanetomo, 176
Miner, Earl, 19
"Mirror for Virtuous Women,"
197
Miscellaneous taxes (komono-
nari), 8
"Miscellany of Filial Piety," 197
Mitford, A. B., 38
Miura Meisuke, 22, 240n.69
Miyahiro Sadao (Miyaoi Yasuo),
129
Miyata Noboru, 13
Miyauchi Yoshinaga, 129
Morris, Ivan, 38
Morris, Mark, 33
Mother, 64, 112–13, 125, 161,
201. See also Chiyo

Motoori Norinaga, 256n.23
Mountain priests (yamabushi), 12–
13, 68–69, 124
Muchembled, Robert, 225

Nagamitsu Norikazu, 78, 193
Nakasendō, 119–20, 134
Nakazawa Kidayū, 121, 125
Namakubi (freshly-severed head),
143–44
Nanbu Sanhei uprising, 224,
240n.68
Naokichi (father), 194, 196, 200,
202, 205–6, 209, 210, 220–21
Narrative, 2, 28, 218–19, 255n.2
Nativism, 14, 121, 126, 128, 196–
97, 209
Night visits (yobai), 195
Ninomiya Sontoku, 15
Nonpeople (hinin), 3
Norito, 39

Obasuteyama, 229
Oda Ujiharu, 177, 190
Official calligraphic style (o-ieryū),
5
Ōhara Yūgaku, 15
Ohnuki-Tierney, Emiko, 248n.25
Ōkubo Gorōzaemon, 176, 191–92
Ōkubo Hikozaemon, 78, 236n.33
Ōmori Hikoshichi, 81, 116,
249n.37
"One Hundred Biographies of
Oriental Advocates of People's
Rights" (Tōyō minken
hyakkaden), 173, 238n.54
Ong, Walter J., 34, 79
Ōno Kichiemon, 125, 160–62
Ono Masaji, 44
Ooms, Herman, 15, 83, 85
Oral culture, 17, 33–34, 39, 43,
79, 124, 126, 238n.58,
243n.12, 244n.30

Index

Origins: of place-name, 26, 174; of shrines *(jisha engi)*, 1, 39, 40, 42, 45, 74, 176
Ōshio Heihachirō, 82
Outcasts *(eta)*, 5, 246n.47

Palmer, Bryan, 2, 219
Peasant consciousness, 30, 217, 229, 231, 247n.15
Peasant heroes, 19, 23, 29, 32, 38, 219–22
Peasant martyrs, 16–17, 29–30, 169, 242n.7; in modern Japan, 230–31
Peasant uprisings, 3; over famine relief, 1; numbers of, 1, 233n.1; peasant assembly before, 142; reasons for, 7, 35, 48, 90; over taxation policies, 1, 3, 35, 48, 77, 137–38, 200, 205
Peasants' representative *(hyakushōdai)*, 7
People's army, 103, 109, 116
People's commander, 91, 102, 105, 107, 109, 110, 111. *See also* General
Plutschow, H. E., 41, 218
Poems: in "Record of How the Four Orders of People in Mimasaka Ran Riot," 87, 88; in "Tale of a Dream from the Fox Woman Plain," 190; in "Tale Told in a Dream of a Eulogy to Filial Piety," 205, 212, 215; in "Thousand Spears at Kitsune-zuka," 131, 146, 147, 157, 159
Poor peasants. *See* Tenant farmers
Post station riot 1764, 1, 9, 14, 119, 121, 123, 124–25
Post station riot 1804, 1, 9, 169, 177–78
"Precepts for an Encouragement of Farming" *(Kannō kyōkun roku)*, 22
Proto-capitalism, 122
Punishment: of peasants, 113–14, 166, 185–86, 207, 221; of women, 199–200, 209

Rani Lakshmibai of Jhansi, 198
"Record of How the Four Orders of People in Mimasaka Ran Riot" *(Mikoku shimin ranbōki)*, 16, 17, 22, 217, 221, 227, 229; battles in, 82, 107–9, 224; defeat of peasants in, 106–9; description of, 77–83; Japanese literature in, 78–79; military strategy in, 86, 101, 104–6; names in, 82, 91–92, 96–97, 105, 111, 112, 114–15; officials in, 89–90, 94–95, 100–101, 102–3, 115–16; and peasant heroes, 220; punishment of peasants in, 111–15; riot in, 90–94, 99–100; text of, 86–118
"Record of the Beggars' Riot in Mimasaka" *(Sashū hinin sōdōki)*, 24
"Record of the Great Pacification of the Peoples' Disturbances in Inaba and Hōki" *(Inbaku minran taiheiki)*, 22
"Record of the Kurume Uprising," 24
"Record of the Rise and Fall of the Minamoto and Taira" *(Gempei seisuiki)*, 24
"Record of the Watanabe Doheiji Riot," 20, 22, 220
Renga (linked-verse poetry), 170
Ritual literature, 219, 246n.4
Root, Hilton L., 6
Ruch, Barbara, 38, 42

Rural elite, 10, 126, 128–29, 222, 228, 230; and shōgun, 139–40

Sabean, David Warren, 222
Sakai Iwami no kami, 69–71
Sakura Sōgorō, 125, 217, 220–21, 230; and community values, 225; crucifixion of, 45, 46, 63; illness of, 44, 51; in kabuki, 37–38, 40, 41–42; in modern times, 42; as peasant hero, 1, 35, 37, 38; as Shintō deity, 36, 37, 39; stories about, 17, 35, 36, 37; in "Tale of a Dream from the Fox Woman Plain," 191; verdict on, 61–63; in woodblock prints, 40–41
Sakura Sōgorō den, 37
Sakura Sōgorō shrine, 36, 40, 41, 43, 47, 242n.6
"Sakura Sōgorō Story" (*Sakura Sōgorō monogatari*), 28, 229; appeal to officials in, 49–50, 51–52; dissemination of, 43–44; modern version of, 257n.28; petition in, 57–60; Senior councillor in, 53–55; shōgun in, 35, 37, 44, 55–57, 62, 69, 71; text of, 47–75; variant versions of, 21, 43–46; and village officials, 29–30
Samurai, 4, 73, 75, 89–90, 149, 182–86, 202, 229
Sanshō the bailiff (Sanshō dayū), 122, 129
Sasaki Kyōichi, 224
Sekkyōshi (itinerant storytellers), 43
Semimaru, 42
Semi-proletariat, 200
Senior councillors (rojū), 5, 44, 46; Matsudaira Ukon no Zō, 134–35, 140, 142, 165; in

Sōgorō story, 53–55, 62; in "Thousand Spears at Kitsunezuka," 144
Sensō-ji, 245n.40
Seven Samurai, 38
Shares (*kabu*), 6
Shibusome uprising 1856, 22
Shima (daughter), 204, 207–11, 214, 228
Shimabara Christian Rebellion, 17, 79, 81, 82, 85, 119, 123, 127, 149, 173, 236n.38, 237n.39
Shimazaki Tōson, 120
Shinkei (poet), 170
Shinobi-koto, 18
Shinpū Kenchiku-ō, 16, 26, 77–80, 82, 118
Shinshi (Gentleman believer), 254n.19
Shintō, 84–85; beliefs, 12, 182, 201; practices, 180, 182, 207–8; shrines, 11–13; deities, see *Kami*
Shōgun, 4, 120; and rural elite, 139–40, 220; and Sakura Sōgorō, 35, 37, 44, 46, 55–57, 62, 69–73; in "Story of the Beggars' Riot in Mimasaka," 194; in "Thousand Spears at Kitsunezuka," 144, 145, 161–62; and Tsuyama domain, 80
Shōhei era, 153
Shōmonki, 24, 40, 243n.17
Sima Qin, 247n.8, 252n.8
Smith, Thomas C., 6
Songs, 36, 191
Spufford, Margaret, 18
Status system, 233n.5
"Story of the Beggars' Riot in Mimasaka," 193–94
Story of the Sōga Brothers, 78

Sugawara Michizane, 20, 127, 153, 244n.22
Sugiura Minpei, 29
"Sumō Rankings of Conspicuous Villains" *(Kanzoku midate sumō bansuke-hyō)*, 20
Sun tzu, 101
Sutras, 11; Daihannya, 41–42, 69, 244n.26; Lotus, 79
Suzuki Bokushi, 15, 17, 176, 256n.17
Suzuki Hisashi, 175

Taiheiki, 24, 78, 79, 226, 239n.65, 240n.71, 246n.5
Taira no Masakado, 17, 24; in "Record of How the Four Orders of People in Mimasaka Ran Riot," 81, 98; and Sōgorō, 39, 40, 41, 47, 220; in "Thousand Spears at Kitsunezuka," 127
Takahashi Jinzaemon, 122, 155, 159, 165
Takasago (Noh song), 215, 254n.21
Takeda Shingen, 177, 191
"Tale of a Dream from the Fox Women Plain" *(Onnabake hara yume monogatari)*, 3; comparison with other texts, 171; contradictions in, 171–72; description of, 170–72; documents in, 178, 185–86; leaders in, 184–85, 221; response of government officials, 182–86; riot in, 179–82, 224; text, 177–92; variant versions of, 17, 171, 173
Tale of Genji, 33, 42, 79, 246n.4
Tale of the Heike, 18, 23, 30, 38, 44, 79, 245n.37, 246n.4, 253n.6; and angry spirits, 39

"Tale of the White Stones Used in Great Battles on a Go Board" *(Go taiheiki shiraishi banashi)*, 198–99
"Tale Told in a Dream of a Eulogy to Filial Piety" *(Kōkō wasan yume monogatari)*," 23, 24, 84, 221, 227, 228; comparison with other texts, 194–95; description of, 194–201; leadership in, 205, 208; reasons for riot, 194; riot in, 202–4; text, 201–15; variant versions of, 209
"Tale Told through the Night at Nayadera" *(Nayadera tsūya monogatari)*, 25
"Tale Told through the Night at the Shrine to Jizō" *(Jizōdō tsuya monogatari)*, 21
"Tales of Filial Children in Higo," 197
"Tales of Filial Piety from Geibi," 197
Tales of Old Japan, 38, 44
Taxes, 7–9
"Tea Canister in the Rain" *(Uchū no kanzu)*, 21, 227
Tenant farmers, 9–10, 27, 200, 223, 224, 225
Tenpō taiheiki, 25
"Thousand Spears at Kitsunezuka" *(Kitsunezuka senbon yari)*, 3, 217, 229; battles in, 139, 143, 156; deaths in, 158; description of, 122–29; documents in, 135, 136, 142, 159, 164; filial piety in, 160–62; and Japanese traditions, 15, 20, 27; reasons for riot in, 123, 136, 137, 164; riot in, 143–44, 146–50; shōgun in, 161–62; story of

earlier uprising in, 137–39; text, 129–67; variant versions of, 141, 151
Tōkō-ji, 50, 65, 67
Tokugawa Ieyasu, 139–40, 141
Tokyo International Airport, 35
Totō (conspiracy), 123
Toyotomi Hideyoshi, 85
Transportation assistance *(sukegō)*, 120–21, 132, 134–36, 165, 168, 177–78, 184, 185, 249n.3
Traveling proselytizers *(oshi)*, 43
"Treasury of Loyal Retainers" *(Chūshingura)*, 20, 44
"True Account of Endō from Western Bizen" *(Seibi Endō jikki)*, 24
Tsuna (nursemaid), 197
Tsuyama domain 1727, 1, 7, 9, 77; administrative practices in, 80; comparison with other riots, 119, 200; description of riot, 80; taxation policies in, 94–95
Tsuyama domain 1866, 2, 9; description of riot, 193, 194–95
Two sisters from Adachi, 198–99, 229, 253n.11

"Ueda Broken Plaid" *(Ueda jimakuzure gōshi)*, 25
Underground heroes, 16–17
Underground literature, 15–16
Utte Myōjin (punitive shining deity), 143

Village, 6–7
Village headman. *See* Village officials
Village officials, 1, 7, 230; as authors of histories of peasant uprisings, 32, 44; and literacy, 27; and local history, 176; in

Sōgorō story, 48–50, 51–54; and "Tale of a Dream from the Fox Woman Plain," 172; in "Tale Told in a Dream of a Eulogy to Filial Piety," 210, 212, 214; and taxes, 9; and "Thousand Spears at Kitsunezuka," 124
Village schools (terakoya), 197, 240n.77
Villains, 23, 31, 48, 80–81, 89–90, 110, 122, 129–34, 177
Vlastos, Stephen, 30
Vocal literature, 42–43

Walthall, Anne, 31–32
War tales *(gunki monogatari)*, 18–20, 23–40, 79, 219, 220, 239n.65, 253n.6; and Kuribayashi Yoshinaga, 174; tellers of, 23–24, 77. *See also Tale of the Heike, Taiheiki*
Warrior histories of peasant uprisings, 24–25, 193
Watanabe Masaka, 26
Way of heaven *(tendō)*, 83–84, 93, 98, 99, 113, 115, 117
White, James, 5
Widow, 87–88, 227
Wife, 66, 126, 163, 187–88, 227–28
Women: consort, 67; daughters, 12, 63, 98, 206–15; in histories of peasant uprisings, 23, 226–28; mothers, 45, 64, 84, 112, 125, 161; in "Tale Told in a Dream of a Eulogy to Filial Piety," 197–200; in warrior histories of peasant uprisings, 25; widow, 87–88, 227; wife, 46, 66, 126, 163, 187–88, 227–28. *See also* Fox wife
Wu tzu, 101

Yasumaru Yoshio, 28–29
Yokoyama Toshio, 29, 221
Yonaoshi (world rectification), 30,
    241n.86

Yoshida Kenkō, 127, 130
Youth association, 195, 197, 204,
    206, 225, 228
Yui Shōsetsu, 17, 86, 87, 199, 239